The Wedding Planner

The Wedding Planner

DIANA BRIGHT

Nash Publishing
Los Angeles

My thanks to Diane Bolz, Jill Brauner,
Fay Landau, Kay McRee and Nancy Roaman who worked
long and hard to help make this book.

Library of Congress Catalog Card Number: 75-95370
Standard Book Number: 8402-1116-3

Published simultaneously in the United States and
Canada by NASH PUBLISHING, 9255 Sunset Boulevard,
Los Angeles, California 90069

Printed in the United States of America

Second Printing

To my husband
whose understanding and love
make my life a joy...

"We deserve to be happy"

Contents

The Wedding Planner

A Note of Introduction

Welcome to the Wedding Planner. In its pages you will find the answers to everything you need to know about planning the wedding you've always dreamed of.

My book is different from any other you may have seen. First of all, it is not an etiquette book. I tell you about etiquette and traditions, of course, but not as ends in themselves. Your wedding does not have to be like the weddings of your parents and grandparents —certainly not like the weddings held in the Victorian Era when self-appointed wedding authorities first came on the scene. And it need not be like the other weddings in your town or like the ones that your friends have had. Certainly it is easier for caterers and consultants to "sell" you on their standard-package wedding, but your wedding should be a reflection of your tastes, your values, your fondest hopes. Even your parents should understand that the wedding ceremony is your celebration, not theirs, and that you will live with its memories for many years to come.

In this book, many styles of weddings are explained; and, unlike most other books, I tell you not only what to do but how to do it. If you follow this book chapter by chapter, step by step, you will have the wedding you've always wanted at a minimum of expense and, hopefully, with a complete absence of problems and aggravation. The book covers not only the ceremony and reception, but also the many other areas which will be on your mind during this busy period—registering your china and silver patterns, planning the honeymoon, preparing for your new home—all presented in the same practical step-by-step format.

You'll find even the tone of the book to be different, for I speak to you not as a society snob or etiquette expert, but as a friend giving help to a friend. This book is written in a casual, informal style, as if I were sending advice to a close girl friend.

It was less than a year before I started writing *The Wedding Planner* that I organized and planned my own wedding. With both sets of parents out of town and my fiancé a busy businessman, I literally had to do almost everything myself. The task seemed overwhelming. The lists of things to do seemed to grow longer each day. Unexpected expenses seemed to come from nowhere, and on top of this, I had the usual problems of getting to know a whole new set of friends and in-laws.

I turned to books for help, and was terribly disappointed. The etiquette books concentrated on what was and was not "proper" in some distant age. The more recent books were too short, too superficial. And nowhere did any author provide the kind of step-by-step, detailed advice I needed. With more ingredients than a gourmet dinner, with more steps than building a house, the details of planning a wedding could not be found in a guide-book style.

This is what I have tried to do in *The Wedding Planner*. If you can follow a recipe in a cookbook, you will be able to follow the procedures I have outlined here to make your wedding everything you've always wanted. The book is based not only on my experiences, and my mistakes, but on my observations of the countless brides whom I have had the opportunity to help.

My own wedding was one that people still talk about today and one which I will always remember. It was a great success. I have written this book so yours will be too!

Sincerely,

Diana Bright

Diana Bright

Part One

THE FIRST STEPS

Yes!

THE PROPOSAL AND ENGAGEMENT

YES! IT ALL BEGINS with one small, magical word —a word that means a whole new life for you. Sometimes it's hard to say, but usually it's excitingly easy because you've been waiting and hoping he would ask you. You were so sure that he knew you loved him and wanted to marry him, and that he wanted to marry you, too. Well, you were right. He does love you, and he wants you to be his wife. So he asked and you said yes to his question—and to sharing a life of happiness together. Now you feel wonderful, loved—and probably a little nervous.

Almost all couples feel nervous at the actual moment of proposal—and some for a long time afterward. You may feel this way yourself right now, but this feeling will pass, and you'll start floating on your private cloud—and loving it.

Many couples remember exactly how their proposal took place and some don't. But no matter how yours was phrased, or where, the day of your proposal will probably hold as special a place in your heart as your actual wedding day.

There are any number of ways a proposal can take place. If your fiancé is the romantic type, he may have chosen the most fabulous restaurant in town as the nicest place to ask the big question. Or he may have bypassed these trimmings, and just blurted out over coffee one afternoon, "Will you marry me?", and waited nervously for your reply. Although this type of proposal might have taken you by surprise, it probably seemed very logical to your fiancé—he's the one who had been gathering his nerve and choosing his words for the past three weeks.

There are some proposals that were never made as such, because somehow an unspoken understanding grew. When I asked a friend how her husband asked her, she was quiet for a moment, and then replied, smiling, "...I don't think he ever did. I can't even remember how or when we decided for sure that we were going to be married. I guess we just always knew...."

You may have *always known* too, but sometimes special circumstances can cause you to receive your proposal in a unique way. If your fiancé is in the service or is away at college, he may have asked you to marry him by letter, telephone, or by a special note tucked among a dozen roses. It doesn't matter how it was done—just that it was, and that you said yes. Now that you're actually engaged, you're probably eager to begin planning your wedding. You and your fiancé may have already set your wedding date. Or you may have chosen the year or season and left the actual date for later. But don't worry—it isn't necessary to set your wedding date the moment he proposes. As you'll discover, there are many considerations in

Your proposal is special

"Will you marry me?"

"...we just always knew..."

selecting a wedding date. Making this first choice carefully can greatly enhance the enjoyment of your wedding. So take time—enjoy yourself.

In the movies, the hero just happens to have with him a little velvet box containing a large, sparkling diamond. But in real life many couples prefer to pick out an engagement ring together. Still others may choose to do without a ring entirely. Whether you receive your ring when he proposes, choose it together later, or postpone the purchase indefinitely, the important thing is that you're in love and about to embark on a spree of celebration, culminated by the greatest of all celebrations: Your Wedding Day.

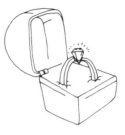

You'll want to tell the world

Now that you're engaged, you've most likely been telling the world, and it's only natural. But when you count all the people you want to tell, you may find you have a huge list. The people to tell first are your parents and his, of course, and then all your friends and relatives, and finally, the people you work with or go to class with and other casual friends.

If you haven't met your fiancé's parents, or he hasn't met yours yet—now is the time. It's nice to ask your parents' permission to marry, and they will certainly appreciate it, but it isn't always possible. If you tell them after you're engaged, your parents should still be the first to know and should meet your fiancé as soon as possible. Then tell his parents and make plans to meet them.

When you do meet his parents, try to be as natural as possible. And keep in mind that this occasion is as important for them as it is for you. They may be more than a little nervous until they've come to know you and love you like a daughter and until they feel you love and accept them as parents, too.

Meeting his parents

Your own parents will also want this reassurance, and they'll want to be certain that your fiancé will take good care of you and that he loves you as much as they do. This reassurance will come with time, but you can help by giving both sets of parents a chance to get used to the idea before you begin discussing your wedding plans or even setting a date. They'll bring up the subject of planning—probably with enthusiasm—when they're ready for it. Your parents in particular may want to consider their financial situation before making commitments about the wedding plans.

Ideally, once they have learned you're engaged, your fiancé's family will call or write your parents to express their happiness. And your parents might respond by an invitation to them—either to plan a party to announce the engagement or merely to get to know one another. Your parents and future in-laws might even become good friends—mine did!

Engagement announcements

Few couples send formal engagement announcements these days, so plan to tell your friends in person or by phone. It's certainly more personal and more fun that way. When you call, try to use a phone with an extension so you and your fiancé can talk together. If long-distance costs are too expensive, write personal notes about your good news. But write only about your engagement in your note, don't make it part of a long "newsy" letter. It's too important for that.

Have a party!

A happy way to break the news to a group of friends and relatives is to have an engagement party. Anyone can host this party, but if both sets of parents live in the same city, they might decide to co-host this affair. Or, if they are far apart, each can host a separate party for family and friends. And you can always plan some small, informal parties of your own to introduce your fiancé to friends and relatives. There are all sorts of parties to give and others that will be given in your honor. The more the merrier on this once-in-a-lifetime occasion.

Although most of the guests have probably found out that you're going to be married and have congratulated you during your party, it still lends a warm note to make a formal announcement of it sometime during the evening.

Usually, the host of the party makes this announcement with a special toast. The toast can always be given by your father, your fiancé's father, or by your fiancé, if you like.

Your engagement party can be a small, intimate gathering at home or a large, lavish affair at a restaurant. The menu can be anything you like—from coffee and cake to hors d'oeuvres and champagne. It needn't be a nighttime event, either. A weekend brunch, luncheon, or late afternoon cocktail party are all good choices—after all, your announcement is what is really important.

If you want to place your announcement in your local newspaper, call the society editor of your paper and ask her how to go about submitting your engagement information and photograph. Your newspaper may have its own way of handling engagements, but if it doesn't, you might want to use some of the ideas in the following procedure.

Newspaper announcements

It's best to send your engagement story on typed, double-spaced, 8½ by 11 inch white bond paper. In the upper right-hand corner of the page, list the name, address and telephone number of the person the newspaper can contact for additional information.

Then in the upper left-hand corner, type the words "FOR IMMEDIATE RELEASE" in capital letters. Or, if you want to delay the story until you've told additional relatives or friends of your engagement, give a definite release date.

Immediately below this line, type a brief headline in capital letters that tells at a glance what the story is about. For example: "JOAN DREW ENGAGED TO ROBERT SMITH." Then give the basic information about your engagement. Sample formats are listed in this chapter for your convenience.

For more ideas, read other girls' engagement announcements in your local newspaper. Notice how they're worded. You'll find it's easy, once you begin. And here's how to begin:

Mr. and Mrs. (your parents' names) have announced the engagement of their daughter, Miss (your name), to Mr. (your fiancé's full name).

If a bride's parents are divorced, however, either parent (or a guardian) can be named. Or she can announce her engagement herself as follows:

Miss (her full name) has announced her engagement to Mr. (her fiancé's full name).

"If a girl has been married before . . ."

If a girl has been married before, she may use either her maiden name or previous married name, whichever is better known to her friends. And she shouldn't hesitate to send in her announcement. It's perfectly acceptable.

The second paragraph lists more information about you. For example:

Miss (your last name) is a student at (an alumna of) (name of your school). [Or, if you are employed, you may wish to say Miss (your last name) is employed by (your firm).] She is a member of (name your club, sorority, or other affiliations here if any).

The third paragraph gives information about your fiancé. It also names his parents or guardian.

Mr. (your fiancé's last name) is the son of Mr. and Mrs. (your fiancé's parents' names) of (their city of residence). A student at (a graduate of) (name of his school), he is employed as a (his job title) at (the name of his company). He was formerly a (past military rank) in the (branch of the military service). He is a member of (name his club, fraternity or other affilations).

The fourth paragraph can mention your future plans. Perhaps they're only general plans: "The couple plan a spring wedding." Or, if you have set the date and reserved the site, you can give more details:

The couple plan to be wed April 12 at St. John's

Episcopal Church in Cincinnati.

If either your parents or his are active in civic organizations, hold public office, or are prominent professional people, this can be added in a brief final paragraph. Here's an example:

The parents of the prospective bridegroom reside in Denver, where the senior Mr. Mitchell is president of the Denver Chamber of Commerce.

If either of the bride's parents is deceased, the word "late" should precede the name in the announcement.

When you send your typewritten story to the newspaper, include a brief note with it. A line or two is all you need:

Enclosed, for release, is the story of my engagement. Please phone me for any additional information you may require. Thank you.
                    Cordially,
                    (Your name)

Some newspapers, such as the New York *Times*, have instituted very brief three-line or four-line announcements. The nice thing about these is their tone:

Mr. and Mrs. Jarvis Kellogg joyfully announce the engagement of their daughter Marjorie . . .

They're simple, sure to be printed, and charmingly worded, too. Some papers will accept this style announcement free or at a nominal charge.

Include a glossy black and white photo of yourself (8 by 10 inches, head and shoulders only) along with your engagement announcement. Print your name on the back of the photo in pencil or crayon—but very lightly, to avoid damage. Also pack the photo carefully when you send it. Hand-delivery is the best way, but if you have to mail it, place a sheet of cardboard on either side of the photo and send it along with your announcement in a manila envelope marked "PHOTO— DO NOT BEND." Few newspapers, if any, will return your

Send a photo

photo, so don't send a valuable shot, or one for which you have no negative.

Like to collect mementos? Start a wedding scrapbook with your engagement announcement on the first page. Add special keepsakes saved from your first dates together, and include photos and other souvenirs of your engagement party. Later you can add items saved from your showers, wedding ceremony, reception and honeymoon.

Along with collecting mementos, you'll probably find you're collecting gazes. You'll be in the spotlight simply because everyone is happy for you. You can relax and enjoy it—but you'll need to be careful in some ways, too.

Be discreet

You'll probably have very little privacy these days. And you may find you have to be careful about the kinds of attention you attract. Warmth and affection are always beautiful to see; but your love for each other is basically a private thing, not meant for the world to witness. So be particularly discreet when you know you're being watched.

Have you been wondering what the words "fiancé" and "fiancée" really mean? It's really quite simple. A "fiancé" is a man engaged to be married, and a "fiancée" is a woman engaged to be married. Both are pronounced in the same way: *fee-ahn-say*. Together they mean the two of you have something wonderful in common: your future.

Yes, you are a fiancée now, and you're soon to become a bride—the happiest bride ever, because you'll get lots of help from the chapters that follow, plus ideas to make this exciting and delightful time in your life perfect in every way.

2

On Second Thought

HOW TO BE SURE

YOU'RE ENGAGED to the man of your dreams and you're walking on air, right? But in recent days, you may also have come down to earth long enough for the startling question "What am I doing?" to have occurred to you. Don't panic. While it's true that you might have thought of it sooner, few girls do. So don't feel alone, or different.

First of all, you have to know what your questions really are. "What am I doing?" can mean many things. If you have been on your own for some time, changing your way of life may be what's worrying you. Some girls worry that marriage is a trap that involves giving up their independence. Or the reverse may be true for you. Perhaps you are fresh from school or college and you fear you'll miss that golden opportunity to "try your wings."

Perhaps your fears lie elsewhere. Do you doubt your ability to cook, keep house and generally take care of someone other than yourself? Maybe it's not marriage itself, but your fiancé you have doubts about. Does he have habits that annoy you? Are his goals different from your own? Is he concerned about matters that seem unimportant to you? These are all valid and important questions, but before you can dispense with your nagging doubts, you must pin them down and make sure they are very clear.

Talk things over

If you find as you think about these things that there are still certain aspects about your future which worry you, now is the time to act. If you are sure they are *real* considerations, discuss them fully with your fiancé. Any couple planning to spend the rest of their lives together must be close enough to discuss their problems with each other. If you can't do it—with honesty and mutual understanding—then now is the time to postpone plans until both parties are sure.

The following list of questions isn't the ultimate in personality analysis, but it can help you and your fiancé learn about yourselves and each other. If you are troubled by doubts, no matter how small, answering these questions might clear up areas that are disturbing you. But keep in mind that matters on which you don't totally agree needn't be cause for argument or despair. There is much to be learned from listening to another person's point of view.

Some questions

Here are the questions for you and your fiancé to answer and discuss:

1. What do I want from life? What brings me "happiness"?
2. What are the things that interest me most (people, books, hobbies, music, sports)?
3. Why do I want to get married?
4. What is the thing I most value (religion, social position, material items)? The thing I value least?

5. How do I feel about family? Close friends?
6. What is my favorite way of spending leisure time (alone, at parties, with a few close friends)?
7. What do we fight about (important disagreements)?
8. What size family do I want (many children, a few, none)? When do I want them?
9. Where do I want to live (city, country, small town)? Am I flexible in this?
10. Where do I stand on philosophical beliefs, both my own and those I would want to hand on to my children?
11. What is my attitude toward sex, both in my own life and in others' lives?
12. What are my financial needs and goals?
13. How do I feel about traveling? What kind of vacations do I enjoy?
14. What do I expect from marriage?
15. What do I find difficult or embarrassing to discuss with him (her)?

These are basic questions and you've probably thought of some of them long ago. But they may touch off other questions, for which you *don't* have the answers ready immediately—personal questions, probably the most important ones for you.

Another interesting and revealing exercise might be this: Write out a simple list, stating your reasons for loving your fiancé. You may discover this causes you to think about him in a totally new way, and it will certainly help you to understand any doubts you may have. Notice, by the way, in what order you list his qualities (be sure to write them down just as they pop into your head); it may surprise you to discover what you value most in him. Don't be concerned if only two or three qualities come to mind. Kindness, honesty and humor don't make a bad list at all!

Chances are that thinking things through will only show you how certain you are that you've made

Make a list

the right choice. But remember, if you had vague doubts and can now formulate them clearly, you are well on your way to solving them. It would be foolish not to share your fears with your fiancé—who, you might discover, has some worries of his own. The engagement period is the best time for such honest discussions.

It's natural for a girl to be nervous about getting married. But she's likely to be even more concerned if she finds herself pregnant before her wedding. This is a very difficult problem and most girls think there is only one solution—marriage.

First thoughts may go immediately to the security of the child. But it is not always the wisest thing, for child *or* parents, to enter a marriage for the sole purpose of giving the baby a name. All the questions, doubts and fears are the same for this girl as for any other, with the single exception of one question: Would I marry him if I were not pregnant?

A concern about "what will people say" is only natural, but, difficult as it may be, it is essential that she put others out of her mind and think only of herself, her fiancé and her decision. She must see a doctor, one who will be compassionate and understanding about the situation. A doctor who in any way makes her uncomfortable or who casts judgment upon the morality of the situation is not the man she needs at such a time. A kind and understanding doctor will be an enormous help.

Also, it's important that she make her decision according to her own needs and wishes, and not those of friends or family, no matter how well-meant their advice. She should marry in spite of her pregnancy, not because of it.

If she decides to marry, she doesn't have to change her basic wedding plans substantially. It might be necessary to set an earlier date but everything else can be the same. The ceremony can be as joyous and beautiful as any other, complete with white gown if she

If a bride is pregnant...

wishes. She doesn't have to discuss her condition or apologize for it. She should look to the future, and plan the wedding of her dreams just as any other bride would.

Now that you and your fiancé have discussed your doubts and fears, you have an even stronger bond of love between you. With this deeper awareness and understanding of one another, you can face the future with confidence. You know you will grow even closer as the years go by, and your love will be young and alive always.

3

With This Ring

WEDDING AND ENGAGEMENT RINGS

YOU MAY BE PROUDLY WEARING your new engagement ring as you read this, but chances are the choosing of both engagement and wedding rings is yet to come. Because they are symbols of your love for each other, the selection of these rings is a romantic and important matter. A wise choice is crucial, for these rings will be jewelry you will treasure always. Your fiancé may find this chapter very helpful, too.

When you select your engagement ring, keep your fiancé's budget firmly in mind. Although he wants to buy you the finest, it's up to you to be sure he can afford your choice. If you can't afford an engagement ring right now, don't feel pressured to buy one. You're better off delaying this purchase than starting out your marriage in debt. Many girls put off getting an engagement ring for some time—often until after they've been married for some years.

19

If your fiancé is a student, fresh out of the service or just beginning in business, he may not have much money to spend on this beautiful, but essentially luxury, item. If you have confidence in him and in your future together, there's no need to worry. Some day, perhaps on an anniversary, you will find a jewel being slipped on your finger, and it will be as meaningful then as now—perhaps more so. Don't allow raised eyebrows —"What, no ring?"—to keep you from doing the wise and loving thing.

Find a good jeweler

If you are buying a ring, however, the first thing you'll have to do is find a good jeweler. If you don't have a friend or family member who can recommend a reliable jeweler, here are some suggestions. Try to select a jewelry store that has been in business for a number of years. Investigate, if possible, the jeweler's reputation, and try to deal with a jeweler who is a certified gemmologist. He will have a certificate from the Gemmological Institute of America, which is the leading authority on diamonds in America.

You can have confidence if a jeweler stocks "brand names." But the store is no better than the particular salesman who is helping you. Don't deal with a man or woman who makes you uncomfortable or seems to be bored with your desire to pick and choose. Don't allow yourself to be pressured—quietly take your business elsewhere.

You need not choose a diamond

Although the diamond is the traditional stone for an engagement ring, for many girls the diamond lacks the warmth of other stones, and is simply not a favorite. Any stone is appropriate as long as you both like it. Some of the more popular stones are opal, jade, lapis lazuli, ruby, sapphire. There are precious stones, such as diamonds, rubies, emeralds, amethysts, and semi-precious stones, such as jade, opal, onyx, lapis; and in both groups prices vary according to size and cut. You may have a favorite color—lapis is a deep blue; jade, of various greens—or a sentimental preference for your

20

birthstone or his.

If you have decided that the traditional diamond is your choice, keep in mind that there are many things to know about making an investment in these beautiful stones. Diamonds are expensive because they are in limited supply—their sale and distribution is controlled by careful production. Though diamonds can literally be picked off the beaches in South Africa, the supply is held down to maintain their value. As long as the number is limited, diamonds will continue to be a good investment—both financially and romantically.

There are as many different kinds of diamonds as there are stars and as many different prices. The most expensive diamond, because it is the rarest, is the colorless diamond. When you look at it in sunlight, it reflects practically all the colors of the rainbow. This is not necessarily the most beautiful diamond for you, however. Often a slight tone of blue or yellow in a diamond can add a touch of warmth and interest—even if this blueness or yellowness is only visible through the jeweler's eyeglass. And it can help bring the price of the gem down to a reasonable range.

Kinds of diamonds

A diamond is flawless when it doesn't show impurities under magnification. Many diamonds have small natural impurities—bubbles or spots of carbon—which reduce their value but are not really noticeable to the naked eye.

Clarity

The cut of a diamond also affects its value. Each tiny surface of the gem, which is called a facet, must be cut at just the right angle. An off-center diamond—one from which a flaw has been removed, making the facets imperfect—can be practically worthless.

Cut

Diamonds are sold by weight, measured in units called points and carats, which are roughly equivalent to dollars and cents. There are one hundred points to a carat, so a seventy-five point diamond would be three-quarters of a carat. Prices are not necessarily in proportion to size. Large diamonds, like flawless and colorless

Carats

diamonds, are extremely rare. A two-carat diamond may therefore be as much as three times more expensive than a one-carat diamond.

If you and your fiancé will shop together for a diamond ring, here are some questions you might ask the jeweler. Is it flawless? Colorless? Is it a perfect cut? And if not, discover the degree of imperfection in any of these categories.

When the diamond you select is supposed to be better than average in any respect or you are paying a higher price, insist that the exceptional-quality feature be written on the sales slip. You will need this for insurance purposes or in the event you discover that the jeweler has made false claims. Insist that the store explain the meaning of the terms they use and put them in writing. If a jewel is presented as "flawless," that should go down in writing. If the jeweler refuses, he is using "flawless" as a purely descriptive term, and price should vary accordingly.

Buyer beware

Even in a famous New York-Beverly Hills jewelry store, the salesmen are not above double talking. Their salesmen imply that "Fine" quality is a very good diamond, without making it clear that it is, in fact, inferior to their "Extra Fine," "Extra Extra Fine" and "Extra Extra Extra Fine" quality gems. Ask the jeweler to break down the cost of the ring into the amount you are paying for the stone, for any other stones in the ring, and for the setting, so you can compare the exact value of the diamond if you choose. And remember: A diamond is quite an investment, so *caveat emptor*—buyer, beware! If you have reason to question the quality of your diamond, have it appraised. Check your Yellow Pages for the name of an appraiser.

A setting for your ring

If you have found a stone in a setting that suits you, well and good, but often girls prefer to choose the stone and setting separately. The same standard that applies to the stone applies to the setting. Choose a setting that you will enjoy as much later as you do now.

Some women have their engagement or wedding stones reset in later years, but it would be nice, in years to come, to know that the ring you're wearing is the same one he slipped on your finger that wonderful day.

Your stone or stones will influence your choice of a setting. A beautiful solitaire, single, diamond should be placed in a simple setting which sets off its own beauty. A collection of smaller stones, on the other hand, could be set in an interesting multiple design like dinner rings.

Next comes the decision about the color of the band. Begin by answering some general questions. Do you generally wear gold or silver jewelry? What color is your favorite watch, and do you intend to keep it? Mixing jewelry tones is not taboo, but if all the jewelry you own is yellow gold, a white-gold band is not the best choice. White gold looks best with smaller stones, blends well with the diamond and adds brilliance to the ring. With a large single diamond, yellow gold gives contrast and sets off its size and shape. With a colorful gem, such as a ruby, the situation is reversed—yellow blends with red tones, while white is the more striking contrast.

There are many different finishes for gold, ranging from the plain smooth finish, which develops a lovely patina through the years, to the textured Florentine gold, which gives the metal depth and interest. If you choose Florentine gold, the design may mellow and the gold become finer as the years go by.

Styles of rings vary from traditional simple gold bands to elaborate and intricate mountings. As a rule, the more beautiful your gem the simpler the ring should be. Some rings are so unusual and decorative that they don't need any gem. Many modern lines include designs with no stones at all, or with very small decorative stones that would produce as many ooh's and ah's as the largest diamond. For the more traditional as well as modern settings, ArtCarved has a fine selection of bands, also reasonably priced.

Wedding bands

Your wedding band should match your engagement ring and, if possible, should be selected at the same time. Many manufacturers design matching engagement and wedding rings. Some even have a tiny hook to keep them close together on your finger. If you're not getting your engagement ring now, select a wedding band that is relatively plain, so that it will go with the ring you may someday be given. Remember to try rings on, don't just look at them in the jewelry case. It's the only way to tell how they will really look on your hand.

If your fiancé is going to wear a wedding ring, too, your ring and his can match. There are thin rings and thick ones, rings with rounded edges and squared. Be sure you choose a ring that he will like wearing and one that suits his hand. If the ring style you have chosen for yourself is too delicate for his hand, select one that is similar though not exactly matching. If you have always hoped for a double-ring ceremony and your fiancé doesn't like the idea of wearing a wedding band, don't take it to mean that he won't want people to know he's married. Some men dislike jewelry or work at jobs where rings would make them uncomfortable. Let him know that it's important to you, but if he persists in not liking the idea, let it drop.

If you do decide on a double-ring ceremony, be sure to take this into account when budgeting. The simplest gold band for a woman can cost between $30 and $60 today, and a larger man's ring may go anywhere from $50 to $100. You might prefer to spend the money on your wedding, honeymoon or setting up your new household.

Special rings

Sometimes a school or fraternity has a traditional wedding ring. West Point, for example, has a special wedding band that can be worn with the West Point class rings which are given as engagement rings. If a custom is important to you, by all means go along with it, but do it because you want to and not because you think you must.

Unless you're experienced with custom-made jewelry and know a good designer, now is *not* the time to experiment. But if you have a particular design in mind or a special jewel that you want reset, investigate designers carefully and plunge ahead.

If you already have a stone, your first thought might be—Do I want it cut? Generally, smaller stones have less value than larger ones, but a defect in a gem can be cut out in reducing the size—perhaps making the stone more beautiful. Be sure, in any case, that you have a detailed sketch of what you want the finished ring to look like. There's too much room for interpretation unless you designate exactly what you want.

When you place your order, be sure it specifies the exact delivery date. You will be anxious to wear your ring, and you won't want to wait. Also, make sure the order states that they have received your gem in perfect condition. When you receive your finished ring, be sure you are satisfied with it in every detail. Don't be afraid to insist that something be changed and that more work be done if necessary.

The care of your ring

Get your jeweler's advice on how to clean and care for your ring. Ask him what solutions should be used to clean it and how often you should clean your ring. Some jewelers invite their customers to bring in their rings twice a year to be cleaned and checked. There's usually no charge, and the jeweler can assure you that your gem is mounted securely, too. So ask him about this.

If your fiancé gave you a ring when he proposed, it may only need to be sized. The band must be small enough so that it won't fall off, but roomy enough to be comfortable. Have it sized immediately, so that you can wear it soon. And if you want your ring engraved, ask the jeweler how long this will take when you go in to have it sized.

Although it isn't necessary, many couples like having something personal engraved on the inside of their engagement or wedding bands. If you decide to do this, ask to see some other engraving work your jeweler has done. Often a couple has the groom's three initials, followed by the bride's three initials, and then the wedding date engraved on the inside of each wedding band. Following that, any phrase that has meaning for both of you is fine—but make sure it will fit! Some popular inscriptions are: "Forever"; "Love and Happiness"; "In Holy Matrimony"; or "Till death do us part." If you're having a double-ring ceremony, perhaps both rings could contain the same inscription.

If your ring is particularly valuable, plan to have it insured. Many insurance companies don't like to insure expensive rings and will only do so if it is part of household or other insurance. They also are known to include clauses in the small print which disclaim responsibility for items like engagement rings.

Some insurance companies will only replace a lost or stolen ring at their appraisal of the value, which results in much less valuable rings as replacements. Be sure that you specify cut, carats, and color of any diamond you are insuring. There is another common loophole. The company will insure the entire ring if it is lost—but if only the stone is lost, the company is not liable. Read the fine print carefully, and if you can't get the coverage you want and need, go to another firm.

Once you have your ring, you will undoubtedly be anxious to wear it all the time. Some old-fashioned etiquette books say you can't until the engagement is "officially" announced at a party or in the newspaper. Unless you want to make a surprise announcement, however, there is no reason in the world why you shouldn't wear your new ring right away.

Ordinarily, the engagement ring is worn on the fourth finger of the left hand. This custom comes from the ancient belief that the vein of love runs directly from that finger to the heart. However, during the ceremony, the engagement ring can be placed on any finger of your right hand and afterward replaced on your left hand, with your wedding ring closest to your heart, so you will be wearing both rings as you take your place in the receiving line at your reception.

If you have decided to buy only a wedding band, it is proper to wear it through your engagement period. Remove it before the wedding so the groom can give it to the best man; it can be blessed if you like and returned to you during the ceremony. This way you can wear and enjoy it both before and after you are married. Your fiancé, however, wouldn't wear his ring until after the wedding ceremony.

Your engagement ring tells the world that you have declared your love and are going to be married. No matter what kind of ring you get, to you it will be the most beautiful piece of jewelry in the world—because he gave it to you. As a symbol of your mutual love, nothing will ever surpass it in beauty—except your wedding ring.

4

Making Cents

PLANNING YOUR BUDGET

YOU'LL FIND IT'S EASY TO SPEND lots of money on something that is as much fun as a wedding—especially when it's your own. The trick is to budget your spending. And that's not always done by spending less money, but by spending your money wisely. *How you spend it* is what really counts. No need to be confused about your financial problems, though. The answer to your questions is right here in this chapter—a brand new budget planner. If you use it to help spend your money, you'll be able to buy—and pay for—everything you need and want for your wedding. You'll have money set aside for the essentials and for the little extras that will make your wedding even more beautiful. Knowing how to spend your money well can make your wedding months even happier for you and for your parents. (They might want to read this chapter, too.)

I've seen weddings where the bride had a magnificent gown, where a small fortune was spent for food and drink, but where there wasn't even a photographer to record the occasion. And I've seen other weddings where everything was done simply, tastefully and economically, but where an unnecessarily large amount of money was spent for an orchestra—one that was so large that it was out of keeping with the rest of the occasion. So you can see it's most important to know how to spend your money wisely—and equally—for all the items that will make your wedding beautiful.

Budgeting is the answer to this problem, as it is with spending any large amount of money. It will help you to set limits for your total budget, so your family won't have to remember your wedding—unpleasantly —with a pile of unpaid bills or bank loan coupons. Also, it will help you to set aside a workable amount of money to spend for each item you'll need. Then you won't have the problem of overspending on any one item at the expense of others.

Budgeting need not be painful. Your wedding— budgeted within your means—can be as tasteful and beautiful as a wedding that costs a fortune. It's not the amount of money you spend but the happy memories that you and your guests take away with you when the wedding day is over that's important. Unusual and tasteful selections like a unique flower arrangement or the wedding gown you designed yourself will be remembered more fondly than wanton spending. The key is good taste. A small amount of the best is preferable to great quantities of the mediocre. There are many ways to make your wedding beautiful—and memorable— while keeping well within your budget at the same time. There are lots of good ideas and helpful suggestions for you in the chapters that follow, so don't worry. Begin making up your wedding budget instead.

*Spend wisely,
spend beautifully*

It's not what you spend ...

30

Your first step is to decide how much you can spend for all your wedding costs—the ceremony, reception, photographs, flowers, your gown, everything that you will buy especially for your wedding. Your honeymoon and the bride's wedding and engagement rings are usually paid for by the groom, so they will not be included in this total.

If you and your family already have an idea of how much you can comfortably spend, then this will be your wedding budget amount. Take this amount as your goal, and work from there to decide either how many people you can invite or how much to spend on a per person basis. The more guests you invite, of course, the less you can spend per person. The fewer you invite, the more elaborate your plans can be. You and your parents should work on this together—and perhaps ask your fiancé to join in if you think that would be helpful.

Figure the total cost

If you and your family are not sure how much to spend for your wedding, you can figure out what the amount will be by taking into account the total number of guests who will attend your reception and the amount you wish to spend, per person, for both ceremony and reception. The total number of guests you expect to *attend* your reception is the number you must work with, not the number you invite. Count only those invited to the reception, not the ceremony. Happily it costs little more than postage and stationery to invite as many people as you like to the ceremony.

Now take the number of guests that you expect to *attend* your reception and multiply it by an estimated cost per person—be sure to count people, *not* couples. First, of course, you will have to decide how much to spend per person. The minimum amount today seems to be about $10 per person, with $30 per person as an average and $50 per person as a maximum. Of course, if you have lots of money available, it's easily possible to spend much, much more. If you read this book carefully and take your budget planning seriously, you can

The cost per guest

have a lovely wedding, well within your means.

The amount you spend may depend on the area in which you live. In most cities, the typical cost per person is $30, although a nice wedding, carefully budgeted, can be had for $20 to $25 per person. In smaller towns, this cost can be cut by 10 to 20 percent. For some high-cost-of-living areas, such as Manhattan and San Francisco, the "average" cost per person is as much as 20 percent higher than anyplace else. Expensive? Yes, and true.

For a budget of $10 a person, you should think in terms of an informal wedding, perhaps in your home or garden. Your friends and relatives can be asked to pitch in and do some of the work—perhaps even helping to prepare the food. But you'll have all the ingredients of a beautiful wedding—including at least one musician (perhaps a pianist, violinist or organist), flowers, photographs, and a fun-filled reception.

If you are fortunate enough to be able to spend a larger amount—say $45 a person—the sky's the limit. You can investigate a first-class hotel or country club as a site for your reception, two orchestras for continuous music, unlimited drinks, imported champagnes, and a dinner right out of *Gourmet* magazine. This kind of super de luxe wedding is easier to plan, but a budget will still be helpful just to be sure you are not skimping in one area at the expense of others.

Spending $50 a person is a pleasant thought; but for most of us, wedding costs will have to be kept to within the $20 to $25 a person range. There is a special chart in this chapter on page 33 to help you find out how much to spend for each of your guests. The chart is called the WEDDING BUDGET GUIDE. It will help you see how adding more guests will increase your budget—and by exactly how much—as well as how decreasing your cost per person will allow you to invite more guests. Just look down the list and find the number of guests you are thinking of, run your finger across the line until you reach the wedding budget you had in mind, and you will see at the top of that column how much you can spend per person. Or you can begin with the total budget amount you had in mind, move your fingers along both columns, and you will see how many guests you can invite and how much you can plan to spend for each.

NUMBER OF GUESTS	COST PER PERSON								
	$ 10	$ 15	$ 20	$ 25	$ 30	$ 35	$ 40	$ 45	$ 50
(up to) 50	$ 500	750	1,000	1,250	1,500	1,750	2,000	2,250	2,500
100	1,000	1,500	2,000	2,500	3,000	3,500	4,000	4,500	5,000
150	1,500	2,250	3,000	3,750	4,500	5,250	6,000	6,750	7,500
200	2,000	3,000	4,000	5,000	6,000	7,000	8,000	9,000	10,000
250	2,500	3,750	5,000	6,250	7,500	8,750	10,000	11,250	12,500
300	3,000	4,500	6,000	7,500	9,000	10,500	12,000	13,500	15,000
350	3,500	5,250	7,000	8,750	10,500	12,250	14,000	15,750	17,500
400	4,000	6,000	8,000	10,000	12,000	14,000	16,000	18,000	20,000
500	5,000	7,500	10,000	12,500	15,000	17,500	20,000	22,500	25,000
750	7,500	11,250	15,000	18,750	22,500	26,250	30,000	33,750	37,500
1,000	10,000	15,000	20,000	25,000	30,000	35,000	40,000	45,000	50,000

WEDDING BUDGET GUIDE

The approach you take to find your wedding budget is up to you, but once you have your total budget in mind, it's a good idea to begin dividing up the money for specific purposes. My researchers and I have checked costs in various parts of the country and have come up with a suggested percentage for each aspect of your wedding. These percentages are explained in the chart called SUGGESTED BUDGET PROPORTIONS, which is the second chart on page 36 in this chapter.

You'll see as you look at this chart that the number of guests is listed on the left side and covers 50 to 400 guests and more. Across the top are listed six gen-

Now to divide it up

eral categories of items that you will have to buy for your wedding. The items for each category are listed at the bottom of the page. Because each bride's wedding is unique, the amount she decides to spend for each part of her wedding can vary. If you want to spend amounts different from the ones listed, make whatever changes you like.

There are six categories covered on this chart. They are Stationery, Photography, Clothing and Gifts, Ceremony, Reception, and Miscellaneous.

Stationery

Each category provides for many items. The first category—*Stationery*—includes wedding invitations, thank-you notes, announcements, and special party invitations. (There's more information in Chapter 11 that will help you choose your wedding stationery.)

Photography

The second category—*Photography*—covers all the photographs that you will have taken during the wedding period. These pictures begin with your engagement photo, used with your engagement announcement (Chapter 1), continue with photographs taken of your ceremony (Chapter 20) and reception (Chapter 26) and end with your bridal portrait to be included with the newspaper announcement of your wedding (Chapter 31). The items in this category are expensive, but all-important, because they are mementos you will keep forever.

Clothing and gifts

The third category—*Clothing and Gifts*—is extremely flexible in cost. Just as everyday clothing and special gifts are available in all sorts of prices, so are wedding clothing and gifts. Besides your wedding gown, going-away outfit, personal trousseau (clothes for your honeymoon and after) and gifts or clothes for your attendants, this section also covers costs for a matching wedding ring for your groom and special engagement and wedding presents for him, too, if you like this idea and can afford special touches. (Chapters 15, 16 and 17 will help you know what clothing and gifts to buy for yourself and your attendants, and

Chapters 3 and 12 will help with gifts and a ring for your fiancé.)

The fourth category—*Ceremony*—includes any rental of your site and fees for such things as someone to ring your wedding bells or to clean up after your ceremony. It, also, includes flowers for your maid of honor, bridesmaids, flower girl—and possibly boutonnieres for the ushers and best man—corsages for both mothers and for special people you might want to honor, plus your bouquet and going-away corsage. (Your groom may pay for your bouquets and others if he likes. If he does, you can deduct this cost from this category.) Other decoration costs for the ceremony will also be included here along with the cost of providing music for your ceremony. (Sometimes musicians will be hired for both the ceremony and reception and the same flowers and decorations used for both, so don't add these costs in both categories unless they are completely different.) The total cost can be expensive or quite reasonable, depending on your choices (See Chapters 18-24).

Ceremony

The fifth category—*Reception*—is usually the most costly. Parties are expensive and wedding receptions can be even more so. This category would include the rental of the site (if different from the ceremony site), flowers and special party decorations that are bought just for the reception. (See Chapters 25-30 for ideas about the reception.) The last items covered are the refreshments to be served: food, drink, wedding cake and champagne. Add an extra amount for any people who will serve guests at the reception and for the rental of party equipment. Finish the list of items with music for your reception. Keep in mind as you work with this category that it is usually the most expensive and, as such, requires close attention—keeping accurate and exact records here is a must.

Reception

The last category—inevitably called *Miscellaneous*—should cover the cost of any additional entertaining you plan for friends, relatives, or out-of-town

. . . and miscellaneous

guests—also, special parties such as the rehearsal dinner, engagement party, or bridesmaids' luncheon. These parties are not absolutely necessary, but they are great fun if you can afford them. (Chapters 32 and 33 will explain the pre-wedding parties.) The final item in this category is a contingency fund, which is purely an amount of money set aside to cover such extra unexpected costs as sales tax, one more toast of champagne or an extra hour of music. It is strictly for extra extras, so don't plan to spend it—save it till later.

SUGGESTED BUDGET PROPORTIONS						
NUMBER OF GUESTS	I STATIONERY	II PHOTOGRAPHY	III CLOTHING AND GIFTS	IV CEREMONY	V RECEPTION	VI MISCELLANEOUS
(up to) 50	6%	11%	30%	11%	30%	12%
100	5%	10%	25%	10%	40%	10%
150	4%	9%	22%	9%	47%	9%
200	4%	8%	18%	8%	54%	8%
250	3%	6%	17%	6%	62%	6%
300	3%	5%	13%	5%	69%	5%
350	2%	4%	9%	4%	77%	4%
400 (and more)	2%	3%	5%	4%	82%	4%

    I   Stationery includes: invitations, announcements, informals
    II   Photography includes: engagement and wedding photos, bridal portrait
    III Clothing and Gifts include: gowns, attendants' gifts, trousseau, ring, groom's gift
    IV   Ceremony includes: rental site, flowers/decorations, music
    V   Reception includes: rental site, flowers/decorations, food/drink, music, wedding cake
    VI   Miscellaneous includes: rehearsal dinner, special parties, contingency fund

A sample budget

Knowing how your money will be spent and keeping track of it are two different matters. Since you'll probably have a million other things on your mind during the weeks and months before your wedding, I've made up a WEDDING BUDGET PLANNER for you that will help you keep track of your finances in an organized and easy way. There's a sample WEDDING BUDGET PLANNER in this chapter, all filled in so you can see how it works, and a blank one attached to the back of this book for your own use. You can take it out, fill it in, and carry it in your purse while you shop. Here's how it works:

The first column—*Category*—lists the six basic categories on which you will spend your money. They are the same six categories that we have just discussed —Stationery, Photography, Ceremony, Reception, Clothing and Gifts, and Miscellaneous—which include all the items that you will have to buy for your wedding. Now, you have to figure out how much to spend for each. For your convenience, I have listed chapter references next to each item, so you can refer quickly to that chapter for ideas about controlling your wedding costs.

The second column—*Percentage Amount*—is where you should write in the percentage amount for your size wedding taken from the SUGGESTED BUDGET PROPORTIONS chart.

The third column—*Dollar Amount*—is for entering the total dollar figure for each category, which you get by taking the percentage of your total budget. For example, if your budget figure is $3,000 and your stationery *percentage* is 5 percent, you multiply 5 percent times $3,000 and get $150. The $150 is the amount to enter in the third column, Stationery. A quick way to figure a percentage is to multiply it times your total budget, then drop the last two digits from the resulting answer. For instance, in this example, 5 times $3,000 which is $15,000, drop the last two zeros and you have the amount: $150.

The fourth column—*Your Adjustments*—is just that—a column for you to use for your adjusted total figures. You will adjust them according to your personal preferences and situations. For instance, if you are planning to use a gown which is a family heirloom, you will need less for the Clothing category. If you want to have motion pictures taken of your wedding instead of regular photographs, you'll have to allot more for the

Your personal adjustments

Photography category. So, you can change the dollar amounts you will spend for each category to suit your personal situation. But remember to keep your wedding budget total the same as you originally had planned. Also, keep in mind that if you add an amount to one category, you'll have to cut down on another—not on the miscellaneous budget though; that's to be definitely saved for extra fun things and emergency expenses. If you are changing any amount, by adding or subtracting, enter the new amount in this column, then enter the final figure in the next column—*Final Wedding Budget*.

The very last column—*Actual Wedding Costs*—is the column where you keep track of your wedding budget as you spend and buy all of the things you need for your wedding. As you make your decisions or place orders, jot down the dollar amount; when you can fill in the total amount for a category, compare it with the amount for the category listed in the *Final Wedding Budget* column. Let's say, for example, you have allowed $150 for photographs, but you have spent only $120; that leaves you $30 to spend somewhere else.

Is this a little confusing? It will be easy to follow if you look at the filled-in WEDDING BUDGET PLAN-NER on page 41. It's exactly like the blank chart in the back of the book, except that it was filled in by a typical bride.

The bride in our example has decided to spend $25 per person and to invite 100 people to her wedding. The WEDDING BUDGET GUIDE shows that her total wedding will cost her and her family $2,500. She fills in this amount—$2,500—at the top of the WEDDING BUDGET PLANNER. Our bride, like all girls, checks with her parents and gets an OK on this amount of money.

Her next step is to consult the SUGGESTED BUDGET PROPORTIONS chart to find out how much she can spend for each category. She finds she can spend 5 percent for stationery, 10 percent for photography,

For example

$25 per person
x 100 = $2,500

38

25 percent for clothing, 10 percent for the ceremony, 40 percent for the reception, and 10 percent for miscellaneous. On the sample chart, we have indicated these figures in the second column, *Percentage Amount*.

She then multiplies these percentages times her total budget of $2,500 and enters these totals in the third column, marked *Dollar Amount*. She takes 5 percent of $2,500, which is $125, and places that amount in the column across from Category I (Stationery). Next she takes 10 percent of $2,500, gets $250, and enters this amount across from Photography. And so on down the list until all the amounts are filled in.

Our girl, like you, has some changes she wants to make. She has a gown that she is in love with, but it's expensive—an extra $100 worth—so she has added $100 to the Clothing and Gifts category to help pay for it. Also, she expects a lot of out-of-town guests, so she adds $200 to the Miscellaneous category to help pay for extra parties and special dinners. This means she has added a total of $300 to her budget. And it also means she is over her budget.

How can she correct this? By cutting back on the amount of money she will spend on the other categories. Fortunately, she finds that her best man has a friend who is a *professional* photographer. He has offered to take all the photos and to provide albums for relatives for only $200—so she will save $50. Also, she decides to have her reception at home rather than at an expensive private club, so she saves $250 in the Reception category. This reception is not only less expensive, it is nicer—because she felt it would be warmer and more informal, and more fun. With these two adjustments she's back on budget: $2,500 again.

The revised totals—showing her economies— are then entered under the *Final Wedding Budget*, and she's ready to begin the actual spending for her wedding.

As she goes along, she jots down the amounts

$2,500 x 5%
= $125

she spends for each category. When a category is complete, she adds up the total and enters it in the last column, *Actual Wedding Costs*. Even at this point she finds things she has to change. For example, she has forgotten to add sales tax to the photographer's estimate, so Photography will actually cost her $210, not the $200 on which she had planned. But, her gown was less than what she thought it would be—$60 less to be exact—so she can subtract that amount from the Clothing category. She finds, as you probably will, that some changes are inevitable. And she keeps track of them, so that she will know whether she is over her budget, or if she will have extra money to spend.

The last column is for these kinds of adjustments. It may not help you keep your costs in line, but at least you, like the bride in our example, will know exactly where your money is going and where you stand.

There are other adjustments you might be making, too. You might be subtracting the costs of some items because your fiancé and his family have offered to pay for them. These costs are still a part of the total cost of your wedding, even though they will most likely be billed to and paid for by the groom's family. Some items the groom's family might pay for are:

1. Engagement or wedding gift for the bride.
2. Bride's wedding and engagement rings.
3. The marriage license.
4. Fee for clergyman or judge.
5. Cost of honeymoon.
6. Costs of furnishing and maintaining your new home.
7. Bridal bouquet, corsages for mothers and possibly grandmothers, and boutonnieres for himself, the best man and ushers.
8. His wedding and going-away outfits.
9. Gifts and accessories for the best man and ushers.

10.   Special pre-wedding entertaining.

You have all the information you need to help you now; and if you use your WEDDING BUDGET PLANNER chart carefully and keep it up to date, you'll have not only a beautiful wedding, but one that is free of financial worry. And that's the best kind—for you —and for your parents.

Wedding Budget Planner

CATEGORY	CHAPTER	PERCENT**	DOLLAR AMOUNT	YOUR ADJUSTMENTS	FINAL WEDDING BUDGET	ACTUAL WEDDING COSTS
I STATIONERY						
Invitations	(11)	5 %	$125	None	$125	$118
Announcements	(11)					
Informals and Miscellaneous	(11)					
II PHOTOGRAPHY						
Engagement	(1)	10 %	$250	— $50	$200	$210
Wedding	(20, 26)					
Bridal Portrait	(31)					
III CLOTHING AND GIFTS						
Gown and Accessories	(15)					
Attendant Gifts	(16)	25%	$625	+ $100	$725	$665
Trousseau	(17)					
Ring	(3)					
Gift to Groom	(12)					
IV CEREMONY						
Rental Site	(18)	10%	$250	None	$250	$250
Flowers/Decorations*	(21)					
Music	(22)					
V RECEPTION						
Rental Site	(25)					
Flowers/Decorations	(27)					
Food	(28)	40%	$1000	– $250	$750	$750
Bar/Champagne	(28)					
Music	(29)					
Wedding Cake	(30)					
VI MISCELLANEOUS						
Rehearsal Dinner*	(32)					
Special Parties	(33)	10 %	$250	+ $200	$450	$450
Pre-wedding Entertainment*	(33)					
Contingency Fund						
TOTALS		100 %	$2500	$2500	$2500	$2443

*Groom or his family may provide   ** You'll find suggested percentage on page 36   © 1970 Diana Bright

5

Set the Date

ADVICE ABOUT TIMING

YOU MIGHT WELL BE FEELING that the best of all possible times to get married is right now. Why wait? Why go through all the effort of planning and arranging a large wedding when you could simply elope and begin living happily ever after? For some couples, this may be the right course to take, but most girls have been dreaming about their wedding for more years than they can remember. Men, be they enthusiastic participants or nervous observers, assume that their fiancées want a wedding that is special and are glad to help that dream come true. The bride's parents usually approach wedding plans with a fervor born of their love and happiness for her. Your wedding and the festivities that go with it may take up a relatively small space in time, but the happy bustle that goes before and the memories that linger after are for most of us the stuff that dreams are made of. It's worth the time and trouble, and it's worth the waiting, too. So—set the date.

Now you can begin to plan. Forget practical things for a minute and write out all you know about The Wedding you've always dreamed of having—where it would take place, what it would be like, when it would be. You might have preconceived ideas about things. Perhaps lilies of the valley always bloom by your house in early April and have given you a particularly nice feeling, which you would like to capture for your wedding. You could indulge yourself and be married the first week in April. Or perhaps you have a lucky number or day of the week. You might even want to consult the stars and be wed at a particular time in the astrological calendar. You'll have your basic ideas down in front of you then, and you can adapt and change as you go. No doubt you'll have compromises to make, but at least you'll start from a firm base.

First, consider the season. Discuss with your fiancé, even before choosing the month, day and time, your seasonal preferences—and take the weather into account. If you're both from the East, you may especially love winter and snow, and a winter wedding may sound ideal. Or perhaps you love summer and have your heart set on a warm-weather honeymoon. If you've always wanted to have an outdoor wedding or a garden reception, obviously it's better to have such a wedding in spring, summer, or fall, even in temperate climates. The season you choose and the month you pick in that season will influence all your other plans, particularly if you settle on a spring wedding and the month of June.

June is the most popular month of the year for weddings—a month associated with brides and romance. I was married in June and I loved it, but remember that many other girls will also want to be married in June, and this can cause problems. Also, a June wedding may conflict with another family affair, such as a gradu-

Your ideal wedding

A particular season

The June wedding

ation. This could cause both emotional and financial strain for your family; thus, if you find yourself in such a predicament, you'd be well advised to pick an alternate month.

But the main problem with a June wedding is its popularity. The prices of various services and accommodations go up because the suppliers realize that June is their peak month, and they must adjust their fees and charges accordingly. Suddenly the hotel you wanted for your reception may cost a little more, and the food and services you need might be more expensive. Many hotels and churches are reserved, florists are busier. The same may be true of the band or the photographer. So you must increase your budget and reserve things even farther in advance for a June wedding.

If you haven't much time for planning but necessity or desire demands a spring/summer wedding, think about marrying in May or July. BUT—if you have your heart set on June, be married in June. Take into account that additional problems can arise, and plan accordingly. Perhaps you could defray costs by selecting a private home for your reception rather than a hotel or club. The "June problem" may only force you to be imaginative and resourceful, and there's nothing wrong with that!

Other decisions will influence your choice of month. If you are in school or college, check dates for graduation and exams, and know exactly when your semester or holiday breaks occur. Will these dates work to your advantage, or will you be having a midterm the night before your wedding week begins? Don't forget to obtain the same information from any of your attendants who are still in school.

If you or your fiancé are both employed, you'll have to consider how much vacation time you can get for your honeymoon and pre-wedding preparation. If your heaviest work load is in the summer, for example, you may want to have your wedding in late spring or

Conflicting dates

early fall. There would be more time for you to take part in the festivities that way and more time for the planning you'll need to do before your wedding day.

Choosing the day

After you've decided on a good month for your wedding, you must choose the day. It's of first importance to check the requirements of your particular clergyman. If you're being married in a Catholic church, for example, you may want to check when a Nuptial Mass can be performed; what time of day is customary; what day of the week is best. During certain holidays the place of worship you need may not be available for a wedding service. You must check if you are to be married by a priest, a minister, a rabbi, or even a judge. Although the latter's preference won't be based on religion, he may be available only at certain times.

Consider your emotional and physical requirements when choosing the day. If you are able to plan with any accuracy, try to establish the dates of your menstrual cycle for that month to avoid tension or "blues" during your wedding week. Knowing this in advance will help you to avoid any discomfort or nervousness during this all-important time in your life.

Site of ceremony

Choosing the site for your wedding may guide you in your selection of the wedding date. If you have your heart set on being married in a particular church or having the reception at a particular hotel, you might consult them in advance and find out how much time they need for planning. What are their heaviest months? Will you be able to get the date you prefer? You may find it necessary to compromise, so be flexible.

Choosing the time

Having chosen the month and the day, you must now pick the time of day. Would you like to have your wedding in the morning, the afternoon or the evening? Here again, consider your personal preferences, the availability of your chosen site for the ceremony, the availability of your wedding party, and any of the requirements of your religion. Check, too, on the customs in your area. (Your clergyman can tell you what

46

is customary in your town.)

If any of your attendants or guests must travel some distance to the site of the ceremony, this must influence your choice. Weddings are quite often held on weekends, but if a weekend date prevents you from holding either the wedding or the reception in a place you have your heart set on, think about an evening wedding during the week. Remember, however, that your guests may not all be able to linger if you schedule a weekday night.

Travel considerations

Consider, too, the lighting, for it can affect the mood and quality of your wedding photos. You'll want your pictures to be as beautiful as possible, of course. Some say that it's best to have your picture taken in the morning because when you wake up you are the freshest and your complexion is the nicest. This may be true, and this may not be true of you; on the other hand, it may be true that later in the day the lighting in the ceremony area is better. You might go to the church or the hotel or wherever it is you've planned to be married and check the lighting at various times of the day to see when you think it the most beautiful.

Another factor to consider is the degree of formality. If you intend to have an informal wedding—perhaps in your church or a small chapel, your home, club, garden, or hotel—you may want to have it early in the day. Then your reception, if you choose to have one, could also be informal. You could serve cocktails and hors d'oeuvres in the middle of the afternoon rather than a formal sit-down luncheon or dinner. A formal wedding might be either early in the morning with a reception-luncheon following, or it might be later, in the afternoon with a full-course dinner served afterward or in the evening. The same would be true of an ultra-formal wedding.

How formal

Money, also, is an important consideration. The size of your ceremony, your guest list and your reception determine your cost and help you in choosing a time: It is much less costly to have a morning or afternoon wedding reception than to have a large evening wedding complete with full-course dinners. It will cost less to serve punch, cocktails and hors d'oeuvres—perhaps finger sandwiches and such—than it does to serve a full-course meal. The general rule is that the later in the day your party, in this case ceremony or reception, the more likely it is that your guests will drink and eat a lot. Let's face it. After a 10 A.M. wedding, not too many people will feel like drinking or eating much; they are really not quite awake.

After you have considered all of these items and decided which are most important to you, you'll be able to narrow your choice down to a particular month, day and time. But, before you make any announcement, check around and see that the things you'll need— services, sites, et cetera—are available.

Telling people

Confirm the date, and you're ready to inform people. First you tell your respective families, then the members of your wedding party. Inform the clergyman or judge and begin to think about reserving the reception site. Next, contact whoever will be responsible for the reception plans (caterer, or banquet manager), florists and photographers. You should, of course, make up your invitation list as soon as possible. Monumental? Sure! And fun.

6

To Thine Own Self Be True

STYLE AND THEME

NOW THAT YOU HAVE actually set the time and date for your wedding and have decided what your budget will be, it's time for you to choose the kind of look you want your wedding to have. Do you visualize it as extremely formal and elegant? Or do you prefer a more informal wedding, perhaps a smaller group of people with a ceremony in your home and a reception for very close friends and relatives? The day of the set pattern and traditional form for weddings is past. Today, all your imagination and originality may be brought into play in planning a wedding and a reception. The style you choose for a modern wedding should reflect your taste, your personality. With so much leeway, the planning of your wedding can be an exciting and creative project.

Before making any decisions, you should know

51

what the different types of weddings are. There is much confusion on this subject, as quite often books will break down weddings into so many categories that they can be difficult to follow. As far as I'm concerned, there are only *three* types of weddings: informal, formal and ultra-formal. Now you may say, "Well, what about garden weddings? Double weddings? Military weddings?" These are merely variations on the three basic types. If you plan a wedding which is a variation, familiarize yourself with the three types here, and then apply one of them to your own special needs.

The formality of a wedding is determined by the number of guests, the number of attendants and the choice of items like stationery, reception decorations and menu. If you wish, you can have a highly informal wedding done in a very grand style—perhaps all your guests very dressy, with you in a floor-length gown with a long, cathedral train. The site you choose for any type of wedding is equally flexible. In this day and age, an ultra-formal wedding need not be held in the largest church in town with fourteen bridesmaids in attendance; it can take place in your own home if you choose.

Regardless of size or how you personalize your wedding, there are three basic styles: informal, formal and ultra-formal. Let's discuss these as a starting point.

The informal wedding

An informal wedding generally has a maid of honor, a best man and one usher or groomsman for every fifty guests, to seat them. Bridesmaids are optional. (See Chapter 9 for hints on choosing your bridal party.) Your ceremony could take place in a church, chapel, synagogue, home, private club, garden or hotel. You could have a limited number of guests, say from fifty to seventy-five people. As far as your invitations are concerned, it's up to you whether you want to send a printed or handwritten type. Generally, it's easier to send printed invitations if you're inviting a large number of people; if you're inviting a small number, you might find it just as easy and as nice to send handwritten ones. (More on invitations in Chapter 11.) Decorations need not be elaborate. You could stay with flowers and paper ribbons which are less expensive to buy and are nice to have as mementoes after the big day is over. A reception for an informal wedding is optional. If you decide you want one, you can have the reception at the ceremony's location or you can move to a different site.

For formal weddings you could have a maid of honor, a best man, one usher for every fifty guests, and approximately four bridesmaids and a flower girl. Your ceremony again can be in a church, synagogue, home, et cetera. You could have a fairly limited number of guests, say from fifty to one hundred and fifty. Most likely for a formal wedding you would want to have printed or engraved invitations with reception enclosure cards. You can have more elaborate decorations and flowers for the ceremony itself; and a formal wedding is generally followed by a reception. This can be as elaborate or as simple as you wish, although usually it's a buffet dinner, breakfast or luncheon.

The formal wedding

An ultra-formal wedding might feature more attendants—a maid of honor, a best man, an usher for every fifty guests, six to fourteen bridesmaids (this number might include junior bridesmaids, though), a ring-bearer and a flower girl. If a church ceremony, it is generally longer and more involved than the ceremonies mentioned above, and the number of guests is limitless: from 150 to 400 or even 500 people. Your invitations would be engraved, as would the reception invitations. If you're inviting enormous numbers you might want to include pew cards in the invitations. These cards indicate the seating for your friends and relatives. (For definitions and procedures involved, refer to Chapter 11.) An ultra-formal wedding would have the most lavish decorations. You might have a church canopy from the church to the sidewalk, pew

The ultra-formal wedding

ribbons, an aisle carpet and decorations limited only by your imagination and your budget.

How to decide   One of the ways to decide whether or not you want your wedding to be large or small, formal or in-·formal, is to ask yourself the question: What kind of parties and occasions do I enjoy the most? Do I really prefer an informal gathering, or do I like something like a formal dance, which is highly structured and organized? How do I enjoy myself the most in an evening with friends? How does my fiancé enjoy himself the most? This may help you decide if you want an extremely large wedding or a small one. Perhaps you're most comfortable at a small informal party. If this is true, then you may want to have an informal wedding in your parents' home.

Double wedding   As far as a double wedding goes, it's more a problem of logistics than anything else. You may be able to have the same number of people and the same amount of food, liquor and decorations, but you will have to consider such things as a double processional and recessional and how to set up your reception lines. (See Chapter 23 for advice.) These are the practical aspects of planning your wedding, the differences that you need to be aware of. The fact that you have a double wedding should not influence the formality decision. You can have any style agreed upon by both brides.

Military wedding   The same choice is true of a military wedding. They also vary in type. I went to one military wedding that was a very pleasant combination of formal and informal. The wedding ceremony itself was held in a small New England church, with no more than eighty people attending. It was very brief, very simple, and very lovely. The groom and the ushers were dressed in their uniforms, and the bride, who had four bridesmaids, was dressed in a traditional white gown. A combination of two types, the wedding was beautifully done, as was the reception that followed. Held in a country garden, the reception had no formal receiving line: The guests came in and milled around and laughed and talked and had refreshments. There were formal toasts to the bride and groom and the guests were dressed in cocktail attire (not tails, et cetera; the men wore business suits and the women were in dressy gowns). So you see, a military wedding doesn't have to be strictly formal. It can be any one or any combination of the three types.

Once you have decided on the formality of your wedding you should begin to consider the *style* that you want. A style is a way of expressing your personality: It's a manner or an expression characteristic of an individual, a period in time, or even of a national or ethnic group.

Choosing a style

In order to make the happiest artistic choices throughout the wedding period, you ought to know as much as possible about yourself, your preferences and your tastes. Plan your wedding around a good self-knowledge. In other words, begin by questioning yourself about the various areas that concern you—the kinds of music you like, the flowers, the gowns.

Know yourself

Are you a romantic who loves laces and frills and the look of the Old South? You may want to have your gown designed after something that might have been worn in *Gone With the Wind*—a very beautiful hoopskirted dress made of yards and yards of Chantilly lace. With your gentlemen dressed in tuxedoes and your bridesmaids in wide picture hats, you can have a formal wedding in a feminine and romantic mood.

You may be a sophisticate who prefers unfrilly, highly stylized lines. For you, a gown very simple in design, perhaps a floor-length toga of classic line, in a soft, elegant fabric.

The all-American you who loves hot dogs and cheerleading can carry American Beauty roses, just right for an American Beauty Girl, and complete the look by using shades of pink and rose throughout.

Elizabethan

Are you a history buff? Why not have your wedding reflect a favorite period? Let's assume that you like the Elizabethan era. How would you apply this to the look of your wedding? Actually, it can be done very beautifully. You might want to use music that would have the quality of that time, perhaps featuring musical instruments such as the harpsichord. You may be adventuresome and have period entertainment at your reception, possibly a couple giving a demonstration of the minuet. Of course, you could have great fun in choosing your gown and those of your attendants: You could use the more regal colors such as violets and purples, also rich dark reds with gold accents; for fabrics, a velvet or a lush, rich satin. To complete the regal look, you could have your headdress in the shape of a crown. Flowers could be arranged in a tapestry effect, like a backdrop for your ceremony, and you might even use actual tapestries as decorations at your reception.

If you do use the Elizabethan style for your wedding, check with the various reference books in the library to see what specialities of food and refreshment were served during weddings in Elizabethan times. Planning a wedding in this style could affect your choice of site for the ceremony; a large cathedral-like church would be apt. You might want to schedule your wedding in the fall so you could make use of heavier fabrics to achieve this Elizabethan look, which is very ornate, very formal, and very regal.

Colonial

Let's say, on the other hand, that you really feel the most comfortable with a Colonial approach to things. Perhaps you like copper pots and cast-iron skillets, cherrywood furniture and marvelous old farm houses with walk-in fireplaces. You may want to have your wedding take place in a small country church, followed by a reception in the garden of a New England-style farmhouse. You could wear a wedding apron of lovely white lace such as the colonial women wore over their wedding gowns, and use wild flowers for your bouquet. A perfect spring wedding, it exudes homeyness and warmth.

Suppose you don't want to go back in time. Let's say that you're quite happy in the era that we live in and your focus is on the future. You're enjoying the beginning of the space age and you want your wedding to reflect the excitement that surrounds us. Why not have a modernistic wedding—clean lines, bright lights, metallic accents. You might design a gown that is utterly simple and futuristic, done in a fluid, silvery material (not lamé) or even a heavy, rich brocade of silver or gold. For your hair, a very stylized ornament, and silver or gold shoes to complete the outfit. Carry this look to the bridal bouquet—plain white flowers (perhaps camellias or a single, large white flower) with silver or gold ribbon streamers—and you'll have an effective atmosphere, particularly for an evening wedding. The total look should be silver or gold, and it should be consistent. Mixing the two together would be too glittery.

Modernistic

The space-age look could be very elegant, and also very easy to achieve. Many party shops have special sections for silver and golden wedding anniversaries where they carry wedding bells and decorations, napkins and a complete line of accessories that you could use for your wedding. This could be particularly nice if you are having your wedding at home and want it to be quite formal and elegant.

Space age

To carry out the space-age look, have a buffet table set with very modern silver or gold pieces, either your own or rented (perhaps belonging to the caterer); avoid tremendously decorative pieces and feature instead serving pieces with clean modern lines to carry out your look. You would want to use cool shades of blue, green and blue-violet. Save the warm colors such as yellow, orange or red for use with gold.

57

Nationality or ethnic style

Another approach to selecting a style for your wedding is to consider a specific nationality or ethnic group—particularly if your family have fond memories of their former country or enjoy various customs begun in their homeland. It would be wise to make sure, of course, that this would not offend your fiancé's family should you be of different backgrounds and heritage. If you would like to give a particular national flavor to your wedding, even though you and your fiancé are not of that particular nationality, this, too, is correct (again, provided no offense is given).

Oriental

An Oriental theme, for example, could be quite effective and very beautiful, and could be incorporated into your wedding plans with ease. A gown which suggests a kimono, perhaps in a white silk brocade, could be combined with characteristics of the Japanese bride's headdress. You might carry pure white cymbidium orchids, and your flower arrangements which decorate the ceremony and reception can be designed simply, in the Oriental manner. You can even use a floral canopy in the altar area, perhaps covered with the sweet-smelling Jasmine blossom which has a lovely fragrance. Jade wedding rings and pearl or jade jewelry as gifts for the attendants would be appropriate here, and your attendants could dress in a pearly tone or in jade green. The Oriental influence could carry over to the reception menu, with a whimsical touch like fortune cookies served with dessert.

Mexican

A Mexican-style wedding can be very exciting. Imagine yourself a Latin lady in a white cotton eyelet Mexican wedding gown. (You can see many examples of the Mexican wedding dress in library reference books.) If you live in the West, you can even arrange to have your ceremony in an old Spanish mission. Your reception could be decorated like a fiesta, with beautiful *piñatas*; have a mariachi band for music; and offer food with a slightly Mexican flavor. You might even have someone demonstrate Mexican dances.

The style of your wedding is up to you, and it deserves a great deal of thought. Try to visualize the total look of your wedding and keep your choices consistent. For example, if you've chosen the Elizabethan look, it would be jarring to have your bridesmaids appear in mini-skirts. If your dominant color is green, avoid using secondary colors that would not be harmonious. A bouquet of light and airy flowers would not look right with a gown that was extremely elaborate and ornate. Decide what your total look should be and check each of the things that you choose along the way to make sure it fits in with your total wedding style. Everything your guests hear, see, eat and drink is part of the total look you're trying to create.

Visualize your style

Be not only consistent but also exercise good taste. In general, it's better to use a small number of good quality items than a large number of the mediocre. For example, a bridal bouquet made up of masses of inexpensive flowers is never as tasteful as a single high-quality flower. It may not necessarily cost more than the other arrangement, but it's in better taste. The same idea applies to music, food and all the other components of your wedding. A small amount of something good can go a long way: Quality, not quantity, is most important.

As you discuss your wedding with your parents, you may find that your ideas are very different from theirs. You'll probably be working closely with your mother throughout the planning stages, and she'll have many wise suggestions to make. But often mothers are guided by the traditions that have governed weddings in the past.

You and your parents

Traditions can be beautiful additions to a wedding, but they are also sometimes based on superstitions that are not very sensible. For example, the bride is *not* supposed to wear a gown of any color but white, nor is she supposed to personally take part in her own wedding rehearsal. You'll see when you come to the chapters on wedding gowns and wedding rehearsals that I don't agree with these taboos. Even in *this* chapter there may be notions which appeal to you but not to your family.

It will require lots of love and tact to discuss your plans and ideas with your parents, for you may meet with opposition. With your help they will be wise enough to understand that you are trying to establish new traditions, and if you sincerely want to use these suggestions to make your wedding special and individual, they will cooperate because they want you to be happy.

Do all you can to make your wedding a happy occasion that expresses you and your personality in every possible way: Pick the type and style *you* like, and your wedding will be uniquely your own special celebration.

Part Two

GETTING ORGANIZED

7

Sitting "Perty"

SCHEDULING AND ORGANIZATION

THERE'S SO MUCH TO DO, how can I possibly find the time to do it all? You wouldn't be the first bride to ask that question. Here you are with a whole book about what has to be done, and it might seem discouraging. If you make up a list of everything that has to be done, it will seem even more overwhelming. You might feel really discouraged and not know where to start. But hold on, this problem, too, can be solved; and the solution is simple. You do just *one thing* at a time, step by step. Start at the beginning, and before you know it, everything will be done.

As with any complicated project, every decision depends upon another one. For example, you will want to know your overall color scheme for your reception before you choose your flowers and decorations. And you will need to know who will perform your ceremony and where it is to be before you hire a band or a caterer. Your wedding gown must be delivered before you have your bridal portrait taken. So, if you stick to the idea of first things first, you won't waste your time and energy on doing things twice or in the wrong order. You won't find yourself boxed-in by time schedules or last-minute choices for things that should have been well planned and leisurely.

Where will you find the answer to your problem? Strangely enough in the business world. Businessmen, for a number of years, have been using an idea that really works to help them solve their problems. Their solution to handling complex problems is a system called PERT. PERT is an abbreviation for Program Evaluation and Review Technique. That's a rather fancy name for a basically simple procedure which makes use of giant charts and, sometimes, computers to schedule everything from sending astronauts to the moon to the construction of huge office buildings. If it can work so well for such tremendously involved undertakings, why can't it work for the planning, organizing and scheduling of a wedding?

The answer is it can and does. Planning your wedding is not nearly as complex as sending a man to the moon, but the problems can seem as great. Particularly if you've never even helped plan a wedding before. Fortunately the solution to your problems is available. The answer is a simplified form of the PERT system.

There's no mystery to understanding and using the PERT ideas. Basically, all it involves is the breaking down of the various large stages of planning your wedding into smaller parts. Each of these smaller parts can then be handled individually, in an organized way until every part (and soon your wedding itself) is completed. All the arrangements will then be finished in the proper order and, most importantly, *on time*.

You can do all of the planning, shopping and arranging for your wedding and not end each day feeling weary and confused. Ready to start? OK. All of the information you'll need to organize your wedding is available in our version of the PERT chart. There's a blank chart in the back of this book, and a sample chart for you to look at in this chapter. The sample chart is on page 68.

As you look at it you'll see that there are seven sections across the top of the chart, each with an amount of time listed. For example, the first section is called *The First Steps*, and has 4 to 8 months as the amount of time suggested for everything in this section to be completed. Along the left-hand side of the chart are listed the general types of activities you will need to be concerned with during each particular amount of time: Ceremony, Reception, Photography, Gifts and Honeymoon. There are many things to be done within each of these categories, and during a certain amount of time.

There are seven sections

Here's where the PERT system comes in handy. Each type of thing that has to be done is listed in the order in which it should be completed. For example: The first box under the column *Getting Organized* contains seven different items. All of them should be completed within 3 to 6 months before your wedding. When they are, you can move on to the next column, called *Moving Ahead*, to complete the items listed in this column, and so on until the *Your Wedding Week* column. That's where things really begin to be fun. You can pretty much take it easy at this point and enjoy your wedding week and wedding day, and beyond.

Now to get organized

It's up to you to decide how much time you have —or is necessary—to complete all the items in each column. And when you decide, you place the times in each of the first four columns on your chart and you are ready to begin.

Your WEDDING ORGANIZER is just like your

WEDGING BUDGET PLANNER. Take out your copy, fill it in and carry it with you as you shop and plan. So take yours and fill in the amounts of time you have to spend as you begin working on your wedding. Check the box after each item as you complete that item, and you'll have a constant record of your progress. Also read the chapter listed after each item for all the information you'll need to know. If you follow the time sections in sequence, you'll automatically be doing things in the right order; and at the same time, you will be making steady and sure progress that you *can see*. And if you have extra time, you can even get ahead by doing something in the next column. Feel free to delete the items that don't apply to your wedding or to add any new ideas you may have. The first main section on the chart for you to consider is the *Ceremony*. This is probably what you will think of first when you think of planning your wedding anyway. You are no doubt engaged right now, and have been for some time, whether you have a ring or engagement party or you just decide that you are now engaged and will soon be married. You may now begin to look for a wedding ring for yourself—and possibly for your fiancé. And even before you set your date, you will have to consider your budget. How much money you can plan to spend for what is crucial. You can't begin even basic plans until you know what you can spend. You will next set your wedding date and that's a lot of fun—after all you are choosing the date that will be your anniversary for many years to come. Now you have finished your basic ceremony plans, and you are ready to start getting organized.

Your ceremony is first

It's time to make up your guest list, which will include all of your wedding party and relatives—both yours and his—in short, everybody that you want to share your happy day with. After that you can begin to select your attendants and your fiancé will do the same. You will choose bridesmaids, maid of honor, and a flower girl if you like. If you feel that you are really

There are lots of choices

bogged down after making these first decisions, you can get the help of a bridal consultant, who can take over from here and handle everything for you if you like. Personally, I recommend that you do your own wedding planning. This way, you're sure to have things the way you want them and to get a good price for the items and services that you need. Plus it's good experience. You're soon to be a home manager, and you'll have new responsibilities—happy ones, true—but many routine. So it's best to get your experience in advance.

You can buy your wedding stationery next—in the styles and colors that you like best—and begin to plan for shopping for that all-important wedding dress. Bridesmaids' dresses to match your gown are your next selection. And once they are selected, you can begin choosing the site where they will be worn.

Choosing a ceremony site and a clergyman or judge to perform your ceremony should be done at about the same time. If you are a member of a congregation, you will probably be married by your clergyman at your place of worship. If not, you may select a clergyman or judge and a site that you particularly like—perhaps one of the unusual ones mentioned in the chapter on selecting a wedding site.

The rest of your ceremony plans will become easy now—they are simply a matter of choosing the special touches that will make your wedding even more lovely. You'll select flowers, decorations and music and begin giving thought to how you want the wedding party to walk in the processional and recessional.

Add special touches

One to two months before your wedding you can mail your carefully-addressed invitations and pick up your gown—or at least check on the delivery date. Plan a formal or informal procession to the church for the members of the wedding party and yourself. Wedding showers may be given for you at this time, so shop for a pretty dress for these first parties—and for the many more to come.

	THE FIRST STEPS 4 to 8 Months	GETTING ORGANIZED 3 to 6 Months	MOVING AHEAD 2 to 3 Months
CEREMONY	Tell friends and relatives about engagement 1 ☐ Buy engagement and wedding rings 3 ☐ Plan budget 4 ☐ Set date 5 ☐ Choose wedding style 6 ☐ Organize ceremony 7 ☐	Make up guest list 8 ☐ Select attendants 9 ☐ Hire bridal consultant 10 ☐ Select/order stationery 11 ☐ Buy gown 15 ☐ Buy bridesmaids' gowns 16 ☐ Reserve ceremony site 18 ☐ Choose clergyman 19 ☐	Talk with clergyman (get marriage license) 19 ☐ Order ceremony flowers 21 ☐ Arrange for ceremony music and words 22 ☐ Plan processional, ceremony, recessional and reception line 23 ☐
RECEPTION	Organize reception 7 ☐	Pick reception site 25 ☐	Order reception flowers 27 ☐ Order reception refreshments 28 ☐ Order wedding cake 30 ☐
PHOTOGRAPHS	Have engagement photograph taken 1 ☐		Reserve ceremony photographer 20 ☐ Reserve reception photographer 26 ☐
GIFTS		Order informals 11 ☐ Write thank you's 12 ☐	Plan new home 13 ☐ Register china, crystal and silver patterns 14 ☐
HONEYMOON	Talk out doubts 2 ☐		Get information and make honeymoon reservations 17 ☐

THE FINAL STAGES _1_ to _2_ Months	YOUR WEDDING WEEK	YOUR WEDDING DAY	AND BEYOND
Send out invitations 11 ☐ Pick up wedding gown 15 ☐ Plan procession to the ceremony site 24 ☐ Attend bridal showers 33 ☐	Schedule and attend wedding rehearsal and rehearsal dinner 32 ☐ Entertain out-of-town guests 33 ☐ Attend more bridal showers and bridesmaids' luncheon 33 ☐	Dress for wedding day 35 ☐	
Confirm number of wedding guests 28 ☐ Choose reception music 29 ☐	Confirm final number of wedding guests 28 ☐	Take part in wedding ceremony and reception 36 ☐ Mail wedding announcements 11 ☐	
Arrange for bridal portrait 31 ☐			Order wedding album 26 ☐
	Move belongings to new home 13 ☐		Return wedding gifts and finish thank you's 12 ☐
Pick up tickets and hotel confirmation 17 ☐	Pack for honeymoon 17 ☐	Leave for honeymoon 37 ☐	Enjoy new married life 38 ☐

Now plan your reception

As you begin your engagement and your basic ceremony planning, your thoughts will naturally go to your wedding *Reception*, so this is the next section on the chart. It's a great party and a great celebration of your wedding ceremony. To begin this planning, you will choose your reception site and reserve it. And then start to think about the food and drink to be served at your party. Also, talk with your florist about flowers and decorations for your reception, and order the little extras like printed napkins and matches for your guests to keep as mementos. All this will be topped off by choosing a luscious wedding cake—maybe even baking one yourself. All this arranged, you can practically forget your reception until your wedding day. The basic planning is best done in the early stages of your wedding preparations, by confirming your plans with your caterer, party rental company suppliers, or with your banquet manager and maître d'. Thus you will be free to enjoy your wedding week and all the parties that will no doubt be given in your honor.

Photographs are a must

The third section is *Photography*. Photographs are not only traditional, they are essential. You must have some kind of photographs of your wedding day— they record an event that is so beautiful and meaningful in your life—and they can never be taken again. This is one item in your life that you can't afford not to splurge on.

Photographs can begin with your engagement announcement. Even if you don't plan to have a formal announcement of your engagement in the newspaper, have some kind of engagement photo taken for your scrapbook. Your major decision about a photographer will come later—when you choose one to take the photos at your ceremony and reception and to take your all-important bridal portrait. The choice of a photographer is very important, so be sure to check the chapters about choosing the best photographer possible. The result will be photographs bound in a lovely album for you to enjoy again and again.

Gifts follow photography and are certainly one of the nicest things about a wedding. And you'll see lots of them as you go through the weeks and months of your wedding—it really gets to be like a giant birthday party, all for you. It's great fun, but there are some things you'll have to do, too. You'll have to write thank-you notes and record each gift. Also, you'll want to register your patterns of china, crystal and silver—three important choices—so guests can buy these lovely gifts if they like. You'll also want to do some basic planning for your new home. Both of these things can be done whenever you have the time, but the sooner the better. Also, it's wise to keep up with your thank-you notes for your wedding gifts so that you won't have a great number to catch up on during your honeymoon or after. Thank you's should begin with your first engagement gift, if at all possible.

Gifts are great fun

The fifth section is your *Honeymoon* and I'm sure it doesn't have to be checked off any list. I'm sure you'll enjoy your chance to be alone together in many weeks and have a lovely time. There will be fun things to do when you return from your honeymoon, too. As a new wife, you have all the pleasure of arranging your new home exactly as *you* and *your husband* like it and, of course, of finishing those last few thank-you notes and ordering your wedding album from the proofs that should soon be ready. When you've returned your last few unusable gifts, you can settle back into your new way of life.

Honeymoon plans

All five sections—Ceremony, Reception, Photography, Gifts and Honeymoon—require basic planning and lots of doing—but they are worth it, because they will lead to the greatest of all weeks, your wedding week.

Your wedding week

Your wedding week will be one of the most joyous and the most busy of all the weeks in your life. It

71

will be filled with fun, parties and anticipation, and may begin with a last bridal shower, your bridesmaids' luncheon or his bachelor party. Mixed in with these parties you may have special parties and dinners with out-of-town guests and close family and friends. Your wedding rehearsal and rehearsal dinner will be a highlight of this special week, and may even be scheduled the night before your big day.

Last-minute checks

Your wedding reception should be in your thoughts this week, too. You should confirm all last minute details with your caterer or maître d'—including giving him the final count of the number of guests that you expect to attend. Check all other plans with your mother and father or any other person you may have appointed to take care of the reception for you. Otherwise, make a last-minute check with the florist, photographer, musicians and baker.

An exciting part of your wedding week is moving all of your belongings and gifts to your new home. Everything but you, at this point. And it won't be long until you move in, too. The last part of your evening before your wedding day is usually spent packing the last-minute articles needed for your honeymoon. And you might remind your fiancé to make the last confirmation of your travel plans, or tell him in person—before midnight, if you're superstitious. And think your last sweet thoughts before you go to sleep the last night alone as a Miss.

Your wonderful wedding day

Your wedding day is like the first day of school, Christmas morning and the moment you got engaged, all rolled into one. It will be a wonderful day for you. Everything you've planned for and worked with become real and meaningful today—and your life will change soon. Time will go by so quickly you will hardly blink before you and *he* are standing together at the altar taking the vows that will make you man and wife.

You'll get dressed and made up with great assurance—ignoring the butterflies in your stomach—slip into your wedding gown, and before you barely turn around, walk down the aisle to meet the man who will soon be your husband.

Others will take over as you go through your ceremony. All the details you have handled will be complete and ready. After your happy ceremony the party will really begin. Your reception will be brimming with happy people—and the happiest of all will be you and your husband. All the merriment will reach a happy crescendo and shouts of "Good-bye, have a wonderful honeymoon." Yes, your wedding day will be over, but your honeymoon will be just beginning.

You can be this happy, organized bride on your *real* wedding day by using your WEDDING ORGANIZER. As you get closer and closer to your ultimate goal, you will see how everything begins to fall into place. You'll be not only a radiant bride, but also a confident one, because you'll know that everything will be beautifully ready and easily completed for your wedding—on time.

8

Who Should We Ask?

THE INVITATION LIST

YOU'LL WANT TO START making up your guest list early, as you will need it when ordering the invitations, planning the ceremony and reception, and sending out announcements. How do you—where do you—begin to do this? First, make up a list of all of your friends and relatives whom you intend to invite. Then add the members of the wedding party, including both sets of parents, and the clergyman or the judge who will perform the ceremony. (Although you may not know his name at this point, you know that you will want to send him an invitation to keep for a souvenir. Of course, he and the others are going to know they're invited, but it is a nice remembrance to send them a formal invitation.) It's easiest to compile this kind of list initially on one long sheet of paper; when you

75

come up with your final list, then you'll find it best to transfer the information to 3 by 5 inch index cards (more on this later).

Your list and his

Once you have started making up your own list, ask your fiancé and/or his mother to begin making up theirs; eventually, both lists will be brought together, compared and, probably, trimmed. There may be duplications and you might have to invite certain people to the ceremony only, rather than to both the ceremony and the reception. Also, you may be sending announcements to people who will not be invited to the wedding.

Have in mind the approximate number of guests you want and give this number to your fiancé. Tell him, for instance, that you expect to invite about two hundred people. This gives his family a guideline. Generally the bride's family invites more people than the groom's family. This doesn't have to be so, but quite often it is the case; thus by telling his family that you expect two hundred guests in total, they know that they might invite roughly fifty to seventy-five friends and relatives.

Check both lists together

Once both lists are completed, you and your fiancé should check for duplications. Adjust these and get an approximate total number. If this number surpasses to any extent the number of people you had originally intended to invite, both sides must meet to decide which names can be eliminated. This needn't be a hassle. The nice way to handle it is for everyone concerned to get together for coffee in an informal atmosphere and talk things over.

The groom's family

If the families do not live near each other, and it's not possible for them to get together, then you and your mother should make up your list first. Make sure you have everyone provided for, and set aside a few extra invitations for anyone you might have forgotten. Compare your list with the total number of guests you want to invite, subtract the number of guests on your list from that number, and come up with the number of guests that your fiancé's family can invite. Write to your fiancé's mother and give her this information. Ask her to send her list to you as soon as possible, perhaps giving a certain date. If it's financially possible, it would be nice to call her on this occasion and talk to her personally. But in either case be warm and pleasant about it. Don't be uncomfortable about having to do this—she'll understand the problems involved.

If when you're working on your list you find that you have too many people, you might consider some of the following ideas on how to decide whom to eliminate.

People may tell you that you *must* invite all your own relatives. I don't think this is necessary. It's nice if it's possible, but if it would be financially difficult to entertain and accommodate all your relatives, don't ask them. The same is true if you are not particularly close to them and have not been for some time. If they are distant, either in lineage or in number of miles, don't feel obligated to invite them. Relatives should be handled like friends. If you would enjoy having them share your happiness, invite them; if not, don't.

When considering friends, ask yourself if you have seen them within the last year. Are you really close? This is not a time to pay back social obligations to acquaintances. Believe me, I made that mistake, and it's not a wise thing to do. If it gets down to a fine line, ask the friends who are close to both you *and* your fiancé in preference to a group of your college or high school friends he may never have met.

It may seem difficult to you to exclude anyone, and you may feel bad and worry about hurting someone. Don't. Frankly, you'll look back on your wedding day and remember the people who were closest to you. These are the people you won't forget to invite, and you won't forget them after you're married either.

Unless you are particularly close to them, friends or business associates of your parents really have no

Relatives

Friends

77

place at your wedding: It's much more important to have your friends and close relatives around to share your happiness. It is embarrassing for the bride and the guest not to know each other as they meet in the reception line—a situation which is not pleasant for the bride or the guest.

Don't overlook . . .   Make sure you haven't forgotten anyone. Is there a teacher from your school days with whom you still correspond and visit? A younger sister of a friend who admires you tremendously and of whom you are fond? People such as these are often thrilled that you have remembered them, and their joy at your marriage will be as great as that of some of your more intimate friends.

When making out your wedding list, keep in mind friends far away to whom you might want to send an invitation. Most likely they won't be able to come, but they will enjoy receiving your invitation and be sure to keep it as a memento. Just be certain you don't include them in your final count.

You might also want to invite the parents of your bridesmaids and ushers, particularly if your attendants are people you've grown up with and you know their parents well. A courteous gesture like this can mean so much.

Your final list   After you've combined both lists, checked for duplications and made sure you've invited people you really care about, you will have your final list of wedding guests which you will use to order your invitations and announcements and eventually to inform all those who will be involved with wedding arrangements. Not every invitee will attend, of course. The number of guests will grow smaller as the wedding day approaches, and as you receive your acceptances and regrets, you'll eventually have a realistic number with which to work. Because of last-minute cancellations, try to estimate carefully how many people will actually attend. Although it's proper to write to the bride to accept or regret her invitation, many people don't. So keep any caterer, banquet manager or person in charge of handling your reception plans informed of both the actual number you expect and the estimated number of last-minute arrivals and cancellations.

When you have your final list, you might want to transfer it to 3 by 5 inch file cards. On each card, list the name, address and phone number of the guest and indicate whether he accepts or regrets. At the bottom of the card, note any gifts received (engagement, wedding, shower) and whether a thank-you card has already been sent. This is a good system and can be kept in alphabetical order in a small file box, providing you with a handy and complete record of invitations and gifts sent and acknowledged. You can keep your card file after your wedding to use for a Christmas or holiday card list for your first holidays together as "Mr. and Mrs." Without guessing, you can send a card to everyone who attended your wedding.

Now that you have a complete list, you can get on to the more engrossing business of selecting your bridal party and planning the wedding itself. And remember: Every step brings you closer to your wedding day!

A handy system

79

9

The Bridal Party

THE BEST MAN, MAID OF HONOR AND OTHERS

CHOOSE YOUR WEDDING ATTENDANTS with care. Since they share a position of honor, they should be people who mean something to you—friends, relatives, anyone you love.

The bride's attendants often include a maid (matron) of honor, bridesmaids, junior bridesmaids, a flower girl, a train-bearer and a ring-bearer.

Your maid (matron) of honor may be your sister, a close girl friend or a particularly dear relative. If you are close to your mother, you might ask her to be matron of honor at a small wedding. This would be lovely, particularly if you have planned your own wedding and she won't be heavily burdened with last minute details. If she is free and you want her to be part of your wedding party, choosing your mother as matron of honor could be both beautiful and meaningful.

Maid of honor

A problem that sometimes arises is whom to choose as maid of honor when you have both a sister and a very close friend. How do you handle this situation? You can have two maids of honor, or a maid and a matron, who would walk down the aisle together. During the ceremony, one can help lift your veil while the other holds your flowers or gloves. Both girls would thus be honor attendants and both would be pleased to be a part of your wedding.

Bridesmaids are usually your close friends or relatives, and you might, as a courtesy, invite the sister or sisters of your fiancé to be bridesmaid(s) in your wedding; a simple thing, it shows your friendliness toward your in-laws-to-be. If your fiancé has more than one sister and you want to ask only one to participate, go by the rule of inviting the sister who is closest to you in age. But don't ignore the others. Ask them to assist you in some informal way, such as taking care of your guest book at the reception. If your fiancé has many sisters, it will be difficult to include them all, but if there are only two or three in the family, extending these courtesies is not only a possible, but an extremely kind gesture.

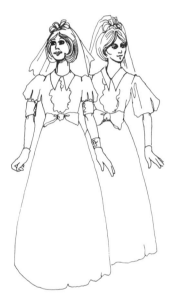

Junior bridesmaid

A junior bridesmaid is usually a young girl— friend or relative—whom you want as an attendant, but who is younger than your other bridesmaids. As a member of the bridal party, she would perform the same duties as the other maids and attend the same festivities. She is differentiated only by her age.

Flower girl

If you have a young sister, a small cousin or niece, or if you are particularly fond of the daughter of a friend, you may want to include her as flower girl. The ring-bearer, though usually a boy, can be any young child. Generally he is a brother or cousin of the bride or groom. Although children are cute and always seem to produce "ahs" from the guests, be sure you think through the idea of having a child in your wedding party before saying, "How lovely! I'll ask Susie." Consider the hour of the wedding and the child's personality before you get carried away with the notion of including any young person in your wedding party.

The groom's attendants usually include a best man and ushers. His best man can be anyone he is fond of—his brother or a close friend, a cousin or an uncle, even his father. If your fiancé and your own brother have become close, your brother might well be invited to fill this role.

Best man

The ushers are generally friends of the groom, although there is usually at least one usher (often called the "bride's usher") who is a brother or relative of the bride. For a large wedding, have approximately one usher for every fifty guests, or one usher per bridesmaid if you want to pair them off for the processional and recessional. Although pairs are attractive, it is not essential to have one groomsman or usher for every bridesmaid. There are ways of grouping an odd number of attendants for the processional and recessional no matter what the total number might be. Keep this in mind if an usher or a bridesmaid has to decline at the last minute, perhaps even after ordering the tuxedo or gown for the occasion. There are always ways to rearrange the processional and recessional to accommodate this emergency. (See Chapter 23 for specific suggestions.)

Ushers

The number of attendants you select is, of course, up to you. As a general rule, the larger and more formal your wedding, the more bridesmaids and groomsmen you would have. But be sure, before you make your selections, that you consider the cost. After all, it *is* more expensive to buy gifts for ten or twelve attendants than it is for four or five. If you intend to purchase the bridesmaids' gowns as a gift to them, you might want to have fewer maids than you would if you were expecting the girls to buy their own. Check the finances with your parents and choose a workable num-

How many attendants?

ber of attendants who will add to the joyousness of the occasion.

After you have decided what kind of attendants you want and who they will be, draw up a list of the wedding party, making sure you have forgotten no one, and discuss it thoroughly with your parents and your fiancé (and his parents whenever possible). If you have too many attendants, different unofficial duties can be assigned to some of those you've put on your original list. Once you have discussed all the possibilities and settled on your final choices, you can begin inviting your attendants.

Inviting them

It's most courteous to invite your attendants in person, but if this is not possible, call them on the phone or send them a special letter. Be sure that you do not "sort of ask" someone to be in your wedding. Make it a definite thing. Don't rush out the day you get engaged and ask the first girl friend you run into to be in your wedding; it may work out that you don't want to invite her after all and you have already made a commitment. Make up the list of your bridesmaids first, and then invite them. (Your groom should follow the same procedure in inviting his ushers.) It's wise to include possible alternate attendants on this original list in case your first-choice attendants cannot accept. Begin asking people right away. Give them the approximate date and tell them as soon as possible if you expect them to buy or rent their own apparel. If you intend to buy the bridesmaids' gowns, it's also good to inform them of this as it may influence their decision to accept or decline your offer.

Expenses

Traditionally, the attendants are expected to pay for their wedding clothes and accessories and their travel expenses. If any one or all of your attendants are coming from out of town, where will they stay? Can they afford lodging in your area? Can you have them stay in your home? Or would you be able to provide a place for them with a friend or relative of yours? These problems must be given thought.

The duties of the attendants are explained in Chapter 34. Remember for now, though, that you should communicate well with your attendants all through the pre-wedding period. Tell them exactly what help is needed in the days preceding the wedding, and let them know what is expected of them in regard to parties and spending money—especially if they live some distance from you. Remember: You are in the hometown where all the plans are being made, and you are aware of the total scheme of things. But unless they are part of the immediate family, your attendants are probably not. Keep them posted. It's even a nice idea, for example, when you make up a list of people to invite to your shower, to include the names of your bridesmaids as well as your mother and your mother-in-law-to-be so that, even if they cannot attend, they will feel they are part of the wedding festivities. You might have the hostess write on the invitation, "I just wanted you to know that if you were here, we'd want you to attend."

If you make your attendants an integral part of your wedding, you will find yourself on your wedding day surrounded by devoted assistance—the very reason for the existence of "the wedding attendant."

Good communications

10

Getting Help

SHOULD YOU USE A CONSULTANT

IF YOU ARE WONDERING how you are going to get everything done in time for your wedding, you may want to consider seriously taking advantage of the services of people who can help you plan your wedding and take many of your responsibilities onto their shoulders. One such person would be a bridal consultant.

Bridal consultants are women who can be found in the bridal salon of a department store, in smaller stores featuring bridal stationery or bridal gowns, or even in a church office. They also sometimes maintain their own offices solely for the purpose of planning and supervising weddings.

The bridal consultant is just that: a consultant to the bride. She can advise you on the various aspects of the wedding—everything from choosing your wedding gown and attire for the wedding party to selecting invitations. She can actually come to your wedding to assist you, helping you to dress or even overseeing the reception.

Where to find her

How she can help

Often, the bridal consultant is a saleswoman who specializes in a particular area. In the stationery department of a large department store, for example, you may find a bridal consultant to advise you regarding your choice of invitations, announcements and personal stationery. In the housewares or home furnishings department, they may have a bridal consultant who can help you determine your requirements for a new home. Another consultant might be in the lingerie department, available to help you plan your personal trousseau, select undergarments, peignoirs, et cetera. A bridal consultant in the linen department will offer advice about coordinating and buying sheets, blankets, towels, tablecloths and all the other paraphernalia needed for setting up housekeeping. The point is, a bridal consultant can be found in many areas of a department store as well as in the many smaller stores that specialize in planning weddings.

A bridal consultant can help you in three different ways. First, she can guide you and help you in choosing the items that she deals with, whether they be gowns, lingerie, housewares or, in the case of a bridal secretary, the religious arrangements. Second, she can help by referring you to other suppliers, such as photographers or florists. Even for such things as a band, decorations, someone to make up headpieces for your bridesmaids, or a service for renting tuxedoes she is bound to have her contacts.

Third, she can plan your entire wedding. If you decide to go to a bridal consultant who handles complete wedding arrangements, you can leave to her everything from choosing invitations and having them mailed and addressed to arranging the ceremony itself (coordinating with the church; choosing the dresses, flowers, photographer, music; and managing the reception). This service can be an enormous help, or it can be a disaster. It depends upon the bridal consultant—her abilities, her personality, her knowledge—and whether or not she has a lot of time to devote to your wedding. You must decide if she will devote the proper time to detail and the careful planning of your wedding.

A bridal consultant can help you with many aspects of your wedding, but keep in mind that she can be only as helpful to you as her capabilities allow. You must judge the consultant by your standards. Decide if the woman really has the knowledge, background and experience in the area she's advising you about. Do you like her taste? Or does she seem to be merely agreeing with you and saying yes to any choice you make? In other words, you must determine if the advice she is capable of giving you is of real value.

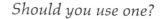

Should you use one?

The decision to use the services of a bridal consultant is completely up to you. No store will force you into it. Usually you don't have to pay for her services if she is in a specific department of a store; her fee is included in the price you pay for any articles you wind up buying from her. A private bridal consultant who oversees many aspects of your wedding may have a set fee, perhaps a certain percentage of the total cost of the wedding. But you should be warned about the consultant's extra source of income, which may be coming directly out of your pocket without your knowing it.

A bridal consultant may casually advise you to use a certain photographer or florist. You may think it's very nice of her to help you with this problem, but what you don't know is that she is probably receiving a percentage of the order you place with the supplier she recommends. On the recommendation of the bridal consultant, you work with a particular wedding photographer and contract to use his services for your wedding. If you place an order of $200 with him, your bridal consultant may be receiving anywhere from 5 percent

Hidden costs

to 15 percent of the sale. And *you're* paying the extra. If the photographer's work makes the recommendation worth that to you, fine. But keep in mind that you are paying extra for this type of referral.

If time's a problem

Using the bridal consultant as a reference service can be helpful to you if time is a problem and it would be impossible for you to check various bands, florists, photographers, et cetera. I wouldn't recommend that you have a bridal consultant handle your wedding completely, unless you have a real time problem and a good deal of money to spend. Even if you are unsure of your taste, you must be very certain that the bridal consultant has good taste and that her choices appeal to you. Remember that if you plan your wedding on your own with the help of your mother, it is sure to reflect you and your personality. Be guided by that instinct which tells you whether or not you *like* a particular bridal consultant. If you "click" with one another in taste and attitude, chances are she will serve you well. If not, she won't do. *Never* allow a bridal consultant to talk you into buying something for your wedding that you don't really like.

Your friendly bridal salon

Special note: A bridal salon located in a department store is not necessarily a part of that store. Many bridal salons are concessions, specialized departments rented by a private retailer. In the event that you have difficulties with the bridal salon within a department store where the bridal salon is a concession, the department store is not actually responsible. It has merely leased its space to the salon and is only a landlord. If you find yourself disappointed by services rendered, remember that you will have to deal directly with the bridal salon in question: you cannot count on the support of the store.

As I have said, a bridal consultant is someone who can be a tremendous help to you, giving advice, referring you to others, or handling your wedding completely. Be very sure that you are choosing the right person if you ask her to do any or all of these things. Remember that the suppliers she recommends often are paying her to do just that, so her recommendation alone is no guarantee of satisfaction. Although my personal suggestion is to do as much of the planning and make as many of the choices as you possibly can for your wedding yourself, you should know that there are wise and useful consulting services available should you need to take advantage of them.

11

The Honour of Your Presence

INVITATIONS AND STATIONERY

ORDERING INVITATIONS, announcements, enclosure cards and informals—all of the wedding stationery that you will be buying—need not be the big problem most people think. It's true that you must settle on number, style and type of wedding stationery, but if you deal with the selection systematically, it won't be a chore. Once you have compiled your list of wedding guests and have set the time and date of your wedding, you are ready to begin.

Basically there are three types of stationery to consider: invitations, to invite guests to your ceremony and/or reception; announcements, to inform guests that your wedding has taken place; and informals to be used for thank-you notes and/or informal invitations or announcements.

Let's begin with wedding invitations since they will probably be your biggest and most important purchase. Wedding invitations are like party invitations in that they contain much of the same information. They tell who is giving the event, what the event is, who it's for, and the day, date, time and place. You will be sending wedding invitations to everyone on your guest list, all members of your wedding party, your officiating clergyman or judge and your family. Plan to keep one for yourself, too.

The wording on a printed or engraved wedding invitation is pretty standard, with a few variations for special cases. For handwritten invitations, see the section on informals. For information about reception invitations (as opposed to ceremony invitations), see the section on enclosure cards.

Wedding invitations   Here is an example of typical wording for an invitation to a wedding ceremony:

Mr. and Mrs. Walter Jones

request the honour of your presence

at the marriage of their daughter

Ellen Deanne

to

Mr. Anthony Brown

on Sunday, the tenth of January

nineteen hundred and seventy

at five o'clock

First Methodist Church

Bowling Green, Ohio

The first line contains the names of the sponsors of your wedding. If a married sister is sponsoring you, the line would have her name, possibly combined with her husband's, and the word "daughter" would be changed to "sister." If your sponsor is an aunt, the first line holds her name, and "daughter" becomes "niece." The word "honour" is spelled in the English manner with an additional *u*. As far as your name is concerned, you may use your first and middle name only, or if you are being sponsored by someone with a different last name from your own, you may have the invitation read "Ellen Deanne Jones." Never use nicknames or pet names. A formal occasion requires formal usage. The next line names the date, and the use of the year on the following line is optional. If you are to be married in a special chapel or a specific room in a large hotel, the name of that chapel or room follows the time line and precedes the name of the cathedral or hotel. If many of your guests are from out of town and might have difficulty finding the ceremony site, a street address may be included on a separate line between the name of the place and the city and state.

Possible wording

In general, you will notice that everything— numbers, middle names and times—is spelled out in full. This is the customary procedure for wedding invitations. The only abbreviations used are Mr., Mrs., Dr. or St. (Saint). If your address has a very long street number, such as 1122 Main Street, you need not write out the number. If your ceremony is to begin at six-thirty, the invitation reads "at half after six" or "at half past six." (Note: You can list the time on your invitation half an hour earlier than you actually plan to begin if you want to make sure all guests will be there on time. If you do this, though, be sure to inform your wedding party and the person who will be officiating at the ceremony, so they can be guided accordingly.)

Everything is spelled out

If your wedding and reception will both take place at the same site—another hall in the community center, another room in the hotel—the same basic form is used with certain minor changes. After you list the time, place and city, add: "and afterwards at the recep-

For ceremony and reception at same site

tion." Include your return address on the outside envelope if you have an R.S.V.P. on the invitation. This is particularly important for out-of-town guests who may not have your parents' correct address.

Some wedding invitations, instead of reading "request the honour of your presence," have a blank line after "of"; and the name of each individual guest is written in by hand. This is more personal, but it also takes much more time. It can be an elegant touch, presuming that your handwriting is neat and pleasant or that you plan to hire a secretary to assist you. Order extra invitations if you plan to have them printed in this manner, as there is a greater chance of error when working by hand.

Guests R.S.V.P. to reception

The R.S.V.P. on an invitation requests a reply to the reception, *not* to the ceremony. The phrase "R.S.V.P." may be printed in the lower left-hand corner, or "The favour (notice the *u*) of a reply is requested" may be written out. "Please respond to," "Please respond" or "Kindly respond" (with your address underneath) are all equally correct.

You will notice that there is no punctuation at the end of each phrase. This causes the guest to take in the information as if it were one continuous sentence. Punctuation can appear within the body of the invitation ("Friday, the tenth of June") but not at the end of a line. If the place is given as "The Beverly Eton Hotel" there is no comma after "Hotel" even though "Los Angeles, California" goes directly beneath it.

Some special wording

There are some cases to use special wording for a wedding invitation. If your fiancé's parents speak a foreign language, it's thoughtful to have an invitation printed or engraved for them in their language. This is a little expensive, but such an invitation is a nice keepsake for them and would show your consideration. You will have to pay for translation as well as printing, so it would be wise to get several bids for this kind of work. You may be able to save by having the translation done by a student of foreign languages.

If you plan to have a double wedding, and the brides are sisters, the invitation would be standard except for the opening lines:

Mr. and Mrs. Leonard Alexander
request the honour of your presence
at the marriage of their daughters
Joan Taylor
to
Robert Patrick Donahue
and
Judith Ann
to
Michael David Purker

If the brides are not sisters, the sponsor line is altered, listing the families in alphabetical order.

Mr. and Mrs. James Roberts
and
Mr. and Mrs. Andrew Thompson
request the honour of your presence
at the marriage of their daughters

And the names of their respective daughters and *their* respective grooms follow. This approach is quite proper, but if the brides are not sisters, you would probably be better advised to send out separate invitations.

If you plan a military wedding, there are some variations to consider for your invitations and announcements. An enlisted man's name and grade can be given two ways:

Staff Sergeant Samuel Morgan Jones
United States Marine Corps

or

Samuel Morgan Jones
Staff Sergeant, United States Marine Corps

Both ways are correct, but never omit his military association or list him as "Mr." Samuel Morgan Jones.

If your fiancé is a reserve officer on active duty, you may include his rank or use "Mr." If you use his rank, it would read:

David Simpson Brown
Lieutenant, Army of the United States

The phrase "Army of the United States" is used only for a reserve officer on active duty.

If he is a regular officer of the Army, Navy, Merchant Marine or Coast Guard, his military rank would appear *instead of* the "Mr.":

Captain Orville Scot
United States Navy

If he wants to list the branch of service, this is added to the second line: "Artillery, United States Army."

A bride in the service would also use her grade or rank, following the same rules that apply to men.

. . . a Catholic ceremony

If you plan a Catholic ceremony, you may want to include certain religious wording in your invitation. The phrase "at the marriage of" may be changed to: "at the marriage in Christ of." The line below the groom's name might read: "and your participation in the offering of the Nuptial Mass." Information about the mass and the fact that the guests may join in would go on a separate card (see the section on enclosure cards). Ask your priest for guidance about proper wording.

Who will be listed as
your sponsor?

Often there is a special situation regarding the wedding sponsorship. Wedding announcements and invitations are issued by the bride's parents if they are living.

If one parent is deceased and the surviving parent has not remarried, he or she alone issues the invitation. When the mother is the sponsor, her married name appears on the first line in full:

Mrs. Horace Swift
requests the honour of your presence

Note that "request" has become plural because only one person is listed as sponsor. When the father is issuing the invitation, the wording is the same, including the change of number. If the surviving parent has re-married, the invitation is issued jointly. When the mother has remarried, the invitation reads:

Mr. and Mrs. Robert Watkins Sterling
request the honour of your presence
at the marriage of Mrs. Sterling's daughter
Susan Anne Seaforth

When the father has remarried, the invitation is identical to the first sample given in this chapter, except that the third line announces the marriage of *his* daughter.

If the parents are separated, then the wedding invitation is issued in the name of the parent one is living with. It's very nice, if the separation is amicable, to have the invitation issued in both names. This is something to discuss with each before one makes a decision.

If parents are separated

If the parents are divorced and neither has remarried, the invitation is issued by one of them. When the mother issues the invitation, she uses a combination of her first name (Mary) and her former husband's last name (Smith), or Mrs. Mary Smith. Her daughter would then be listed as Helen Jean. If the father issues the invitation, his name appears on the first line, and the rest of the information remains the same.

If your legal guardian is sponsoring your wedding, you might have your relationship line read, "at the marriage of their daughter," if your relationship with them is like that of a daughter to parents. You may also omit the relationship line, and have your name written as "Susan Anne Brown" or "Miss Susan Anne Brown" if you prefer.

If you have a guardian

To make it perfectly clear *who* is sponsoring your wedding, include as much of the name as is necessary on the first line. On the second line adjust the number of the word "request" and on the third line list the relationship of the sponsor of the bride.

If you are living away from home and have set up a life of your own, you and your fiancé may want to issue your own invitations:

The honour of your presence is requested
at the marriage of
Miss Cynthia Ann Hamilton

with all other information identical to the first sample.

If you use a professional name and plan to send invitations to people who know you by this name, there are two ways to handle it: (1) You may use both names. If your parents are sponsoring the wedding their names appear on the sponsor line. On the bridal line is the bride's real name, and immediately under that, in parentheses, would be her professional name. The word "Miss" need not be used. (2) You can have your professional name printed on some of the invitations and omitted from others when you place your order with the printer.

If this is the second marriage for the groom but the first for the bride, the wedding stationery is printed and prepared as if it were a first marriage. If it is the second marriage for the bride, whether widowed or divorced, certain changes may be made to avoid confusion.

If you are widowed, you or your parents may sponsor the wedding. On the bridal line, in either case, you may use just your first names, such as "Nancy Ann," or you could use "Nancy Ann Kenning," your previous married name. Don't include the word "Mrs." or use your first husband's given name on an invitation. You might want to use your married name if you are known by it and are sending invitations to friends who do not know your maiden name. If it doesn't matter to you, and you would rather not include your former married name, it's equally proper to omit it.

If you are divorced and are remarrying, you may be sponsored by your parents if you choose, and the bridal line may have your first names only. For purposes of identification you may wish to use your previous married name—the choice is yours. If you think it's wrong to invite some of the same guests you had at your first wedding again, exclude them from the guest list.

It's perfectly proper for a woman who has been married before to have engraved invitations. If someone takes offense, they need not attend your wedding. It's a happy occasion, and if sending out invitations pleases you then send them. It can be very meaningful to a bride who has been married before to have a formal wedding —particularly if her first ceremony was an extremely informal or civil one. This ceremony can properly be as large and lovely as she wants.

Engraved invitations are proper

Your wedding should reflect you, so let your stationery be a part of the wedding you've always wanted.

Now to consider the use of enclosure cards. Enclosure cards list special information that is not already included in the wedding invitation proper. They serve a great variety of purposes and are included along with the wedding invitation. Typical enclosure cards are: a reception card, a bus or plane card, a pew card, a response card, an at-home card, a church card and a Communion card. All the enclosure cards should be printed or engraved on the same paper using the same type face as that of the invitations.

Enclosure cards

If your invitation does not mention the reception in its body—the usual form if you will not invite all guests to both the ceremony and reception—a reception card is enclosed with the invitations of those invited to the reception. A formal reception card might look like this:

. . . for the reception

Mr. and Mrs. Mark Adams
request the pleasure of your company
on Thursday the tenth of October
at three o'clock
at the Hawthorne Hotel

or this:

Dr. and Mrs. Avner Feldman
request the pleasure of your company
at the wedding breakfast
following the ceremony
Belmont Hotel

In the lower left-hand corner, the phrase "R.S.V.P." (or a similar reply phrase) would appear above the home address of the sponsors. Often the reception card is in more simplified form:

Reception
immediately following the ceremony
Olympic Hotel

This reception card is about half the size of the invitation and would not bear decoration or a family crest.

... for the ceremony

When your wedding ceremony is to be very small or private, you may want to send out a large invitation to the reception and enclose a ceremony card. The copy for an invitation to the large reception is only slightly different from the invitation to the ceremony. The second line may read, "request the pleasure of your company," rather than "the honour," as you're inviting them to a social occasion rather than a solemn ceremony. The following line then reads, "at the wedding reception of their daughter," et cetera. The kind of paper used and the information given are identical with that of the ceremony invitation; you're just reversing *where* the information appears. The enclosure then reads, "request the honour of your presence at the marriage of."

... for complimentary transportation

A bus or plane card is used only if you are providing transportation for guests from a given area to the ceremony. If, for example, many guests will fly to New York and the wedding is in Connecticut, you may want to provide them with transportation on a chartered flight from Kennedy Airport to a Connecticut air field. The card would read: "A special plane has been reserved and will be leaving Kennedy at 5 P.M. on the third of June.

102

The flight returns at 11 P.M. on the same day. Please present this card." The same arrangement with adjusted wording would be used if you were to provide a private chartered bus.

A pew card is about 2 inches wide by 3 inches long and is best used for very large weddings. If the invitation is going to your relatives or friends, you might have "within the ribbon" entered on a plain card. If it's for the groom's guests, "groom's reserved section" would be printed on the card. Your mother can either sign her full name on a pew card or substitute one of her calling cards with all the necessary information written on the back. If you are assigning an actual pew number, you would wait, of course, until a guest accepts.

. . . for special seating

A response card may be included with the invitation at your discretion. It is a printed card which asks each guest to check whether or not he will attend the reception and to return the card to the bride's family. Such a card is unnecessary as most guests have the good sense to send their acceptance by handwritten note. If you use the response card, then you should also include a stamped, self-addressed envelope and pay for the reply you're requesting.

. . . for response

The at-home card gives out your new address. In effect, you're telling people where you will be located when you return from your honeymoon and that you are settled in your new home. It is generally smaller than the reception card but in the same style, and it should not include any kind of decoration—merely your new address. If you are sending these cards to friends out of town and it is important for them to have your mailing (as opposed to visiting) address, include the zip code on the same line as the city and state.

. . . . for your new address

Although it may be included with the invitation, the at-home card is most often enclosed with the announcement. (More on announcement styles later.) It should be a small 3 by 4 inch or 3 by 5 inch card. If included with the invitation it would read:

After the first of August
3909 Summerlea Avenue
Pittsburgh, Pennsylvania 15232

If included with the announcement it would read:

Mr. and Mrs. Arthur Stern
after the tenth of October
909 Mendlow Drive
Melrose Park, Illinois 60164

...for admission
A church card would be used if your ceremony is to be performed in a church or cathedral that is usually open to the public. If your wedding might attract tourists, the church would be closed to the public during the ceremony, and your guests would need church cards for admission. A church card would read:

Please present this card
at St. John's Episcopal Church
Saturday, the twenty-eighth of June

...for Communion service
If you are going to have a Communion service with your wedding, you may want to include a Communion card. About the same size as a reception card, it would read:

You are invited to share fully
in the Nuptial Mass
by receiving Holy Communion

or:

You are cordially invited
to join the wedding party
in receiving Holy Communion

Enclosure cards are very useful, but they lose their impact when overdone. Don't include more than two enclosures with a wedding invitation; if an at-home card would be the third, send it with your announcement or send out your address informally after the wedding. Remember that you want to inform your guests, not deluge them.

Invitations and enclosures give the necessary information to those persons whom you want at your wedding. Often, however, you will want to tell others of your marriage, and that brings us to wedding announcements. Wedding announcements are sent out after your wedding ceremony has taken place, to inform friends of the facts concerning your wedding. They may be sent out to announce a first marriage, a second marriage, or an elopement.

Wedding announcements

You may or may not choose to send written announcements that your wedding has taken place. If you do send them, they should be sent only to people who have not been invited to the wedding or reception, and they should be mailed on the day of your wedding. You would address and prepare them for mailing before the ceremony and then entrust them to someone to mail after you've left for your honeymoon.

...do you want them?

Send announcements if you were unable to accommodate all the guests you would have wanted at the reception and/or ceremony. If you had good reason—usually financial—to leave out friends who live in your town, you may send them announcements. If you excluded them from your list simply because you didn't want them to attend, don't send them an announcement; it looks as if you are saying, "We don't like you well enough to invite you to our wedding, but as an afterthought we decided we'd let you know that it did take place."

...who should receive them?

The wedding announcement is printed or engraved in almost the same style as the invitation:

Announcement wording

Mr. and Mrs. Harrington Ford French
announce the marriage of

The change in wording occurs in the second line of information. You may also say, "have the honour to announce the marriage of" or "have the honour of announcing the marriage of." The rest of the copy is the same, except that you always give the year, written out completely: "One thousand, nine hundred and sixtynine." Naming the site of the ceremony is optional, whether you were married in a religious or civil ceremony. If, however, you were married at City Hall, this is never included. Use your own judgment with regard to site.

Informals have many uses

Last on your list of wedding stationery are the multipurpose informals. Generally small, plain notes that fold over once, they are used for writing thank-you notes for engagement, shower and/or wedding gifts and can also double as informal handwritten wedding invitations or announcements. Informals are available in various colors, sizes and styles and can be monogrammed with one large initial for your last name or with your name engraved in full. Order your informals when you order your other wedding stationery if at all possible. It's a nice idea to keep the type face and paper stock consistent for all your wedding stationery.

Informals may be used instead of engraved invitations for small weddings. A sample of such an informal invitation might be:

> Dear Connie,
>   George and I plan to be married at five o'clock, Friday the second of June, here at home. It will be a small wedding followed by a reception. Please let us know if you can be with us.
>   Affectionately,
>   Karen

The invitation should be written in good quality ballpoint or the traditional fountain pen with blue or black ink.

You may also invite your friends to an informal wedding by telephoning or sending a telegram. If you phone, it might be a good idea to follow up with a friendly note—restating the time and place—just to make sure the factual information didn't get garbled in your excitement.

. . . for invitations

Informals may also be used to announce your wedding. This is a warm and personal way of informing friends, but it requires a good deal of time if you have many to send.

. . . for announcements

Informals are quite useful for the many thank-you notes you'll have to send as you thank guests for wedding, engagement and shower gifts. They are also good for special thank-you's to members of the wedding party who have been particularly helpful to you. Here are some sample thank-you notes:

. . . for thank you's

For an engagement gift:

Dear Aunt Audrey,
    Hugh and I were thrilled with the pewter bowl! The Early American design will be absolutely perfect in our new home. Thank you so much for this thoughtful remembrance.
        Love,
        Alice

For a shower gift:

> Dear Jane,
>
> The nightgown you gave me at the shower is gorgeous! It's carefully packed among my honeymoon things now, but I just had to tell you again how much I love it.
>
> Love,
> Diane

For a wedding gift:

> Dear Mr. and Mrs. Lowell,
>
> The copper chafing dish you sent us is one of the first and most beautiful additions to our new home. John and I thank you again for your elegant gift.
>
> Best,
> Joan

The degree of informality in your prose and your closing (Love, Best, Affectionately, Cordially) depends, of course, upon how well you know the person who sent the gift.

The bride always writes thank-you's but is sure to state how both she and her fiancé like the gift. For all

108

gifts except those meant for your personal use, you should mention your fiancé's name in the body of the letter, but sign only your own name to the note. Thank-you notes needn't be lengthy, but they must be sincere. If the only thing you like about Cousin Emily's plate is the color, then mention the color.

Order your wedding stationery in the stationery department of a large department store, a stationer's shop or a jewelry store. Avoid ordering your stationery in such places as drug stores, where printing is merely a sideline; they have to send out to have the work done anyway, and you have no guarantees about time and quality of the work. It's always better to deal with a reputable shop or department that specializes in this work. Judge the shop in the same way you judge a grocery store or a dress shop. Deal with a reputable company that has been in business for a number of years— preferably one recommended by a friend who has done business with this company before. Always check samples of their work carefully.

Places to order wedding stationery

You will want to order your invitations two to three months in advance of mailing (see the end of the chapter for when to mail them). If possible, have the salesman give you the approximate delivery date in writing.

Once you are assured of a good selection and delivery on time, you can proceed to the questions at hand.

What color will your wedding stationery be? Traditionally, wedding paper is ivory or ecru in color, and it is engraved or printed in black. Pastel stationery and discreet, modified designs are also nice choices. Colored ink may be used on wedding stationery which is also colored. For example, light green ink on a dark green paper would be an attractive combination, but a colored ink would not look good on a white invitation.

Choose a color

Ivory or various pure-white tones are always appropriate. Pure whites may be rose white, with a pinkish cast, or blue white, which has a bluish cast to it. Choose one color for all the wedding stationery, using it consistently for your invitations, announcements and informal cards. If you decide to have your wedding in fall colors, for example—the yellow, orange and brown tones—you might want to choose one of these three colors for your wedding paper. It's nice to pick a color that will match the color scheme of the ceremony and reception.

Pick the size   What size would you like your wedding stationery to be? The size of your wedding stationery is a matter of personal preference. It is not proper, however, to purchase extremely large invitations of poor quality. It is better to send a small invitation of good quality than to send a large invitation of poor quality. How do you judge quality? By feeling the type of paper and asking about the rag content. Many papers are made of 100 percent rag fibers and bear a watermark. You can see the watermark on the paper if you hold the paper up to the light: The name of the company is marked into the paper. The quality of the paper goes down as the percentage of rag content goes down.

Avoid thin papers   Avoid paper that is thin and slick to the touch; try to purchase paper that is sturdy, even to the point of feeling like construction paper. Such paper, even if not very high in rag content, is perfectly acceptable for a modern invitation.

Will the size you have chosen accommodate the amount of printing that you want to appear on your invitation or announcement? It's best to see a sample of an invitation in the size that you have in mind—one with the same amount of printing on it that you want to have. If, for example, you intend to have anything printed in the lower left-hand corner of your invitation, such as reception or at-home information, then you might need to order a larger invitation. This is also true for announcements.

The sizes of invitations vary from the very small

which is 4 by 4¾ inches to one of the largest which is 8¾ by 6½ inches. The average size runs about 5 by 6½ inches. It's wise, of course, to see as many samples as possible in the various sizes. In addition to considering the amount of printing that will appear on your invitation or announcement, decide if you want a panel on your invitation or announcement. A panel is an indentation that runs around the sides of the paper, forming a frame around the printing much like a picture frame. It looks quite elegant and gives a finished look to the invitation or announcement, but you must allow for additional space if you use this style.

The average invitation is 5 by 6½ inches

What quantity of wedding paper do you wish to purchase? The quantity is determined by the number of guests that you are inviting, plus an additional ten invitations for every seventy-five guests. The additional ten will allow you to invite those persons you may have forgotten on your original list; you may make mistakes, too. Another reason for ordering an additional amount when you place your original order is that it is less expensive than buying more later. Printing costs go down as the quantity of items printed goes up, so order your extra invitations and/or announcements at the time you place your original order. Don't forget you'll need only *one* invitation per couple—not two.

How much will you buy?

What image do you want to have for your invitations? Do you want your look to be modern? Traditional? Religious? Perhaps very ornate? The style should be in keeping with your total plan for your wedding.

A modern look for your invitations and announcements is easily achieved by choosing paper in a rich color or by selecting an invitation of an unusual size or design. Use a simple, bold type face and omit all decorative touches from the front of the invitation or announcement.

. . . a modern look

The traditional look is best achieved by using the average-size wedding invitation in an ivory, off-white

. . . a traditional look

color and script type, which is quite fancy. There would not be any decoration on this wedding stationery either. If you decide to use a panel, you may want to choose another type style, as the script and the panel do not combine well. To blend the traditional and modern elements, consider having a traditional script with an unusual paper stock.

...a decorative look

If your wedding is going to be highly decorative, you can get wedding stationery with fine designs stamped right into the paper. This process is called embossing, and though it can be done in different colors, the best look is achieved by pressing a color design on the same color paper. The "blind embossing" raises the design without ink and without added color and creates a pattern of white-on-white or ivory-on-ivory or even blue-on-blue. It is quite attractive and much more suitable for wedding invitations than embossing with a second color. Gold or silver, for example, tends to look inexpensive and gilty and detracts from the information; black is too stark. For appealing, elegant design "blind embossing" is really the best.

There are other decorative touches you might select to make your wedding invitations distinctive. Some invitations have hearts and cupids and flowers in the white-on-white design which fold in unusual ways. One has two hearts joined together, and in the center is a wedding ring which is the clasp that closes and joins the invitation. You must keep in mind, however, that if you get an invitation that is very, very decorative, your printing will have to fit proportionately. So be sure to see examples of printed invitations or announcements and establish that the print does not look too crowded on the page.

...an Old English look

There are some invitations and announcements which have one edge of the paper looking as if it has been torn. They are not much in use currently, but can be quite attractive in combination with high-quality parchment paper. This gives an Old English look to your stationery. Don't mix the styles on this, though, and have block lettering if you are trying to achieve an Old English look. The block style is more modern and wouldn't complement the torn-edged parchment look.

You may want to consider a style with religious symbols for decoration. The symbol can be embossed on the front of your invitation with the information printed inside, or it may appear at the top of the page with the information below. There are many designs with religious symbols now, very stylized and modern. You might want to investigate these and choose a design for blind embossing.

. . . a religious look

Do you want your return address to appear on the wedding invitation and/or announcement? This can be helpful in case the invitation does not reach the party you're sending it to. Usually your return address is embossed on the outside of the envelope or written there by hand in the same ink used for addressing.

What kind of lettering do you want? In selecting the type face you want, you must be guided by the various printing processes. There are three basic printing methods: engraving, printing, and a kind of plateless engraving often called thermography.

Decide on lettering

Engraving is the most expensive process. The letters are in relief, raised on the front and depressed on the back. They are actually stamped into your wedding stationery. This is the de luxe method, expensive but elegant.

Engraving

Printing goes on the paper much as if you had taken a paint brush and painted the letters on. The paper feels completely smooth to the touch. Quite often printing comes in different color inks. Printing with black ink on white or ivory paper does not look as attractive as engraving or plateless engraving, but if you are having modern invitations done in colors, printing is a good selection. As printing is by far the least expensive method, it is an easy-on-the-budget choice.

Printing

Plateless engraving is very popular now and very

attractive. Sometimes printers call this process by their own particular name, such as novagraph or thermograph. All of these processes are the same thing, so if you are confused by the term that your printer is using, ask him if he means plateless engraving. By running your hand over the print on the wedding stationery, you will be able to feel the letters raised on the surface of the paper. Unlike actual engraving, however, you will feel nothing but the smooth paper if you run your hand underneath. It is very proper to use plateless engraving processes, and it's not much more expensive than printing.

Once you have chosen the process you prefer, you must next select the type face by looking at the selection of type styles that your printer or stationer has available. Keep in mind that you want this first impression to carry through the style of your entire wedding.

If you decide that you haven't time to order your wedding stationery yourself, keep in mind that a bridal consultant could order these items for you. Quite often the banquet manager of a hotel where your reception is being given can order many items you need (see next section). But keep in mind that if either of these people does order things for you, you may have to pay for their services.

If you're going to buy wedding stationery yourself, as most girls do, be sure to get bids from a variety of shops, if possible. The bid should include not only the price, but also the length of time they estimate to complete your order.

You may also wish to order various mementos and decorations for your wedding at the same time you order your wedding stationery. There are good reasons for ordering them from the same place at the same time. First is convenience, for you place your order all at once and are done with it. Second is that many of the items you order must be printed or engraved, and this way you can have the work done consistently. Third is that if you place a large order with the shop it may result in a discount to you (ask about this). It would also probably result in better service.

Other items you might want would be photo albums (less expensive than when purchased from the photographer), napkins with your and your husband's name on them, matches with your names, paper items like streamers or even cake decorations. You may want to order some kind of program of the various events during the ceremony, with the printed list of the bridal party. The store may also have items like engraved cake knives or champagne glasses that could have initials put on them. If you are going to use paper cups, paper plates and tablecloths, you could buy them at this time. Your stationers might also have small boxes to use as cake boxes for your guests, who will want to take home a piece of the wedding cake. You may want to order coasters or place cards for your reception or even an inexpensive replica of your invitation. They might be able to take your invitation and have it pressed into a tray or some plastic item so that you could preserve it and use it. In addition, they may have such items as small bags of rice with your name printed on them or little favor cards saying something like, "Thank you for making our day a happy one," to go at each place setting.

. . . special items made of paper

When you purchase your stationery, you will receive envelopes for your invitations and announcements. Each invitation comes with two envelopes. The invitation goes inside the smaller envelope, and written on the outside, by hand, is the name of the person for whom the invitation is intended. This envelope is not sealed but is placed inside the larger envelope (name side up); the larger envelope is sealed, addressed and stamped.

There are two envelopes

In addressing the outside envelope, abbreviations are not used except for titles like Dr., Mr., Mrs. and Jr. When addressing invitations to servicemen, the only acceptable abbreviation is of the word "Lieutenant" when it is in combination with another word, as in "Lt. Colonel." The names of cities, states and streets are written out in full, though numbers are not. Words like "Boulevard" must not be abbreviated. The addressed envelope should look like this:

Mr. and Mrs. Allen Thomas
1767 Hood Avenue
Bloomington, Indiana 11735

The phrase "and family" is not used. If there are children in the family over the age of sixteen, send them a separate invitation. If they are under sixteen and you want to include them in their parents' invitation, the outer envelope is addressed to the parents; on the inner envelope, write:

Mr. and Mrs. Thomas
Barbara, Sherry and Jim

When sending the separate invitation to the older children, the outside envelope reads:

Misses Alice and Joan Benson
2323 Doheny Drive
Los Angeles, California 90069

For males, the proper form of address is "Messrs." For both sexes, you would write "The Misses and Messrs. Hall." On the inside envelope you would write "Misses Hall" or "Messrs. Hall" or "The Misses and Messrs. Hall." Any members of the family who are not living at home should receive separate invitations, of course.

It is entirely proper to write on the inside envelope more personal forms of address such as "Aunt Mary" or "Grandmother" when the people are particularly close to you. It is not proper to write notes on the envelopes or on the invitations or announcements, nor may you enclose photographs or notes.

...add a personal touch

It's wise to obtain the outside envelopes from your printer ahead of time, so that you can begin addressing them well in advance. Then you can add the inside envelope with invitation and enclosure cards at the last moment and merely write the guest's name in the middle of that envelope before mailing.

The return address may be embossed or written by hand. When embossed it goes on the back of the outside envelope; when written by hand it goes in the upper left-hand corner. The use of stickers with your name and address printed on them is not attractive. Nor should you write on the invitation or the announcement themselves, or print anything on the outside except, perhaps, a very simple decoration in blind embossing.

...the return address

Extra long invitations which are folded in half before mailing will come to you prefolded. Some printers will even insert enclosure cards correctly, with the tissues in place to protect the engraving. If they do not, place them face up on top of the invitation, cover them with the protective tissue and then put the invitation in the envelopes.

It's very important to get help from someone to address your wedding invitations and announcements, particularly if you have many of them or if your handwriting is very poor. The people to ask would be friends, bridesmaids or other members of your wedding party. Women are more suited for this task because they usually have better handwriting and more patience for this kind of work. Your mother or her friends or any of your relatives would probably be willing to help out. This is certainly a good way to include the person who asks, "What can I do to help?"

Ask friends to help

You might consider having a bridal consultant or secretarial service take care of the entire process of addressing and mailing your invitations and announcements. There would be a fee, of course, but if you have a large quantity it can be a valuable, if expensive, service.

Have an "address the invitations" party

Perhaps you would like to consider giving an "address the invitations" party. Before deciding which of your friends and relatives to invite, however, subtly check their handwriting. Make sure you have all the necessary equipment at hand: wedding stationery, black or blue ball-point or fountain pens, any and all enclosure cards and tissues, envelopes, postage stamps and a moistened sponge for putting on the stamps and sealing the outer envelopes.

Serve refreshments for this party, but wait until after the work has been done. Put all stationery safely out of the way, and then bring on the food and drink. You must be very protective of your wedding stationery: if it is ruined, it's time consuming and expensive to replace it or order more.

. . . use first-class postage

Plan on using first-class postage, airmail for cross-country mailing. If you're sending an invitation to someone in a foreign country, check the postal rates before stamping his invitation. Stamps, by the way, can be quite beautiful these days, so you might want to choose a specific commemorative stamp for your wedding invitations. Several have religious themes and some have beautiful flowers. This lends an individual look to your invitations. Be sure to place your stamp carefully; there should be nothing messy about the look of this envelope.

. . . send one to yourself

It's fun to address and mail an invitation to yourself in your maiden name. You'll be able to check to make sure your invitations are arriving safely, and it's a unique souvenir to have of the wedding for a scrapbook.

Your invitations should be mailed four to six weeks before the ceremony. If you plan to have a formal ceremony and you're concerned about getting replies, send your invitations out one month in advance. If your wedding is fairly informal and you don't require a strict count of guests, you may send your invitations out two weeks before the actual ceremony. This is usually the minimum, however. If you expect guests from far away, it would not be improper to send them their invitations as far in advance as five or six weeks. Use your own judgment.

. . . mail invitations 4-6 weeks before

Your invitations go out in several groups. The first group contains invitations which will take longest to arrive, anything going to a foreign country. The second group goes to people across country. The third group goes out last to the people who live in your immediate area.

The mailing of your announcements usually takes place on the actual day of the wedding; you can have someone do this for you. If you have had a secret marriage, or if for some reason you have not announced your marriage for about a year, then you may still mail out announcements.

Soon after your invitations are mailed, you will begin receiving replies. Guests who are invited only to the ceremony need not reply, but you should receive replies to reception invitations, whether or not "R.S.V.P." is printed on the invitation. Acceptances are usually handwritten on informal stationery and use the same style as your wedding invitations.

Replies you may receive

A formal acceptance would read:

Mr. and Mrs. Hall
accept with pleasure
Dr. and Mrs. Armitage's
kind invitation for
Sunday, the second of
March, at six o'clock.

119

An informal acceptance might read:

Dear Susan,
I will be at your
wedding with bells on!
I'm delighted for you!
Fondly,
Nancy

This kind of acceptance is as proper as the formal kind, and is the kind you might receive from someone in the bridal party.

A regret follows the same form as an acceptance, but the second line will read, "regret (or regret exceedingly) that they are unable to attend." Sometimes a regret will state the reason that the person is unable to attend: "regret that their absence from the city prevents their accepting." A regret that is formally written out does not repeat the place or the hour of the reception, but it does repeat the date. The person writing the regret also follows the style of the invitation.

If you plan to keep the 3 by 5 inch planning file and use it throughout your wedding, you will want to mark acceptances and regrets on them as you go along.

You may receive a telegram on the day of the wedding congratulating you and perhaps saying that the person is sorry they could not attend. It's not necessary to acknowledge this telegram as if it were a gift, but it is certainly a considerate thing to do. Most certainly you will be keeping the telegrams you receive on your wedding day to put in your scrapbook.

Once you have finished your wedding stationery project, sit back and not only breathe a sigh of relief, but also congratulate yourself. You've made quite a few choices, learned a great deal, and are well on your way to becoming an excellent social secretary in your new home.

12

Thank You for Your Lovely...

GIFTS AND HOW TO HANDLE THEM

AFTER YOU SEND OUT your wedding invitations, and in fact after you announce your engagement, you may start receiving gifts. People will send you engagement presents and wedding presents. They'll send gifts if they're invited to the wedding and plan to attend, or even if they can't. (It's not necessary to send a gift if they can't go to the wedding, but often close friends will.) If you send announcements after you are married, many friends who weren't invited to the wedding may also send you gifts.

Be prepared to receive unexpected gifts from people. This happens to many engaged girls; they receive a gift from someone they have not invited to their wedding. Don't become alarmed if you do get a gift like this and don't rush out and send the donor an invitation. Merely accept the gift and send the proper thank-you note. The gift is sent with all best wishes and is given sincerely. Very often, too, someone who is not particularly close to you will give you a small gift. Accept all such tokens as the joyful offerings they are, and don't feel guilty about invitations unsent.

Engagement gifts

Occasions for gift-giving that arise throughout the wedding period are numerous. First comes the engagement. Quite often engagement presents will be personal gifts for you, the bride-to-be, though they may be gifts for your home or personal gifts for both you and the groom. If you and your fiancé choose to exchange engagement gifts, they should be items of a personal nature, like jewelry or some special thing that means a great deal to both of you.

Wedding gifts

The wedding, of course, is the occasion on which most gifts are given. You will be receiving gifts from your guests, your friends and your relatives. You and your groom may choose to exchange gifts, too. He will probably want to give something to his best man and ushers and you, traditionally, should give gifts to your members of the wedding party. (For more information on gifts for the wedding party, see Chapter 16.) Your bridal party, in turn, may get together, collect a certain amount of money from each person, and buy you a joint gift for your wedding, so don't be surprised if no wedding gifts arrive from the individual attendants.

Special party gifts

There are other occasions for gift-giving. One is the bridal shower, which is a party usually given for you by one of your attendants or a close friend. (See Chapter 33 for details.) Another, during the wedding week, when you might expect to receive gifts, is the bachelor party for your fiancé. And still another is any special party held in honor of the bride and/or groom.

Kinds of gifts

What can you expect to receive as gifts? Well, almost everything and anything. Your gifts may be old or new, a recent purchase or an heirloom passed down through generations. Someone may give you a gold-plated, engraved cake knife to cut your wedding cake.

Perhaps a friend or relative who hasn't a great deal of money will send you a prized piece of silver or china. You may also receive gifts that have been made especially for you—a piece of embroidery or a hand-knit item. Many of your gifts, of course, will be sent to you directly from stores.

Expect to receive many household items for your new home, anything from furniture to accessories: ashtrays, glass bowls, paperweights, bedspreads, linens, kitchen utensils, serving pieces. You will also get many of the items you register for: crystal, china and silver. It's very sensible to plan your total needs for your new household and to check off the items that you receive as gifts. After you have opened all your presents you will have a list of all the items you still need to purchase. (There's more information on planning your home in Chapter 13.)

Many people will tell girls who have been married before, whether widowed or divorced, that they should not expect any gifts. As you know from the chapter on wedding stationery, I do not agree that a previously married bride should not send out invitations. If she does send out invitations she will doubtless receive gifts, and this is perfectly proper.

If married before

If a friend asks you directly what you would like as a wedding gift, the best answer is, "I'm sure I'll like anything you give me. I have some items registered at (name of store) and those are things I know I'll need." Some people are very apprehensive about choosing a gift. They want to make sure it's the right thing for you. It's best to tell your maid of honor and your mother what you would like to have, or give them the names of the stores where you are registered, so they can guide friends and relatives.

You'll most likely be receiving checks, cash or bonds as wedding gifts. You should keep in mind that it's a wise idea to open a checking or savings account so that as the wedding money comes in you can safely

Cash gifts

deposit it; if you receive bonds, it's advisable to rent a safe-deposit box.

You may want to keep a large amount of wedding gift money in an account separate from your household money. One couple I know did, and every so often when they wanted to buy something special, they would use the wedding money and, in effect, give themselves a gift. They took a short vacation and purchased a few necessary items. They had received lovely linens, but they didn't have a plain tablecloth to use every day, so they used some of their wedding money to purchase this. They used it quite sparingly throughout their first year of marriage as a "buffer" account. If you decide to do this, open a savings or checking account before you're married in the name of Miss Susan Stone and Mr. Ted Field, a joint account. When you are married, change it to Mr. and Mrs. Ted Field. That way, if you need the money before you're married, either one of you can draw from the account, and the same is true after your wedding.

Monograms

You may receive gifts which are monogrammed. If you like monograms, it would be to your benefit to list the style of monogram you prefer when you register your linens. If someone wants to give you towels, he will use the combination of initials or the single initial you have chosen and know you like. You will likely receive gifts from people who purchase from stores where you are not registered, and they may make up their own monogram. Unfortunately you cannot return a monogrammed item. The store will not accept it because they cannot resell it, so usually you must keep this kind of gift. Monograms are usually either the single letter of your new last name or a combination of your first-name initial, your maiden-name initial and your married-name initial, woven in a pattern. It's also proper to use your first-name initial as a monogram. There are many styles of monograms, from Grecian to script. Since it is best to have all monograms consistent, you may want to save all of your linens, silver and any other items for monogramming all at once after you're married. If you decide to do this, it's wise to inform your mother and your maid of honor that you would prefer to receive gifts without a monogram, and let them pass the word along.

If it is before the wedding, gifts are sent to you at your parents' address, directed to you in your maiden name. Gifts sent to the bride's new home are addressed to Mr. and Mrs. John Jones if they are to arrive after the wedding has taken place. These gifts may also be sent to Mr. and Mrs. John Jones in care of the bride's parents if the guests have not been informed of the couple's new address.

Where gifts are sent

Expect to be given gifts at your reception. If you have not received the majority of your presents up to the day of the ceremony, you might anticipate receiving some then. You may want to appoint someone to be in charge of receiving gifts, making sure that the cards are kept with each package and generally seeing that they are safely stored. Don't open your gifts at the reception unless this is the custom among your friends and family. If it is always done, plan for it. But generally it is not done, as it takes time and you risk hurting someone's feelings by not being able to summon enough enthusiasm in front of all the onlookers.

It's very important to be kind and gracious to all who give you gifts. Each person has spent his time, money and effort to buy you something he hopes will please you. It's little enough to ask in return that you thank each person promptly and warmly. This should be done in the form of a handwritten thank-you note. It's best to name exactly what the gift is, or to use a general term to describe it. Perhaps you received a dish which could be a vegetable dish or an ashtray. If you're not sure, you may be able to check at the store where the gift was purchased. If this isn't possible, refer to it as the lovely piece of glass. You might tell them what

Thank-you notes!

127

you plan to use it for: "It could serve so many wonderful uses, but it happens to be *just perfect* for a particular dessert that John adores."

It's easiest to write your thank-you note as you receive each gift. Not only does it save you having to write notes frantically on your honeymoon or right after you return, but it's also easier to write them in the first burst of enthusiasm you experience when you open the box. Your thank-you note will then be sincere and spontaneous, always the best kind.

Shower thank you's   At showers it's customary to open all gifts as your guests sit around and watch you. You will be thanking all your friends on the spot, but I think it's a nice gesture to send a thank-you note, too. Although many authorities don't feel it's necessary, I think it's both necessary and thoughtful.

You should also acknowledge the receipt of checks or money the way you would acknowledge any other kind of gift. It's a nice idea to mention in the thank-you note what you intend to use the wedding money for, such as finishing your settings of china. Send all thank-you notes promptly, particularly to people who send money or gifts from far away; they tend to worry about its safe arrival.

A handy card file   It's wise to keep a careful record of your gifts. The 3 by 5 inch file card system mentioned in Chapter 11 gives all information about each guest—at your fingertips. You list the gift on each card, and you can check it off when the gift is acknowledged.

Printed or engraved thank-you cards which thank the guest in a general way for "your gift" are absolutely improper. They are rude and show no consideration to someone who has taken great care in buying you a gift. Even if your wedding is enormous, never send one of these.

Exchanging gifts   If a gift you receive is not useful to you, you should exchange it, either for credit or a new item. Your close friends and relatives want more than anything

128

to make you happy with their presents and may make a great point of telling you that if you don't like the gift, they hope you will exchange it. But for some people, a little white lie may be needed to save hurt feelings. Quite often you'll have to keep an item that you consider a white elephant, and bring it out when the aunt who gave it to you comes to your house. It will give her pleasure to see it in your home, so use your discretion on exchanging. If the gift comes from someone who will visit you often, you may want to keep it, just to please him. This is particularly a good idea if the item is small and you would only receive nominal credit if you returned it. The china or silver store where you register your patterns will often be able to take back gift items for credit even if the gifts were not purchased there. It's worth it to them because you will probably apply the credit you receive toward additional purchases in their store.

If you have exchanged an item that was sent to you by someone who lives far away, and he suddenly turns up, you may tell him that the item is out being cleaned, refinished or refurbished, or that it has been loaned or broken. If you say broken, though, add that you've finally located a replacement for it, or he may take it as a hint and buy you yet another white elephant. Be cautious in your wording, and try to save hurt feelings whenever possible.

A little white lie

The custom of displaying wedding gifts on a decorated table in the home is still followed by many people. If you choose to display your gifts, a special day should be set aside; or if your reception is in your home, the gifts should be shown at that time. Although this procedure allows guests to admire the gifts you have received, I am not in favor of it. It takes a great deal of someone's time to set up these displays and a tremendous amount of tact to arrange the table so that people are unaware that you've received seven toasters and three portable mixers. More important, you can't ex-

Displaying your gifts

129

change your gifts until you return from your honey-moon if you plan on such a display.

If you want a guest to see his gift, invite him to your home after the wedding; the gifts are intended for your use and enjoyment in this setting anyway. If it's not possible to do this, write another note sometime during the first year to tell the person how much you continue to enjoy his gift. One girl I know received a case of wine as a wedding gift. She, of course, wrote a thank-you note for the gift and filed the information away. Several months later, after she and her husband had enjoyed a bottle of wine at dinner, she took the time to sit down to write a note to the guests, saying that the wine she and Jack had enjoyed at dinner reminded them of their warm thoughts for the couple who had sent such a gracious gift. This is a lovely extra thing to do, and it's much nicer than taking your time before the wedding to display gifts. True consideration and kindness throughout the year and throughout your life is as much appreciated as is lining up your gifts to show your guests.

If you postpone...

If for some reason your wedding is postponed, you may keep your gifts though you must let your guests know about the postponement as soon as possible. Give them the new date if it's confirmed or tell them you'll let them know it as soon as it's reset. You needn't tell them why the wedding has been postponed if you don't want to, but you must let *all* guests, whether they've sent you gifts or not, have this information.

Insure your gifts

It's an excellent idea to take out special insurance to cover your wedding gifts. Check with your parents to see if their insurance policies will cover the gifts. If not, perhaps they can get a "floater" policy for you.

Large or small, inexpensive or rare, your gifts are given in honor of a special occasion, of a special joy. Accept them with grace, and enjoy them to the fullest. They are for you to use and to treasure always.

Part Three

TIME FOR SHOPPING

13

Looking Ahead

BASIC PLANNING FOR YOUR NEW HOME

HAVE YOU EVER spoken with a woman, middle-aged and comfortably settled in her well-appointed home, about her first apartment? Do you wonder why she talks about it so glowingly, considering what she has acquired since? She looks back on her first home with so much love and joy because it *was* her first home after her marriage, and for that reason alone it is bound to be special.

Your first shopping trip will be filled with pleasure and enjoyment as you plan for your new home—making decisions and choosing all the things that you like, things that you and your husband will cherish throughout your married life. One of the most challenging things you may ever do is decorate your new home. Other homes you have will be decorated with the fruits of this experience, but probably this is the

Do your own decorating

Magazines have good ideas

See model homes

first chance to express your taste since you designed your own bedroom or room at school. Even if you can afford to hire an interior decorator, you really should do the job yourself. You will learn from this experience about buying shrewdly and about decorating. When you're done, you will know what you like and dislike, what is workable and what is not.

Gather information from many sources to help you make wise choices. Magazines such as *McCall's, Woman's Day, Family Circle, Good Housekeeping* and *House Beautiful* can give you many decorating ideas. You may not be able to afford the furniture they advertise right now, but you can pick up useful hints about furniture arrangement and color combinations. Buy a few of these magazines or even subscribe. If you're not sure which ones you want yet, you can always go to the library and read them there. In this way you can also check back and see how color schemes and furniture styles have changed or remained the same in the past year or so.

Tour as many model homes as you can, even if their style or location is not for you or you don't intend to buy a house now. In a real house it's easier to see how different kinds of furniture are coordinated, and how color, space and design are used. You can learn a tremendous amount, especially if you make note of the things that you dislike as well as of the things you like.

For kitchen ideas, don't overlook the water and power company in your town. Quite often they will have model kitchens on display. They also have booklets and salespeople who can offer good ideas. Take advantage of this and ask questions, gathering all the information you can.

You can also get ideas by observing other people's homes. Note the way they use color, the type of furniture they choose. Observation will help you come to conclusions about your own taste and may save you from purchasing furniture you won't enjoy living with. Learn from others' decorating skills and learn by their mistakes.

As you plan, remember the area involved. Will you be living in a one-room apartment or will you be fortunate enough to have a house right away? This makes a tremendous difference in terms of what you will need first. I suggest making up a floor plan of each room in your new home. Use one piece of graph paper for each room and make or buy templates, which are sheets of paper scaled to size to represent the various pieces of furniture that you may be purchasing for each room. On your floor plan, allow space for walking, set areas, make note of your lighting fixtures and where electrical outlets are, and, using the templates, place the furniture as you intend to place it in your room when you have it completed. Plan for the future, and decorate each room as you would *ideally*. List everything that you would put in the room if money were no object. Then you can determine which items you will buy now and which items can wait until later. You can check items off this list as you receive wedding gifts which fill your needs. Wedding money you receive can be applied to these items, too.

Your decorating plan

It's important to begin with a budget. You must know how much money you can spend now (break it down per room) and, if possible, how much of your future income you can allot to furnishings. This will give you a general idea of when you will be able to complete your total decorating scheme. Keep in mind that you will be receiving not only engagement, shower and wedding gifts, but also anniversary and special occasion gifts in the future. Your friends and relatives will most likely purchase items that they know will complete your home, as people generally like to buy gifts they know you like and will enjoy.

A budget is important

Make up a list of everything you will need and want for each of your rooms; then establish priorities. Go through and rate each of the items, perhaps coding

List everything

135

them; for example, *N* for necessity, *L* for luxury. Also mark off the items that you receive as gifts or that you purchase so that you can keep an up-to-date record of the items that remain to be purchased or filled in.

NECESSITIES AND LUXURIES

LIVING ROOM

sofa	chairs
mirrors	end tables
drapes	coffee tables
rugs	lamps

Living Room Accessories:

pictures	wall decorations

ENTERTAINMENT EXTRAS

television	radio

Luxury Items:

piano	stereo
tape recorder	movie equipment

BEDROOM

bed	night table
chest	lamp
rugs	drapes
mirrors	chair

Luxury Items:

dressing table with chair

DEN

desk	cabinet
chair	bookshelves
lamps	clock

DINING ROOM

dining table	chairs
drapes	lamps
buffet	accessories
rug	

KITCHEN

table with chairs	curtains

Kitchen Accessories:

pitchers
spice cabinet
canisters
chopping board
mixing bowl set
measuring spoons
bottle opener
spatula
dish draining rack
slotted spoon
wooden spoon
paring knife (3½″)
chopping knife (8″)
bread knife (10″)
steak knives

towel rack
cookbooks
bread box
containers
measuring cup
egg beater
tongs
meat thermometer
salt-pepper shakers
vegetable peeler
colander
utility knife (5-7″)
carving knife (9″)
tomato knife (5″)
knife sharpener

Pots and Pans:

double boiler
frying pans
loaf pan
roasting pan

saucepans
large kettle
casseroles
roasting rack

Baking Needs:

layer cake pans
cookie sheets
muffin pan
wire cooling racks
flower sifter
pastry board

covered cake pan
pie pans
square cut pan
rolling pin
cookie cutters
pastry brush

Miscellaneous:

garbage pail
step stool

wastepaper baskets
ironing board

SILVERWARE

stainless steel
service for 4-8

sterling silver
service for 8-12

EVERYDAY SERVICE

dishes
service for 4-8

glasses
service for 4-8

KITCHEN APPLIANCES

refrigerator

stove

Luxury Items:
freezer   dishwasher
garbage disposal

SMALL ELECTRICAL APPLIANCES
toaster   mixer
coffee pot   clock
waffle iron

Luxury Items:
hot trays   broiler
can opener   ice crusher
salad maker   meat grinder
griddle   rotisserie
juicer   corn popper
egg poacher   frying pan

HOME MAINTENANCE APPLIANCES
washer/dryer   steam/dry iron
vacuum cleaner

Luxury Items:
electric broom   floor polisher

LINEN LIST

Bathroom:
6 bath towels   6 washcloths
6 hand towels   2 bath mats
shower curtain   6 fingertip towels

Bedroom:
mattress pad   2 pillows
6 sheets   6 pillowcases
2 blankets   bedspread

Kitchen:
6 dish cloths   1 table pad
10 dish towels   hot pads
aprons   padded hot mitt
place mats   tablecloths
napkins   napkin holder

It will be necessary, of course, for you to decide on a color scheme. If you haven't overwhelming favorites or if you've never done any decorating before, knowing what colors go together and what effects they have can be a problem. Invest in a color wheel, the paper variety, and see which colors look good in combination. There are twelve colors on the wheel, with complementary colors (red and green, violet and yellow) opposite one another, and analogous colors (yellow and orange, green and blue) side by side. The analogous colors give a soft, one-color look, while the complementary colors offer more variation to the eye. Cool colors, such as blue, green and purple, are very restful; warm colors, such as orange, red and yellow, more stimulating and active The neutral shades—whites, browns, blacks—go well with any and all colors. It's fun to make out color schemes, to mix and match various tones, and you can learn much from experimenting with the color wheel.

The color scheme can be the same for each room or it can vary. Personally I think it gives more variety to a home if you use a different color scheme for each room, although the rooms should not be drastically different if your house is to have a consistency. It's best to select a range of colors for a room and choose unusual accents in very different colors. Remember, however, that too much color can be worse than no color at all. When you are hunting for your apartment or your house, be sure to ask if you can paint walls, ceilings, appointments, anyway you want so that you can have a home that is uniquely you.

If you will be buying or renting an unfurnished home, you will need to consider the investment of furniture. Even if you take a furnished or semi-furnished place, read on. You'll want to give your home an individual touch, and some of these ideas can be incorporated. You can begin investing in furniture now, in preparation for the day when you will have an entire home to fill.

There are a head-spinning number of styles of furniture available today, and each kind of furniture

Colors that blend

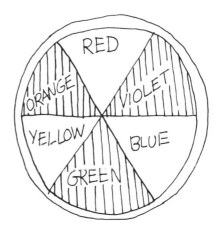

Furniture styles

has accessories that go with it. Within the Modern range alone, there are Scandinavian (or Danish)—sleek woods and abstract or highly-textured upholsteries, clean, low lines; Oriental—black lacquer, straw mats, low tables; Contemporary—unadorned lines, warm woods, interesting, textured fabrics; and the new plastic Mod—unusual shapes in lamps and chairs, chrome, plastic and primary colors. There is French or Italian Provincial, which has more carving and is more ornate than the Modern, and makes use of dark, oiled woods and rich velvet or silk upholstering. The Colonial, or Early American look (also known as Cape Cod), runs to braided rugs, highly flowered prints, pewter and copper accessories, and antique desks and dressers, which are ideal for home refinishing work. The Spanish or Mediterranean style is heavy and ornate; the pieces of furniture are large, and too many clutter a room. The fabrics are rich, and often accessories are wrought iron. These are only a few of the more popular designs available. So again, turn to your magazines, your model homes, and wander through furniture stores to see what's currently available.

Woods and fabrics

In addition to knowing the style of furniture you want, be conscious of the woods and upholstery fabrics that appeal to you. Will they fit in with your overall decorating plan? When you shop for furniture, try it out. Sit in the chair. Make sure that the sofa will be comfortable for you and your husband. Don't buy the first thing that you see and like. Go home and sleep on the idea, and come back the next day to purchase. If you rush out and buy furniture on impulse, you may regret it for many years thereafter. Purchase your items slowly; don't feel pressured, and don't feel you have to have everything for your new home before you move into it. Many couples buy their furniture over several years' time, beginning with just what they need and truly love, and gradually furnish one room at a time. You will be receiving wedding gifts to work into your total plan and wedding money that may change your choices. You will be adding to your home all your life, and your needs will expand as your family grows. So don't feel that you must buy everything now, even if you do make up a list to include everything you may eventually want.

Aside from pieces of furniture, there are floors, walls and windows in apartments and houses to be considered. Floors can be done in wood, slate, concrete or marble and covered with one room-size carpet or with small area rugs. You may take a place that has wall-to-wall carpeting, or you may want to make that investment yourself. Tile can be used in your living room as well as in the kitchen or bath (don't forget that "tile" comes in cork, rubber, asphalt or clay). And the new, easy-care indoor-outdoor carpet is ideal for a kitchen.

The walls of your home can be painted, papered, tiled, mirrored or bricked. Investigate the cork and/or metal textures that can be put on walls, and experiment with the amazing variety of wallpaper, which comes in textured patterns as well as in plain or figured paper.

The windows can be painted, curtained, or shuttered and you can have blinds, shades or hangings (strings of beads, for example) for light *and* design.

The list could go on forever. Always remember that you must take these areas of your rooms into account when you are choosing furniture and accessories. Some of your boldest and most pleasing design accents can be in what you decide to do with a doorway or a wall.

If you need to save money, decorating doesn't have to be a problem, and can even be more fun! The general rule is never buy anything you can make. This is particularly true if you are even remotely handy with sewing—and girls who aren't often learn to be by starting out married life on a budget.

Some fun ways to save $$

Material by the yard can be very inexpensive and small portions of leftover material, called remnants, are always available. There are any number of clever

141

uses for material. Curtains, bedspreads and tablecloths are only the more obvious ideas. You can also take an interesting piece of fabric and cover a lightweight block of wood. Frame it and you have an unusual picture or (if you put it over corkboard) a colorful bulletin board for the kitchen. A long bolt of material hung from the ceiling and draped down into the room can be used as a decorative piece or a room divider (this is often used in the Scandinavian countries). Interesting fabric over a sofa or day bed may hide the fact that the furniture is in poor condition, and the bright colors will lighten your room and your life. Place mats or individual napkins can be made from remnants by turning a shallow hem. Make each napkin from a different material, and give your table an unusual look. As a purely decorative notion, a long and narrow fringed piece of cloth can be run down the middle of your table (about 2½ yards by 1 foot). Place a bowl of fruit or candles in the center, and presto—you've decorated your table.

Accessories are everywhere

Furniture and accessories can fall within the range of your creative talent, too. If you or your husband are at all handy, a wealth of items in thrift shops and inexpensive antique stores should bloom under your loving care. Tables that don't look like much can be restored with finishing or antiquing kits from the five-and-ten, and a chair can be re-covered with relative ease. One couple I know bought a heavily carved door, refinished it and attached legs. The result —a beautiful dining room table, a conversation piece that saved money and looks terrific.

Accessories certainly don't need to be expensive. Often they break, and you'll want to replace them anyway to change the look of your room. Check auctions, fire sales or garage sales for pieces of pottery, vases or unusual sculpture. If you use your imagination, objects can be used for something totally different from what they were intended for. Accessories don't need to be limited to ashtrays and art work. Live plants, ivies and greens—anything you love—can brighten up a home.

Walls, especially plain walls in solid colors, cry out to be filled, and again your imagination can be of much use to you. The collage might have been invented for young people on a budget. A collection of dimensional items affixed to flat posterboard or other lightweight wood, a collage can be made from anything—newspaper clippings, photographs, matchbook covers or bottletops. The postcard collage is made easily and can be especially personal if you have a collection of cards from traveling friends. Simply layer the cards on your corkboard, pasting them randomly with portions showing through. After you apply one layer, shellac it, and let that dry; then paste on another layer. There are many books on collages if you want suggestions, and a collage is certainly one way to collect mementos without having them pile up in a closet. Another wall design can be a photograph, blown up to larger-than-life size and interestingly framed. As you will see, the graphic arts are as interesting as and certainly less expensive than the pictorial arts.

Make a collage

Within this chapter you'll find items listed for the various rooms in your home. You might want to use these lists as checklists for your own needs, but there are certain items, namely your linens, which we can go into in more depth here.

Choose your linens

Your bathroom linens are your towels, and these are available in all sizes, colors, patterns and styles. Although your favorite color may be yellow, you'll have to suit your color choice to the bathroom of your new home; many bathrooms are tiled, at least in part, and that color is something you will have to live with unless you're prepared to go to a great deal of trouble and expense to have it replaced.

It's an interesting and practical idea to coordinate solid-colored towels with patterned ones. This will make your bathroom look entirely different each time you put out fresh towels. The solid color or colors you

Coordinate colors for variety

choose should pick up the least dominant color of your patterned towels. For example, if you have towels with a floral design of pink, gold and red, and the least dominant color is pink, buy solid pink towels to mix and match, the way you mix and match your blouses and skirts in your wardrobe.

Towels come in six sizes, basically: washcloths, face towels, guest towels, bath towels, extra-large bath towels and bath sheets (the largest available and often used as beach towels). You won't necessarily want all six sizes. Choose only those for which you have most need. When you're shopping for towels, buy the best you can afford; they are a good investment because they'll last longer. Once you have them, launder them frequently—white towels in hot water with bleach and colored towels in warm or cold water without bleach. If you buy towels in rich, dark colors, wash them separately the first time to make sure the dye doesn't discolor your other towels—or you.

Four towel textures

There are four basic towel textures. Briefly, these are velour, or sheered terry, which is velvety and luxurious; plain terry, which is rougher and most familiar to us; huck texture, which has a pebbly surface and high absorbency and is most often used for hand towels; and Jacquard, which is very elegant, with a design woven into the actual fabric. Many men don't enjoy using the velour texture, so if you want some sheered terry "for show," combine it with plain terry for family use. And whatever number you feel you'll need, consider buying a few extra hand-sized towels for guests to use.

Your bedroom linens are your sheets and pillowcases, of course, and they, too, are available in a variety of styles, colors, and fabrics.

You will probably buy standard size sheets to fit the bed you first own. Sheet sizes are twin, single, double, queen-size and king-size. I would advise avoiding the queen-size bed, as sheets are often difficult to get. For all four sizes you can buy a fitted bottom sheet.

It's a wonderful time and discomfort-saver that everyone should know about.

Sheets are available in percale, muslin and a polyester blend. Percale sheets are soft and smooth, lightweight and tightly woven. Muslin is more loosely woven and is of heavier cotton. Muslin is not as smooth or soft as percale, but it feels very fine to the touch. The polyester sheets are a new blend of 50 percent cotton and 50 percent synthetic material. They are more expensive than muslin or percale, but can be worth it since they are machine washable and generally need no ironing. They also stay fresh and smooth on your bed and are made of strong fibers which last a long time.

Sheets in many fabrics

Although it is customary to use a top and bottom sheet, you might like to try an unusual practice I discovered while on my honeymoon in Hawaii. The hotels there use a third sheet that covers the blanket and is tucked under the flap of the top sheet. The entire effect is one of beautiful color, and the bed looks and feels very luxurious. The idea is particularly good if you suffer from wool allergies, and it provides excellent insulation.

A general rule about pricing sheets is the more expensive they are, the finer their quality and the longer you can expect them to last. To get maximum enjoyment and use from your bedroom linens, rotate them. Each week put your freshly laundered sheets at the bottom of your stack and use the sheets from the top of the stack to make up your beds.

Sheets and pillowcases are available in all the colors of the rainbow now, as well as in patterns. Many men have a distaste for elaborately adorned sheets, however, and you may wind up compromising with a solid color bottom sheet and a designed top sheet. Feel free to indulge yourself in a variety of colors for your sheets; although it's nice if they coordinate with your bedroom colors, they won't be visible during the day because of a spread, so you might as well go to town.

More expensive, better quality

Don't forget the practical

When planning your new home, don't get so carried away with the fun of decorating that you forget all practical details. Remember to have your phone installed and your utilities turned on before you move in. Also, buy some small unromantic but certainly necessary items such as light bulbs, sink stoppers, bathtub plugs and extra fuses. These small items make life more livable and are easy to forget in the excitement of your wedding and honeymoon.

The last and most enjoyable thing to do is to change your name from Miss to Mrs. on such things as credit cards, charge accounts, checking and savings accounts, social security card, library card, subscriptions, driver's license, safe deposit box and insurance policies. Most important, file your change-of-address form with the post office, so that when you move in, you'll really be "home."

14

The Registry

WHERE, WHAT AND HOW TO REGISTER

YOU, LIKE MOST GIRLS, have probably always wanted to have your own china, crystal and silver. Your second shopping trip will give you the opportunity and happy responsibility of choosing and registering all three. There's lots of information in this chapter to help you, but first, let's explore the word "registry" and see what it really means.

To register means to go to a store and have a salesperson list the items you would like to receive as wedding gifts. This can be a very nice service because many of your friends and relatives will check with the store and buy you the items you have registered for shower, wedding and engagement gifts. This avoids duplication and helps your friends select something that they know you will like. It makes their gift very special, and they don't have to worry about whether or not it will please you.

Let me say at this point that registering is voluntary. If you go into a store and register, you may or may not receive the gifts you have chosen, or you may decide not to register at all. You are also not obligated in any way to buy the items that you register for, unless you make an agreement to that effect—which is the exception not the rule.

How do you register?

When you register your china, crystal and silver, the salesman writes down the name of the pattern and the pieces you have chosen, plus the quantities you would like to receive of each item. The store can then keep track of the exact number of each item that is purchased by your friends and relatives. It's wise to advise the store if someone buys you one of the items in another shop, so that it can be added to the list. And don't be afraid to ask the bridal consultant or salesman if you receive a free gift of some sort for registering your patterns in their store. Many stores will give you a gift—a silver-polishing cloth or an extra goblet of your crystal. It doesn't hurt to ask about this, and you may want to choose a store that will give you a present.

Department stores

Department stores are good places to register your gift preferences. They give advice, offer charge-account service and have many branches for convenience. If you have friends who live in other cities where branches of the store exist, the registry service includes sending your list to the stores you name and keeping a cross-file so that duplications are impossible. If you do register in the branches, be sure to let your friends in those cities know you have done so. You might want to have your mother or maid of honor send the store names to your friends; it is important for members of the wedding party to have this information, so that they can advise guests if the question arises as to what you would like for a wedding gift.

If you would rather, you can register in a jewelry store, a gift shop, or any store you choose as long as it carries the items you want to register. Because you primarily register three basic pattern choices, the gift registry you will be looking for will be located near the silver department. Often this department will have a consultant who will advise you on patterns, but don't allow yourself to be pressured into making hurried choices.

Jewelry or gift shop?

There is one way to save money—but it involves spending money, too. Plan to register in a small china or gift shop, and ask if they might give you a discount. After you have selected your patterns and are assured that the shop has them or will be able to order them, make an appointment to meet with the owner or the manager to discuss your registry. Take your fiancé along, as you will be discussing financial matters involving commitments after your marriage. Ask that, instead of the usual registry procedure, the store owner make a special agreement with you which would give you a 10 percent or 20 percent discount if you agree to purchase either all or part of the total items registered. You are in effect promising to pay for the items that are purchased at this store and not given to you as gifts. Assuming you receive $450 of a $600 set of china, for example, you must make up the difference of $150 and the entire set will be yours.

Arranging a discount

This arrangement works well if you have the money to guarantee buying all these items because you receive a discount and are assured of having your entire set of china when you want it. The manager might also agree to extend this kind of discount to your friends and relatives. He may be willing to give them a partial discount if not the full amount. If you do decide to approach a store in this matter, don't be upset if their answer is negative. If they say they've never heard of such a plan, accept it and leave. Try another store, for some places are delighted to cooperate. And

151

if for some reason you decide to return to the first store, don't be embarrassed about registering your items there in the usual manner: not guaranteeing to buy—just listing your preferences.

If you will be using the discount plan, confirm all details with the store by letter or sales receipt. Both you and the shop owner should have signed copies of such an agreement, which would outline the terms exactly. A business letter will help prevent problems and misunderstanding.

Choose your store carefully

No matter how you plan to register, choose a store with pleasant surroundings and congenial personnel. Keep in mind that your friends will be coming in to purchase gifts, so the salespeople should be courteous and kind. The first thing to do, of course, is to make sure the store has complete place settings in the patterns of your choice, and that these items are on display and readily available. When people come in to purchase a gift, they usually want to see the actual item they are going to buy—not a picture or verbal description of it.

A fun decision

Every bride falls in love with the china, crystal and silver she eventually chooses. And there are so many lovely patterns available that your head will swim when you begin looking. It's overwhelming, but it's a wonderful, fun decision to make. For most girls, this is a once-in-a-lifetime purchase. Choosing your patterns is fun, but you've got to keep in mind that you're making a long-lasting decision, and your future as well as your present tastes should be taken into consideration. Try to visualize what your life-style will be like in the future. If your future husband will be in a business that can lead to lots of entertaining, you're going to want to buy elegant patterns that will be appropriate for this kind of social life.

It's entirely possible to do a lot of entertaining in an informal style. Having people over for formal dinners doesn't mean you can't use informal styles of china, crystal, silver and serving pieces. The reverse is also true. You can have someone over for a snack or dessert and serve it on elegant china. An informal life-style doesn't necessarily mean plastic plates any more than a formal taste dictates solid gold china.

It's important to blend your three basic items—china, crystal, silver—in such a way that there is a total look for your table. There are many different looks, from the modern, which features extremely understated china with heavy bold lines, to the rococco, which uses highly ornate patterns in all three items. It's also possible to obtain flexibility and a variety of looks for your table by combining several of these styles. As you begin your search for the perfect patterns, you might need to answer some very basic questions.

Combining patterns

Do you want one set of good china and one set of everyday china? Two sets of good china and one set of everyday china? You need to decide on color, size and whether you want imported or domestic brands. And, of course, you must consider the cost of each place setting.

To help you choose a pattern, the Spode Company has sets of cardboard plates available, which are replicas of their different designs; and they will send them to you for a dollar. This way you can spread the samples out at home and see what patterns appeal to you. On the back of each demonstration plate is complete information about the entire line in this pattern, and there are line drawings of the available serving pieces. The cost is also listed, of course. This information can be helpful, as it gives you plenty of time to think and choose.

Another approach is to make a list of the kinds of entertaining you plan to do. Write out exactly what you will need to serve each meal you have listed. For example, I made a list of occasions I could anticipate, noting lunch, dinner and coffee or informal entertain-

How will you entertain?

153

ing. I listed the china, silver and crystal I would want for each occasion and added a coffee pot and extra cups. This is the way I knew exactly what service I needed, and I could then concentrate on the pattern.

It makes sense to choose your china pattern first, because it is the item that takes up the most space on your table, visually and literally. Unless you deliberately plan it otherwise, china is the focal point of the table.

Most people use the word china to mean all kinds of dinnerware. Dinnerware includes all items classified as ceramics. A ceramic is a clay that is fired at varying temperatures and then glazed, or coated, with glass and baked until hard. This glaze makes the clay waterproof. Fine china is the highest grade of dinnerware. It is fired at the highest heat in a kiln and baked until extra hard. It is made from highly refined clays, often white clays, and is extremely translucent. There is also bone china, which is made not only of clay but of bone ash as well. It has a chalk white look rather than the ivory look associated with many chinas.

There are many types of dinnerware, and the quality depends on the temperature used for firing the clay and the amount of handwork which appears in the pattern. You will most likely be choosing "fine china" for the dinnerware to be used for entertaining and for formal occasions, but you may want or need other types of informal dinnerware such as earthenware.

Earthenware is medium-to-low priced dinnerware, not as expensive as china. It is clay fired at lower temperatures, and its texture is thicker and heavier than china. The designs available in earthenware are often very modern and dramatic. If you ask for earthenware, you may be told the store carries ironstone. Ironstone is another kind of earthenware, but stronger. It might be an even better choice for you if you're concerned about breakage.

One of the other grades of earthenware is semi-vitreous ware. It's different from regular earthenware in that it's made partially from refined clays and is fired at higher temperatures, making it harder and thinner than earthenware. Ovenware is yet another grade. This is strong, stronger than ironstone, and can be used in most home ovens. Be careful to read the information provided by the manufacturer to find if this means that you can cook in your ovenware or only warm food at low temperatures.

You may also want to consider choosing a plastic dinnerware. Many of the patterns in the very hard plastics, molded by heat, are quite attractive. They are chip-and-break-resistant, inexpensive, and useful for informal entertaining. Although they do not crack or chip as easily as earthenware, they do have one draw-back: They tend to discolor and pick up coffee stains.

Choosing fine china need not be a complicated process. There are some tests to be sure you are getting quality merchandise. The traditional and time-honored test of china is to hold a plate up to the light and see if you can see your hand through it. This tells you if the china is translucent and of good quality. Some chinas are not as translucent as others, but this doesn't mean they aren't as fine. Check the thickness of the plate. Make sure that it is not heavier on one side than on the other, that it is consistently thick or thin. Color should also be consistent and uniform. For example, on a plate with a garland of flowers around the outside, each flower should be uniformly designed and painted. There may be some slight variation if your china is hand-painted, but a gross difference between one part of the pattern and another devaluates the china.

You needn't be overly concerned about the quality of your china pattern if it has a good manufacturer's name or trademark on the bottom. You can be assured that you are buying a fine brand. It is wise to ask the salesman who is assisting you which patterns

How to judge quality

are of the best quality and why. He will be able to advise you of the differences and tell you the best quality items. It's an excellent plan to read the manufacturers' brochures on each of the patterns that you are considering, so you can get their comments in addition to those of the salesman.

How many place settings?

You may be buying or registering as many as eight or twelve place settings of your fine china. A place setting consists of a dinner plate, a dessert or salad plate, a bread-and-butter plate and a cup and saucer. The number of place settings you want will naturally depend upon the number of people you would eventually like to serve. If you're really on a budget but you want china anyway, and you don't receive your pattern as a gift, buy two place settings for you and your husband. They will add great beauty and pleasure to your table and you can always add to them as your income increases.

"Open stock"

When you are choosing a pattern, be sure to find out if your preference is on "open stock." This term means that if you want to buy additional place settings a week, a year or five years from now, this particular pattern will still be available. Otherwise, you may buy a pattern with plans to add to it later, and you'll find that your choice is not being made any more. The same is true of choosing crystal and silver patterns.

In addition to the place settings you require, you may want to choose and register additional serving pieces. Some of the following are items you may want and need:

sugar bowl	12" platter
gravy boat	2 or 3 vegetable
coffee pot	dishes
demitasse cups	cream pitcher
and saucers	soup plates
	fruit saucers

If you receive extra coffee cups or dinner plates, keep

them. They are quite often the first pieces to be broken; and they are useful extras for entertaining.

To judge whether or not china serving pieces are a good purchase, you might ask yourself some questions. Are they strong enough to fill with food and carry comfortably? Will they conduct heat or cold and not crack? Can you put them in the oven to warm foods? If you are planning to order the serving pieces that match your china, keep these questions in mind.

Serving pieces

Be sure to look at all the serving pieces. Many girls register for a complete line in a pattern without seeing more than a picture of the serving items. You don't have to buy them if you don't like them, but do try to see them before you make up your mind.

If you are considering purchasing serving pieces in other materials, you might want to think about silver, silver plate, pewter or copper. If you decide on one of these alternatives, be sure to see these serving pieces with your china, crystal and silver to make sure they harmonize.

If you just can't make up your mind, or you love a great variety of china, choose a variety of patterns. Have your dinner plates in one style, your dessert plates in another, and your serving platters in still another; and combine them beautifully with simple, neutral butter plates, silver and crystal to set an unusual table.

Be sure to ask when selecting your china if it can be washed in a dishwasher. This may not seem important now, but after you have been married for some time you may have a dishwasher, and the more place settings you have, the more of a chore it will be to wash them by hand. Decorations that are under the glaze are usually indestructible, but those painted on top of the glaze must be hand-washed. Salesmen can tell you about the best care of your china, and you might check the manufacturer's brochure for further hints.

Care of china

Be sure to consider more than just the dollar amount charged for each place setting of china. If you are going to buy serving pieces, add their cost to the total cost of your place settings. You may want to purchase your china if you don't receive it as a gift. And if you break any piece you'll have to replace it yourself, so don't invest in an expensive set of china if you cannot assume replacement responsibilities in the years ahead.

Some girls register two china patterns. This is done frequently, and there are pros and cons for doing so. If you want a particularly ornate design and your fiancé prefers simpler patterns, it's a nice compromise if you are able to have two. Unfortunately, if you register two patterns, your friends may buy a larger quantity of the less expensive pattern, for they'd rather give you several settings than just one. A reasonable amount to expect a wedding guest to spend on china is $20 or $30.

Basic styles

When you look at china patterns you'll find that the shapes vary tremendously from set to set. Dinner plates come with and without rims, flat or with gently sloping sides, swirled from the center and on the border or fluted on the border. Coffee cups have different-shaped bowls and handles, and saucers, too, come in all sizes and shapes. Generally, the more angles, swirls, flutes china has, the more ornate the look will be. China that is Colonial or English in inspiration is often very ornate. Modern china, on the other hand, is generally very clean in lines, some without design completely.

Do you want china with a decorative design? China patterns range from no design at all to designs featuring a rim or band of design or covering the entire plate. Subjects are often taken from nature—leaves, flowers, butterflies or the sun. These designs may be highly stylized and simplified or very realistic and ornate. Earthenware is generally decorated with heavier designs and has brighter colors than fine china. Fine china tends to have delicate designs and muted colors. Your pattern can be one color, one color with white, or multi-colored. Some chinas are available in solid colors with decoration in platinum or gold. If you do get gold, be sure it is 24 karat, as this will wear better and longer.

When you are deciding on a china pattern, keep in mind that there are three different basic styles available. First there are the patterns which lend themselves to combination with almost any crystal or silver. Understated and with simple decoration, they are white or ivory in color with perhaps a gold or platinum rim. Second are the patterns with the informal or country look. They blend well with Italian or French Provincial decor, as well as with Colonial or Spanish, are usually casual looking and often make use of floral designs. Third are the more sophisticated and ornate patterns, which combine well with a more formal decorating scheme. Often striking and dramatic, the designs use dark, bold colors. They would combine well with Eighteenth and Nineteenth Century furnishings.

China companies are aware that it is sometimes difficult to coordinate china, crystal and silver, so many of them have wisely made up various lines in matching patterns. The Rosenthal China Company of Germany makes a Studio Line, which has several completely different patterns. Each item—china, crystal and silver —is decorated with the same design element. For the Romance Pattern, they use a circle in combination with stylized leaves and repeat the pattern on each. The design is also beautifully realized on their serving pieces, and the set has a lovely, integrated look.

The Lenox China Company in the United States has many lines of china and crystal which blend well together, and its brochures list ways of combining these patterns. In addition, the accessory pieces for your table in basic ivory with gold trim combine with all Lenox china and other patterns, too.

If you like, decorative tablecloths, lace or splashy

Getting help

flower designs, if you like centerpieces of flowers or fruits, if you serve gourmet food or you cook food that is unusual or especially attractive, then you may want china with a small amount of decoration. If you feel that your china should be the dominant element on your table, then you can choose to play down table-cloths, centerpieces and colorful foods. These are things to consider when you visualize what your dinner table will look like.

Crystal, too, is important to consider. You've probably heard that you can judge whether or not a piece of glass is good crystal by taking your fingernail and tapping it lightly. If there is a bell-like tone, it's fine crystal. This is true, but there's more to judging crystal than just this simple test.

Fine crystal is composed of a high quality of lead and is often called lead crystal. Lower quality crystal without lead is not as lustrous or strong, nor will it have a bell-like tone when you tap it. Lead gives crystal its quality of brilliance, If you compare lead crystal with lesser crystal, you will notice that the former sparkles much more.

A glassblower makes fine crystal by hand, shaping it carefully so that no two pieces are exactly alike. Lesser quality crystal is machine-made. The more brilliant crystals feature a great deal of design. The finer the quality, the more likely that these designs are hand-crafted.

Check that the edges of your crystal are smooth, that they are polished with no bumpy edges. Sometimes there are small bubbles in crystal if they are hand blown. If the bubbles seem too large to you, don't purchase the glass; make arrangements to the effect that if a piece comes to you in this condition, you can return it for a replacement. And look for the manufacturer's signature on fine crystal. This is your guarantee of quality.

A set of crystal for one place setting includes

NOW FOR CRYSTAL!

one goblet or water glass, one champagne glass, and one wine glass. You might also want a cordial glass, a cocktail glass or an iced-tea glass. Some patterns have red and white wine glasses. The red-wine glasses have a shorter stem because the wine is served at room temperature; the white-wine glasses have longer stems so that the heat from your fingers won't warm the wine after it has been chilled. These are nice luxuries but by no means necessities. One basic wine glass is all you'll really need.

It's better to be able to serve a larger number of people with three pieces of crystal per person than to be able to serve fewer people with five or six pieces per person. You can always add to your pattern later.

Although you order a set of crystal for each place setting of china and silver, you may want a few extra glasses because they are so breakable. Water goblets tend to break the easiest. Champagne glasses are nice to use for serving desserts like sherbet or puddings, so you may also want more of these.

Generally, you will want to buy a matched set of crystal, but you can use crystal in a variety of designs, too. For example, you may buy water goblets in one pattern and wine glasses in another. If you decide to do this, it's best to choose your goblets first. They are the largest and most outstanding pieces of crystal on the table, so your other pieces should coordinate with them. But try to keep the general styles the same, choosing patterns for interest and variety, not just for difference of look.

Mix and match

Consider your crystal for its appearance in daylight as well as by candlelight. You might choose an intricately carved pattern if you will be entertaining mostly in the evenings, but try to keep your crystal in lines similar to your everyday glassware. In this way, if you have a large number of people over, you can combine the two sets and still maintain harmony.

Many crystal companies are now making beau-

161

tiful accessory pieces to match crystal patterns. Punch bowls and glasses, ashtrays, cake trays, decanters and many other items are available. Ask when you register if there are additional pieces available in your pattern.

Styles

In choosing your crystal, be aware of the tremendous variety now available. Crystal comes in colors, muted and bold. The designs can be ornate or very plain, and the shapes vary from tall stems with round bowls to short, thick stems with octagonal bowls. If you are after a very modern look, you might want a relatively plain design, a glass that is entirely free of molding or one with a thin platinum ring. If you select gold or platinum trim, though, be sure it goes with your silver and china patterns. To achieve a Spanish or Mediterranean effect, you might choose a heavier crystal with an ornate bowl and a short stem. A Renaissance look might have a tulip-shaped bowl and a stem with subtle and elegant carving.

Crystal, unless heavy and ornate, is the most "invisible" thing on your table. This is true because you see through the clear glass and your eye focuses on the china or silver. So if you buy exquisite crystal, you'll want very simple china and silver so that the crystal is the focal point of your table.

Once you've chosen china and crystal, you're ready to purchase your final item—your flatware or silverware. You may want sterling silver, stainless steel or the new and increasingly popular gold plate.

SILVERWARE IS NEXT

Flatware means eating utensils, and doesn't include serving pieces like large spoons or forks. Nor does it include hollow ware, the term for coffee and tea sets, candlesticks, and ice buckets. Flatware is the basic place setting of silverware you give each person who sits at your table.

You will need one set of flatware for each place setting of your china and crystal. A place setting of flatware includes a dinner fork, a dinner knife, a salad fork and either an oval soup spoon or a butter knife.

The butter knife is a nice luxury, but it is not a necessity. In addition to these, you may want such pieces as cocktail forks, demitasse spoons or iced-tea spoons, as well as larger forks and spoons and ladles for serving.

It's expensive

The value of silver has skyrocketed lately, so the price per place setting has gone up. Because it's expensive to invest in silver, you should think carefully before you choose a pattern. A five-piece place setting of sterling silver flatware can cost from $30 to $130! Stainless steel and gold plate will cost you considerably less.

Stainless steel is much less expensive than silver, and it is a good choice for daily use. Stainless steel is heavy and not quite as shiny as silver, but it has a "silvery" look. It is available in many patterns, some of which are nearly as ornate as certain sterling silver patterns.

How about gold plated?

Gold-plated flatware, which is given its gold color by a process called electro-plating, is another alternative to sterling silver. Gold-plated flatware might be a particularly nice choice if you have china or crystal with gold trim. Your flatware would pick up this accent, and you would have a very dramatic and well-coordinated table.

You may want to consider registering two sets of flatware—one set of sterling silver for entertaining, and one set of stainless steel for convenient, everyday use. But it is wise to use your silver. Most manufacturers will tell you that the more you use it, the more beautiful it will become. With much use and proper care, your silver will develop a lovely patina over the years.

Select your silver the way you select crystal and china. You'll want a reputable store to deal with, and you'll want to buy brand names that you can trust. There are many well-known American and European manufacturers of silver; ask your salesclerk to show you the different lines.

Be sure to test your silver for weight. In general, the heavier the silver, the better the quality. Each piece should bear the stamp "sterling silver" or perhaps just the word "sterling." This means that it is silver, rather than silver plate. Sterling silver is composed of 925 parts silver to 75 parts copper. (The copper is added to make it harder, since silver is a very soft metal.)

Also check the balance of your silverware. If, for example, you have a dinner knife which has a hollow handle and a heavy blade, your knife could be top-heavy. Or, if the design of the silver is such that it is heavily ornate in the handle portion the reverse would be true.

Consider the balance of the design as well. When you look at the individual pieces of flatware, is the design symmetrical? Is it pleasing to you? If the handle is very ornate and of an unusual shape, does it balance with the prongs of the fork or the bowl of the spoon?

With each specific pattern, the shape and the design are important. Examine the different parts of a piece of flatware—the handle, and the bowl, tong or blade—for beauty and consistency of style.

The handle of a piece of flatware comes in three basic shapes—round, square, pointed—with the end decorated or plain. If the piece of silver has design, is the same design that appears on the front of the silver repeated underneath? Is it necessary that it be repeated? In very modern designs there may be no decoration at all; the design is in the shape of the flatware, and this shape may be repeated on the back.

Is the handle solid silver or is it hollow? Is it heavy or light? In general, the heavier the silver, the better the quality. Is the handle thick or thin, flared or gently sculptured? Is it squared or highly carved? Handles can have a cutout design or come perfectly plain, so that you can monogram the handle with the initial of your new married name. (If you plan to monogram your silver, I would recommend that you wait until after the wedding and have all your monogramming done at once. This way it will be done by one craftsman and will be consistent.) Some of the modern handles are even made of wood, bamboo or ceramic.

The style of the handle generally determines the style of the bowl, tong or blade. If the handle is modern, the bowl of the spoon would probably be exaggeratedly round or almost square, the tongs of the fork most likely wider and fewer in number, and the blade possibly of an unusual shape. The traditional handle would require traditional shapes, with the bowl pointed or oblong, the tongs slender and uniform in number, and the blade long and graceful.

Keep in mind, if you decide to choose sterling silver as well as stainless steel or gold plate, that if your two patterns are similar in look you can combine them to entertain large groups.

If you want a formal, elegant look for your flatware, you can achieve this by choosing a pattern that has a lot of swirls on the handle—possibly a design which flows into the bowl. It would be a very rich design, most likely quite rounded and symmetrical in look.

If you have chosen modern china and crystal and you like bold patterns and texture combined with strong bold lines, then you may want to choose modern flatware that is equally stylized. Such flatware would have a small amount of design and might merely repeat a style pattern. A good example of this modern flatware is the Romance pattern by Rosenthal, which would, of course, blend beautifully with their own Romance china pattern.

Be sure to keep the overall look of your table in mind. Don't buy small-scale flatware if the rest of your items are quite large. It's essential to see all three items together before choosing or registering any one

Selecting sizes

165

of the individual items.

Be sure to see the other pieces that come in your sterling or stainless pattern—the hollow ware and the serving accessories. Check items like steak knives and all of the serving pieces. Try to see the real thing rather than just a picture, because this is too expensive an investment to suddenly find that you don't like the pieces that are available in your flatware pattern. Generally it is a better investment to buy serving pieces rather than additional luxury pieces like iced-tea spoons to add to a place setting. The large serving spoons and forks and knives are necessities, not luxuries. So keep in mind what is needed to serve a meal, and make a list of the items that you want in your order of preference, so the bridal consultant or saleswoman can advise your friends accordingly.

Types of hollow ware

You may want to take a look at the various pieces that are available in hollow ware—platters, punch bowls, decorative accessories, candlesticks, ice buckets—and see if you want to register some of these items. This would be wise to do only if you think your guests can afford and will buy the items.

You will be coordinating all three of these items —china, crystal and silver—with the total look of your home. Some people can artfully mix and match different styles, using modern tableware, for example, with Mediterranean decor. But this is difficult to do, so keep working toward a consistent harmonious look for your three items.

One harmonious look

Thin crystal, for example, will look more attractive with fine china that has a delicate hand-painted pattern. On the other hand, thick, chunky glassware will combine best with pottery or earthenware. Because you want to coordinate a total look, it's necessary to see all your items together. Be cautious about this. Don't just look at a dinner plate on a display rack and decide that it's the pattern for you. Insist that the china be taken down, and shown on a real table. Take a lot

166

of time with these decisions. You may want to buy a cup and saucer or a spoon or a glass to take home and decide if you like living with them. Determine if they are comfortable, if you like the way they feel in your hand. Be certain that you want these three items to become part of your home and your life.

When you have narrowed your selection down to two or three patterns, invite your fiancé along to help make the final decision. He'll probably defer to your taste, but many men have surprisingly definite and valuable opinions in these matters. And since he has to live with your choices, it's nice to share this experience with him and give him a chance to offer his opinion.

A word of congratulation is in order here. You've successfully chosen three major items that you're going to be living with and enjoying for a long time; and I know you've given your selection a lot of time and thought. I hope that the total look of your china, crystal and silver will be as pleasing and as beautiful to you in the years to come as they are today.

Now to buy the most special of all items—your wedding gown.

15

Looking Heavenly

CHOOSING YOUR WEDDING GOWN

ONE OF THE MOST MEMORABLE shopping trips you'll ever take is the one you now take to buy your wedding gown. It's a pleasure that comes once in a lifetime. You will be buying the most important dress you'll ever own. And you, like any other girl, are going to want it to be the most beautiful dress imaginable —the ideal wedding gown.

Every girl dreams of a certain kind of wedding gown that will be hers especially and will reflect the very essence of what her idea of a wedding gown is. Gowns nowadays range from dainty mini-dresses to high-fashion harem pants. The range in gowns is as wide as the range in any other kind of dress.

To be sure that your gown is as beautiful and appropriate as it can be for your wedding, you

169

might want to refer to Chapter 6 again, with its suggestions for wedding styles. As you begin your third shopping trip, keep in mind the total look you want for your wedding.

Ultra-formal

Take into account the *type* of wedding you plan. If you are going to have a very formal ceremony, a very large one with a large reception, it's very appropriate to wear an ultra-formal gown. Within the ultra-formal range, you can express your taste in a variety of ways. Traditionally the ultra-formal gown is long, with a long veil and train. Select the color and fabrics you love most, and choose styles and cuts of dresses that suit you best. A high-fashion, sophisticated look is particularly appropriate for the ultra-formal wedding, incorporating very simples lines with heavy brocade or satin materials.

Formal

If you are planning a less formal wedding, you might want a simpler gown, perhaps with no train at all, which features a lovely, full veil that frames your face. The gown for a formal wedding is much the same as that for the ultra-formal wedding, except that the train and veil are usually less opulent, and the gown itself is less extravagant.

Informal

An informal wedding can take place in the daytime or the evening, and it is usually a smaller ceremony than the formal or ultra-formal wedding; as such it offers an even larger choice of dress. A floor-length gown (or shorter version) and headdress, a stylish suit or an afternoon dress are all equally good possibilities.

What will he wear?

The groom's attire, briefly, harmonizes with the bride's degree of formality. At an ultra-formal evening wedding, the groom usually wears white tie and tails. An earlier wedding of equal formality might have the groom in a cutaway coat and striped trousers. For formal weddings, the groom is attired in a black, white or dark blue dinner jacket (white for summer weddings) in the evening. In the daytime he might wear an oxford jacket, which is styled like a suit jacket and is combined with striped trousers and waistcoat.

For an informal wedding your groom might wear a dark gray or navy business suit, or, in summer, a white linen jacket with gray trousers. Naturally, the more elaborate the outfits of the bride and her attendants, the more elegant the attire of the groom, even at the most informal weddings.

All of this information is offered to you merely as a guideline. Most brides choose a gown they find beautiful and work the rest of their wedding around this. If you don't want a cathedral train, you can as easily wear a floor-length dress with a long veil trimmed to complement the gown. In other words, there are no hard and fast rules governing "correct" wedding attire. And although in general the dress of both bride and groom should coordinate, I attended a military wedding once in which the groom was in super-formal full regalia, while his bride wore an informal gown with a short veil. They looked perfect together, not the least bit contradictory. So you must decide for yourself the kind of look you want, and whether or not it combines well with your groom's outfit.

What you want is what is correct

Wedding gowns do pick up the fashion trends and thus are going to change each year, so it's up to you to go and seek the one that is most beautiful to you. You may find one that fits the image you have in mind for your gown, or one that has an image all its own—a beautiful new look that you couldn't even imagine—but whatever your preference, once you fall in love with a particular gown that is the gown in which you should be married.

...the style you like

The color of your gown can range from a pure white to pastels to vivid colors. It's no longer necessary for you to buy a gown that is pure white—or one that is a color, if it's your second marriage. These rules are outdated. It's now proper to wear a gown in any color that you prefer. Colonial brides wore white, which

...the color you like

is probably the way the trend began in this country. White was worn because it was all girls had—not because it had any symbolic value. They would have preferred pastels, which were highly prized during this era, unlike the bleached muslins which everyone wore of necessity. So began the tradition. But modern brides set their own traditions by wearing the colors they love best.

...but be tactful and considerate

However, a word of caution. If you are planning your wedding on your own, well and good. Most girls plan their weddings with their mother's help, and some mothers are not likely to be greatly taken with the idea of a wedding gown that breaks the traditional mold. If you think you might like a wedding gown in a color other than white, you may meet with resistance. And it's only fair to the others concerned that you think through your decision carefully. If you feel that white is an unflattering or unsuitable color for you, or if you plan a wedding in an unusual style which cries out for a color other than white, you will have good points in favor of your decision. But if it's the novelty or shock effect you're after, and you find that your decision is causing unhappiness, then perhaps you should reconsider.

A color for your gown

If color is what you want, be sure to select one that is flattering to you. If you are a redhead, for example, a green gown might be particularly lovely. If you have light brown hair and a fair complexion, you might consider the cool tones of blue, green or purple. The red, orange or yellow tones look ideal on girls with warm complexions and dark hair. Very brown hair and dark skin are flattered by the deeper blues and greens or rich, vivid reds.

There is a wide range of whites. Girls who are tanned or who have dark olive complexions look striking in a pure white-white gown because of the contrast. Ivory is a good choice for a girl who is very fair, as it has more of the pinkish tones in it and will compliment

172

you as beautifully as candlelight. I didn't believe this myself, frankly, until I tried on an ivory gown. I thought the gown stunning, but I was reluctant to try it on because, like most people, I thought ivory to be a dingy color. Yet it looked so beautiful when I had it on, that I knew I had found my dress.

You, as the bride, are the focal point of the wedding, so whatever gown you choose must be set off by the outfits worn by your attendants. If you wear white, you have a great range of colors to choose from for dressing your bridesmaids; if you select a wedding gown in a color, why not reverse and have your bridesmaids wear white. The effect would be unique—and certainly attention-getting. (Chapter 16 gives more information about costuming bridesmaids.)

As you look at bridal gowns, keep your budget clearly in mind. The cost of a wedding gown can be $20 if you make it yourself, or it can range as high as $2000! The average girl pays about $150 to $200 for her gown and veil. Gauge the cost of your wedding gown by how much you would be willing to spend on an ordinary formal gown for your wardrobe. Whether your funds are unlimited or not, remember that this gown is usually worn only once; it's rarely passed on to your sister or saved for a daughter. You may be offered a family heirloom gown, but most girls buy gowns of their own. If, on the other hand, you will be wearing your dress again (for a cocktail outfit, perhaps), an additional amount could be added to the cost of the gown.

A budget for your gown

There are any number of ways to obtain and accessorize your wedding gown. If there is an heirloom gown in your family, or, more likely, an heirloom veil, you might want to wear this for your wedding. Be sure, however, that you leave ample time for alteration and proper cleaning, as you will want the gown and veil to be fresh and beautiful for your wedding.

Where to find your gown

You can have your gown custom-made, from a

173

. . . a custom-designed gown

designer's sketch or your own design. If you do, seek out an experienced seamstress, preferably one whose work you know. This is not the time to experiment and take chances with results. The same is true if you decide to make your gown yourself or have it made by a talented friend. You want to be sure of a quality look, and you don't want to cut corners if the results might be inadequate.

. . . a ready-made gown

You may want to shop for a ready-made gown, to buy "off the rack." Some evening gowns, white or colored, can be ideal for formal weddings. Check dress shops, large and small, for a ready-made gown that you like. Don't, however, buy a gown on sale. Why? Quite often materials and/or colors of sale items are seasonal, and will be outdated by the month of your wedding. Styles, too, change rapidly. And if you aren't satisfied, sale items can't be returned. If you would not normally buy this dress for your wedding gown but are tempted to just because it's on sale, think twice.

. . . a rented gown

It's even possible to rent a wedding gown—a nice thing to know if you plan to be married quickly. Many shops which specialize in renting wedding attire for men are now displaying gowns for brides and bridesmaids, as well. This can be a good solution if time is a problem, but it's more fun to buy your own gown, no matter how modest it is: It's a dress to treasure always.

A bridal salon gown

Perhaps the most common way of buying a wedding gown is to choose one from a bridal shop or the bridal salon of a department store. When you go into the shop or salon, the saleswoman takes your order from a style number and has a gown made up to your measurements. These gowns are, then, in their way custom-made. If you do decide to purchase your gown in this way, there are some pointers you'll find helpful. And these apply whether you decide to buy your gown ready-made, custom-made, or custom-ordered from a sample.

Begin by making an appointment with the bridal salon of your choosing. This is particularly important to busy brides and to busy salons, and it assures you their time and attention. Make your appointment early, for you will need to allow at least two months for your gown to be ordered and delivered to the salon. It's wise to begin shopping as far as six months in advance of your wedding—if possible, even sooner.

...make an appointment

Because this is an important and highly personal shopping trip, try to leave friends and relatives at home, at least during your preliminary excursions. If you do want to take someone along, take one person only, and preferably someone whose taste you know you respect.

Shop around, try on many gowns, and tell the saleswoman or consultant that you're "just looking" at this point. Pick out two or three favorites, and come back to see them again. When you go back to try on these gowns, be careful to supply yourself with the same undergarments, shoes and hairstyle (if possible) that you will be wearing on your wedding day. This is the critical trying-on time when measurements will be taken, and you want everything to approximate actual wedding conditions.

...try it on

When measurements are taken, consider what happens to you in times of stress and excitement. Do you tend to lose or gain five or ten pounds when things get pressured? Also, if you plan to take birth control pills, don't forget to allow for the possibility of weight gain and a change in measurements.

Talk freely about your requirements for a gown. If you have color, style or length set in your mind, tell the saleswoman immediately. Also tell her the dollar amount you can comfortably afford. Since the saleswomen in these salons often work on a commission basis, they will begin showing their most expensive lines first if you don't take the initiative and set the ground rules. They know all too well how irresistible their more costly creations seem to young brides. It's

Talk about your gown

terribly hard to put back a dress you've fallen in love with, so don't tempt yourself by looking in the first place. In order not to go over your head, tell the consultant what your top figure is—and you might consider naming a dollar amount a little below that which you really want to spend, just in case. Don't tempt yourself beyond your means.

If you are buying a gown to match an heirloom veil, bring it along to match up. These veils are often an off-white shade because they have aged. You can't whiten or lighten such delicate material, so you'll have to look for a gown that will blend with it—usually an ivory or pastel shade.

...a little white lie

An excellent tip, which can save you a lot of worry, is to tell the saleswoman a "little white lie" about the date of your wedding. Give her a date that is a week or two *earlier* than your actual wedding date. When she orders, it's common practice for her to give the manufacturer a date even earlier than the one you state. This duplication gives you a leeway of two or three weeks rather than the usual one week, which the manufacturers often ignore because they know the saleswomen's tactics and thus work past given deadlines thinking they have plenty of time.

A friend of mine gave the consultant her correct wedding date and wound up not receiving her gown until four days before the wedding—too late for her bridal portrait—and her veil exactly one day before. The result was unnecessary worry and anxiety. It's far better to use the "little white lie."

The bridal consultant

When you are buying a gown by ordering from a sample, you will most likely come in contact with a bridal consultant or saleswoman who specializes in selling bridal gowns. Be sure during your first "just-looking" trip that you not only see what gowns are available, but that you also judge the bridal consultant or saleswoman who will be assisting you. It's most important during this time, when you're choosing the

176

gown of your dreams, that you deal with a person who is nice—someone who likes weddings and who enjoys the whole idea of getting married. It can be very frustrating and unpleasant to deal with a bridal consultant who is jaded and for whom wedding gowns have long since lost their appeal.

However, the bridal consultant who is pleasant understands the style you like, and respects the amount of money you have to spend, can be extremely helpful. Usually she brings out sample gowns to the main showroom for you to choose from. Ask to see everything she has, and don't allow her to limit your choice by showing you only one line. After you have selected some gowns, you'll most likely be taken to a small dressing room to try them on. If it's difficult to get a perspective on a dress in this small area, move to a larger area where the lighting is brighter and less flattering. Study yourself from every possible angle, and be particularly sure that you like all views—front, side and back—of any dress you buy.

Walk around the room in the gown, and see if it is comfortable, as well as beautiful. Do you like the weight of the gown? Is the length good? (A floor-length gown should be two to three inches off the floor in the front.) To judge the fit of your gown, watch yourself as you try it on. If you have to pull, tug and constantly adjust it as you move, it doesn't fit you properly.

Judge your gown carefully

Will you be dancing at the reception? Can you dance in this gown? Many saleswomen will show you a loop sewn into an underneath seam of the train. You can put your wrist through this loop for dancing, and thus keep the train off the floor. But in reality, when you pick up your dress and train by using this loop, you will expose your slip to all present. Consider the alternative of draping the gown over your arm or holding it comfortably with your left hand. Some gowns have detachable trains which can be removed after the ceremony to make dancing easier for you.

For added comfort, arrange to have dress shields and lingerie straps sewn into your gown. Dress shields prevent perspiration stains from showing. Lingerie straps neaten a cutout neckline or a standaway collar. Bra and slip will be securely snapped into these straps and you'll be completely free of worry.

Plan to buy a slip for your gown, particularly if it is quite full. As you try gowns on, the saleswoman will no doubt supply a slip, but you'll need your own for the wedding day. If you wait until you pick your dress up, you may wind up buying a costly slip from the bridal salon; if you plan in advance, you can have one made up inexpensively for you. Select a material that won't rustle when you move, and have an elastic waistband sewn in so your comfort is total.

Practice for confidence

Practice how to move and sit and stand on your wedding day so you will feel even more comfortable. You probably won't have your gown for practice purposes much before the wedding, but that needn't hamper you (you probably won't want to wear your wedding gown anyway, as it might soil). Actresses can't practice in costume until right before a show opens either, so they use rehearsal skirts. These are usually old skirts or slips—far different from the costumes they will wear, but long and of the proper weight to help them learn how to move. Wear an old slip, or even a long bathrobe, and move, sit, climb in it. Wear the undergarments and shoes you'll be wearing at the ceremony, and put something on your head that is a facsimile of your headpiece. See what adjustments you have to make, how you have to shorten the length of your steps, and how much you must lift the skirt to go up and down stairs. This is particularly necessary if you're going to have to kneel during any part of the ceremony.

Your bridal accessories

When you select shoes to wear with your gown, make sure that they are comfortable. The heel need not be too high, particularly if your bridegroom is not much taller than you. Even though the shoes won't always show under a long gown, they should match in color and go with the material as closely as possible. Again, comfortable shoes are not just nice, they're essential. If your feet are hurting, don't think it won't show up in your wedding pictures. It will!

Add gloves if you like. Select a length to match the sleeve on your gown. A short-sleeved or sleeveless gown can be worn with gloves that come to the wrist bone, or finished off with longer gloves for a more formal look. An informal gown may not require any. Choose gloves in a harmonizing color or white—styled as plainly or ornately as your wedding outfit demands—or dispense with gloves altogether.

You may want to carry a muff, a unique touch for a winter wedding. If you are presented with a pin to wear during your wedding, decide if it can be worn with your gown before committing yourself to wear it. To prevent pin marks in your dress, place a square of material underneath your gown and pin through the dress *and the piece of material*—to hold the pin more securely in place and save the dress from being pulled out of shape. Flowers and jewelry may be worn with your wedding gown, if your religion permits, but should, of course, be chosen with your gown in mind.

Remember that your flowers are accessories to your dress and should be chosen with this in mind. If you have beautiful detail on the front of your gown, for example, you might want to carry a single flower or a light, delicate bouquet which will allow the detail of the gown to show through. (More on this in Chapter 21.)

Select your veil or train next. Buying a veil is like buying a hat. You may see one that looks elegant, but when you try it on, it isn't "you." A large hat can dwarf a petite face, and the same is true of a large headpiece or a too-full veil. Your veil and headpiece should flatter your hairstyle, face and gown. They should be easy to place and easier still to keep on your head with-

...your bridal bouquet

179

out the addition of pins and lots of worries.

Veils are often attached to headpieces. These can be combs, bows, garlands of flowers, tiaras or simple trimmed and embroidered "crowns" shaped like small hats.

...a veil of lace

The veil itself will be available in a variety of materials and can flow to the shoulder, waist, or floor, as desired. Shorter veils are generally worn at more informal weddings or when the detail of the back of a dress is particularly lovely and the bride wants it to be visible. Sometimes a long veil, doubling as a train, will be transparent so that the bride can have elegance and formality and still show the design of the dress.

You can achieve a delicate effect by sewing tiny fresh flowers like lilies of the valley (delicate yet strong) hit and miss on your veil, minutes before you walk down the aisle.

Now to decide

Before you order your gown and all accessories, go home and sleep on your decision. Give yourself a chance to think it over and make sure that this all-important choice is the right one. When you do order your gown ask if there will be any additional charges for alterations or whatever. For future reference hold fast to your copy of the sales order which includes all the items, colors, styles and sizes that you are ordering. Ask the saleswoman to list "who" pays for alterations, too.

When your gown arrives in the store, you'll be called in for a final fitting—and bridal portrait, if you like. (More information about bridal portraits in Chapter 31.)

Now that the gown of your dreams is safely tucked away in your closet, your only problem is to find the patience to wait for the day when you will proudly wear it down the aisle.

16

Pretty Bridesmaids

SELECTING APPAREL FOR THE WEDDING PARTY

SELECTING OUTFITS for your wedding party to wear will be your fourth, but easiest, shopping trip. Easy because you've already chosen your own gown, which is the focal point of the wedding and which sets the style. Now all you have to do is decide what your various attendants will wear and suggest styles and colors for both mothers.

There is a handy chart in this chapter which gives you capsulized advice on what clothes go with what degree of formality, but here are more complete details about choosing outfits for each of your attendants.

Bridesmaids, senior and/or junior, and the maid or matron of honor should wear gowns which complement your own dress and enhance the total picture of the ceremony. If you're wearing a floor-length gown,

183

Gowns for your bridesmaids

your bridesmaids can wear the same if you wish; if you're wearing a short, informal gown, you will want your bridesmaids to wear suits or dresses. They wear outfits that you choose in a color that blends with your ensemble.

Follow your wedding style

To set a certain style for your wedding (see Chapter 6), everyone in your wedding party should wear outfits that carry out this style. A romantic wedding gown with lots of lace and frills would be complemented by bridesmaids in long gowns with wide-brim garden hats, perhaps delicately embroidered, and carrying baskets of garden flowers to complete the look. Or if you want an Elizabethan style, your bridesmaids can wear crocheted bonnets without a veil and gowns of chiffon, unbelted and free-flowing. A recent bride modeled her wedding after *Romeo and Juliet*. Her gown and those of her bridesmaids were Elizabethan in look, and she had twin ring-bearers who wore black velvet knee breeches and white crepe shirts, white hose and black velvet shoes. The men in the wedding party wore traditional morning suits. If you're having a very formal winter or fall wedding, you might select gowns in velvets of rich regal colors, with long white puffed sleeves. Whatever your style or theme, you should choose a material and a look for your bridesmaids' gowns that will reflect the desired image.

Choose gowns that flatter

As you are selecting the gowns, think of colors and styles that are flattering to the girls who will be your attendants. Consider the height, figure type and coloring of each girl, and try to select something that will be complimentary to all of them. For example, an empire bodice suits a slender figure but is not as flattering to a fuller-busted figure. A long gown with a train requires much poise and grace, and a short gown requires attractive legs.

Comfort is important, too. If your bridesmaids will dance at the reception, try on one of the gowns to be sure it's easy to move around in. You will want your

184

bridesmaids to enjoy the reception too.

Try vibrant colors for your attendants' dresses. There's no need to choose neutral shades that are uninteresting as the men in your wedding party will be wearing neutral colors and so will blend with any color you pick for your bridesmaids. If you are wearing a white or an ivory gown, you can choose any color of the rainbow for your bridesmaids to wear. If you have a gown that is colorful, you will have to coordinate colors more carefully. You might in this instance have your bridesmaids dressed in white gowns; this switch will be interesting and will also ensure that you are still the focus of the occasion.

Use colors you like

If your bridesmaids range from fair-haired girls with pale complexions to olive-skinned girls with dark brown hair, you're going to have to choose colors that are flattering to all of them. Blue might be a good compromise. But if your bridesmaids have similar complexions, you can choose colors that flatter their particular coloring. Your situation will be unique and you'll have to choose colors accordingly. Gowns in multicolored fabrics can solve this problem nicely. Multicolored pastels blend nicely with spring bouquets, for example, and create a lovely, unified wedding look. (See Chapter 21 for further help in color selection.)

Think of each girl's coloring

Don't make the mistake of trying to choose a unique outfit for each bridesmaid. The bridesmaids' costumes should be matching so that your gown and accessories stand out. Trying to do too much with their clothes will only detract from you. The only exception to this rule is your maid of honor, who should in some way be distinguished from the other bridesmaids.

Don't attempt to have each girl wear a gown of a different color. Even though you buy the gowns from the same manufacturer, it's unlikely that they will match well. It's difficult to blend different colors, and this will make your wedding photographs look strange—as if the wedding party is not all one group.

The same color for each girl

185

All the bridesmaids should wear the same gowns in the same color. If you want to distinguish the maid of honor by dress, she can wear a different shade of the bridesmaids' color—i.e., a dark green to go with the bridesmaids' light green—or she can wear the same color but with an additional, special trim. But the best solution is to have all the gowns identical and differentiate with changes in bouquets—making the maid of honor's larger or more elaborate.

Whatever color or combination of colors you use, be sure to consider the background hues. If you're going to be married in an elaborate church, decorated perhaps in golds and reds, orange gowns for your bridesmaids are not a happy choice. The careful combining of colors for your bridesmaids' gowns will help give your wedding a complete look and will result in prettier wedding photographs—particularly if they will be in color.

It's traditional to give your attendants a present for assisting you, so in place of a piece of jewelry or some other memento, you can provide each bridesmaid with her gown. This is a particularly nice gesture if you have reason to suspect that someone you would like in your wedding party may refuse because the outfit is too costly. Often the gown that you select is not what these girls would buy for themselves, so this saves each girl the expense of buying a gown she'll wear only once.

Will you pay for the gowns?

If you're going to pay for one girl's gown, you should pay for all. If it's within your budget, and it's something you want to do, be sure to set aside and plan for the total amount of money needed and tell the girls that you will be giving them their gowns as gifts.

The prices of bridesmaids' gowns can vary as greatly as does your own gown. They run from approximately $35 to $65, with the average gown at $45—the price for a floor-length gown in attractive style and fabric that is custom-ordered from a bridal salon.

Bridesmaids' outfits come from the same sources

as wedding gowns, so check Chapter 15 for detailed information. The gowns should all be made by one seamstress or shop, not by several different people. This will ensure uniformity and consistency of workmanship and style.

Bridesmaids' gowns from many sources

Ready-made gowns are an interesting idea. Often you can find a selection of cocktail dresses or evening dresses that are suitable for bridesmaids' outfits. This would save you and the bridesmaids much time and trouble—perhaps dollars—so shop around to see what's available.

If you order your bridesmaids' gowns from a sample gown, remember the tips about dealing with saleswomen or bridal consultants. And be sure to use the same ruse of giving them a wedding date which is two weeks before the actual date.

You might want to consider using an outfit that the girls already own, if you're having only one or two attendants and the wedding is to be small and informal. Suggest this to them and ask to see what they have; let them know as soon as possible if the outfit is appropriate. This saves you or the girls the expense of buying a totally new outfit.

Perhaps you might like to rent bridesmaids' gowns. This is a nice solution if you're getting married very quickly and time is a problem. You could rent gowns for the girls and have them ready right away. Be sure that you rent all the gowns from the same shop or chain of stores, however, so that they match exactly.

Gowns can be rented

In addition to choosing gowns for the girls, you're going to choose a headdress and all accessory items: jewelry, gloves, shoes and bouquets. You should choose these accessory items after you have selected the gown, as you'll want them to match.

The bridesmaids' headpieces can be more colorful than yours, and they can wear a long or short veil to match their gowns. When you're considering headpieces for your bridesmaids, keep costs down whether or not you are paying for this item. They are seldom worn again and, unfortunately, are very expensive.

Quite often it is possible for you to make your own headpieces for the bridesmaids. A wedding that I was in featured simple but attractive headpieces that had been made by the bride's mother. She took a base of light plastic wiring and sewed a fabric doily on top; to this she attached yellow ribbons finished with tiny crocheted daisies on each end. She sewed a comb to the base of the netting to hold the headpiece securely in the hair. The headpieces were the talk of the wedding and yet so inexpensive.

Make your own headpieces

No time to make your bridesmaids' headpieces? Order them custom-made. You might ask the seamstress to keep some of her leftover ribbons or lace materials so you can give them to your florist; he can work them into the design of the bridesmaids' bouquets, so that the bouquets will match the headdresses perfectly.

If you will be married in a suit and hat, your bridesmaids can also wear hats—or ribbons and/or flowers in their hair. Flowers give a fresh and lovely feminine look which your florist can help create. If you do use fresh flowers, select those that are either completely without fragrance or with a light, pleasing scent. Some flowers have an unpleasant odor that is too cloying or irritating, and you won't want your bridesmaids to wear something which will bother them all through the wedding day.

Add fresh flowers for a feminine look

Also, it's perfectly proper for you to request that all girls wear their hair in a similar mode, though not drastically different from their usual styles. If, for example, they all have long hair, you can choose to have them wear it long and flowing, or in a sleek upswept style. This way it will be consistent and attractive with the headpieces you choose.

Once you have determined the total outfit for each girl, make up a list of all the different items she will need. This list should include the dress itself, any special undergarments, shoes (color and heel size), gloves, if you want them (color and length), flowers, jewelry, headpieces, veils, or hats.

In addition to listing the various parts of the outfit, designate who will be paying for what items. Give each girl complete information about where and when to go to be measured and when her final fitting will be. If the girls go alone to these fittings, carefully advise them of any changes you have made in the dress; give specifics, such as length of hem, placement of waistlines, et cetera, so that the dresses will be the same. You can avoid errors by making sure that each girl knows what needs to be altered on her dress.

Give each girl all the details

Tell your bridesmaids what accessories and undergarments to take to the fittings, particularly mentioning correct shoe style and heel size. Give them all this information in writing, especially if your bridesmaids are coming from a distance. If they're not around to see your gown, or even the gown you have chosen for them, it's even more important that you communicate well with them so that when all are gathered together they will indeed be wearing the same outfit.

Both your mother and your fiancé's mother will want to begin shopping for their dresses or arranging to have them made, so it's wise to recommend a style—including accessories and colors that will blend with your total color scheme—as early as possible. Most older women look elegant in floor-length gowns, and you may prefer this attractive and appropriate look for most weddings. You can also suggest street-length dresses or suits for less formal weddings. As far as color is concerned, the lighter hues are generally more flattering to the mature woman; you may want to have them wear a pastel shade of a color that you will be using in your wedding. Ask you mother for her ideas. She can be very helpful and perhaps even come up with additional alternatives you hadn't yet considered.

Once you have decided what is appropriate, your

Floor-length gowns an elegant choice

189

mother should choose the color she will wear. Then tell your future mother-in-law what the various outfits will be like and recommend what you think would be a good color for her. It's a nice gesture to give this information to your fiancé's mother in person. If this isn't possible, call her on the phone or write a warm and friendly letter explaining all the details of the gowns and colors the others will be wearing. In the same letter, it would be nice to ask for her flower preference—to help you pick her corsage. In other words, do your best to let her know that she is an important part of your wedding.

A dress for your flower girl

If you have a flower girl, you can dress her to match the clothes of the train or ring-bearer, or you can have her in a "junior" version of your bridesmaids' gowns. You might use the same fabric for her dress and a somewhat similar style, but have a dress made that is appropriate for her youth. Keep the cost of a child's outfit reasonable, as children outgrow their clothes quickly. Be considerate of her parents, who will have to pay, perhaps checking with her mother to see if the child already owns an appropriate dress. You may want to pay for this outfit and give it as a gift, or you may know someone who could make this dress easily. Decide if you want your flower girl to wear gloves, and select as simple a headpiece as possible. A flowered tiara is nice. If you are going to have her wear a long gown, be sure that she will be able to walk well while wearing it. Perhaps you might make it a trifle shorter than floor-length so that she doesn't get tangled up in it.

The chart will help

As you look at the chart on the wedding party that appears in this chapter, you'll notice it mentions three different types of weddings: ultra-formal, formal and informal. These types are then divided into daytime and nighttime varieties (anytime after 6 P.M. is nighttime). For the women in the wedding party there are suggestions as to the dress, headdress and accessories; for the men there are suggested suits and appropriate accessories for each type of wedding. There are also ways, particularly for the men, to coordinate outfits with changes in season or weather. The chart will help you keep your wedding consistent in style. Don't feel bound by any suggestions given you. Decide what you want for your wedding, exercise your own good taste, and the end result is sure to be a pleasing one.

Just as your wedding gown sets the tone for what will be worn by the women in your wedding party, so your groom's outfit will influence what the men will wear. It's a little easier with men because all of them will wear identical outfits. The only exceptions are the officiating clergyman and military men. If your husband-to-be is in the service and is wearing his uniform for the wedding, all members of the wedding party who are also military may properly wear their uniforms, too. Those who are not, wear outfits that blend with the uniform worn by your groom. Your clergyman will wear his usual attire; some religious orders have special robes to be worn at weddings, and you may fear that the colors of these robes will not go with your color scheme. You should ask your clergyman what he will be wearing if you think this might be the case.

Men are easy

It's wise to discuss the choice of outfits for the men in your wedding party with your fiancé and your father, and with his father, too, if possible. The chart will give suggestions about what is appropriate and will indicate what goes well with your gown.

Go to a reputable shop that rents wedding attire for men to get some ideas of what is available and appropriate for your locale. When you do this shopping, take your fiancé or your father along to get a man's opinion; or you might ask your fiancé to take care of this responsibility himself.

To make sure that all outfits have the same detail, rent them all from the same shop. You can have the groom, the best man or your father take care of coordinating with the shop so that your order is placed for the proper number and style of suits.

Each male member of the wedding party should be given a list stating details about their outfit, just like the one for the bridesmaids. This list for the men should include all the items of the outfit you have chosen, where and when each man is to be fitted, and who pays for what. Quite often the groom pays for the accessory items that complete the ushers' outfits: gloves, spats, et cetera. Your groom might consider paying for the rental of the entire outfit instead of giving his ushers and best man the traditional gift—an arrangement similar to the one outlined for brides and bridesmaids.

Make your fiancé's outfit special by selecting a boutonniere which is unique, possibly a blossom from your bouquet. Keep your wedding style in mind for the men's outfits, too. For that highly romantic wedding, the ushers might be in full dress and tails for the evening, or very formal dress for the afternoon. Even something as small as an unusual shirt—ruffled perhaps—can lend an interesting look to their suits.

If a judge will perform your ceremony, you might request that he wear a particular type of suit, or you could rent an outfit for him. In this case, you assume the rental charge, so be sure you want to pay for this before you request that he wear a special outfit.

Small boys, ring-bearers or train-bearers, can be dressed to match the flower girl's outfit or in smaller versions of the men's clothing. These outfits may or may not be for rent, so check in your area. Just as you discuss the flower girl's dress with her mother, give the same courtesy to the mothers of any ring or train-bearers you may have.

If wedding guests ask you what to wear to the wedding, feel free to tell them what styles the wedding party will be wearing and to suggest an appropriate outfit. Wedding guests should generally dress as they would for any kind of formal affair taking place at that hour of the day. If they were to attend church on Sunday morning they might wear a dressy dress or a suit with hat and gloves to match; this, then, is what they should wear to your wedding if it is in church in the morning. A cocktail dress is appropriate for the after-six wedding.

To the question: Can I wear white? say yes, and tactfully suggest that the guest use colored accessories. It is customary that only the bride wear white at the wedding, for no one must be confused with her on this occasion, but the use of colored accents easily solves this problem.

Should guests wear white?

In some areas of the country, in the South for example, formal dress is expected of a wedding guest if the wedding party is formally attired. If this is also true in your area, be sure to let your guests know either by having it indicated on your invitation "black tie" or by making sure that they find out by word of mouth.

It's a custom to give a gift to each of your attendants. If you're buying your bridesmaids' outfits, then of course it would not be necessary to give them an additional gift. But if not, you might buy them a memento of the wedding—like pictures or a tasteful piece of jewelry that will go with their gowns. The gift should be personal, and each girl should receive the same thing. Your flower girl would most likely be delighted with a locket or a bracelet, engraved or accompanied by a special note of thanks from you. A ring or train-bearer would enjoy his own "grown-up" tiebar as his special gift.

Gifts to ushers should be personal items, too, like cuff links or a tie tack; and they should be identical. These gifts are purchased by your fiancé, or he may substitute the rental of their outfits in place of a formal gift. It's not necessary to give a special gift to your mother and father or to his, but it is a nice touch. A small, personal item or even a note, thanking them for their love, understanding and help given throughout the wedding period would be much appreciated.

Gifts for your attendants

You and your fiancé can present these gifts on

your wedding day, being certain to tell your attendants if the gifts are to be worn during the ceremony, or you can give them out at one of the special parties held during your wedding week.

Your attendants will be of great help to you on your wedding day, giving you the support and assistance you need. The choosing of their outfits and their gifts should be handled with care and attention. They deserve the best from you.

STYLE OF WEDDING	INFORMAL Before 6 P.M.	INFORMAL After 6 P.M.
BRIDE	Gown: Suit, afternoon dress with matching coat or jacket, or mini-dress over matching pants. Headdress: Hat or large single bow with or without short veil. Accessories: Single flower, floral bouquet, flowers and ribbons combined with prayer book or corsage; jewelry, purse and gloves (all optional); shoes to match.	Gown: Suit; dressy pants suit, or cocktail dress with matching coat or jacket. Headdress: Hat or small headpiece with or without short veil. Accessories: Single flower, floral bouquet, flowers and ribbons combined with prayer book or corsage; jewelry, purse and gloves (all optional); shoes to match.
BRIDESMAIDS (And maid/matron of honor)	Gown: Suit, afternoon dress with matching coat or jacket, or mini-dress over matching pants. Headdress: Hat or large single bow with or without short veil. Accessories: Single flower, floral bouquet, flowers and ribbons combined with prayer book or corsage; jewelry, purse and gloves (all optional); shoes to match.	Gowns: Suit, dressy pants suit, or cocktail dress with matching coat or jacket to match bride. Headdress: Hat or small headpiece with or without short veil to match bride. Accessories: Same as bride's choice, and to harmonize.
GROOM (Best man and all other men in party)	Winter clothes and accessories: Black tuxedo with matching trousers; white dress shirt with black bow tie; black shoes and socks. Or dark gray or navy business suit; white dress shirt, with conventional tie; black shoes and socks. No gloves or hats. Summer clothes and accessories: White dinner jacket with black trousers; white dress shirt, cummerbund; bow tie; black shoes and socks. Or light business suit; white dress shirt, with conventional tie; black shoes and socks. No gloves or hats.	Winter clothes and accessories: Black tuxedo with matching trousers; white dress shirt with black bow tie; black shoes and socks. Or dark gray or navy business suit; white dress shirt, with conventional tie; black shoes and socks. No gloves or hats. Summer clothes and accessories: White dinner jacket with black trousers; white dress shirt, cummerbund; bow tie; black shoes and socks. Or light business suit; white dress shirt, with conventional tie; black shoes and socks. No gloves or hats.
MOTHERS (Bride's and Groom's)	Gown: Suit, dressy pants suit, or cocktail dress with matching coat or jacket. Headdress: Hat or small headpiece with or without short veil. Accessories: Single flower, floral bouquet, flowers and ribbons combined with prayer book, or corsage; jewelry, purse and gloves (all optional); shoes to match.	Gowns: Suit, dressy pants suit, or cocktail dress with matching coat or jacket to match bride. Headdress: Hat or small headpiece with or without short veil to match bride. Accessories: Same as bride's choice, and to harmonize.
FLOWER GIRL	Gown: Suit, dressy pants suit, or dress with jacket to match bridesmaids or bride. Dressy dress with colored tights and matching shoes good choice. Headdress: Cap or small headpiece without veil. Accessories: Tiny bouquet or corsage, jewelry and gloves (optional).	Gown: Suit, dressy pants suit, or dress with jacket to match bridesmaids or bride. Dressy dress with colored tights and matching shoes good choice. Headdress: Cap or small headpiece without veil. Accessories: Tiny bouquet or corsage, jewelry and gloves (optional).
RING and/or TRAIN-BEARERS	Clothes: Dark or light colored simple suit, blazer with light trousers. Accessories: Black shoes and socks. Note: If ring-bearer is a little girl, she would dress the same as flower girl.	Clothes: Dark or light colored suit, blazer with light trousers, or to match men. Accessories: Black shoes and socks. Note: If ring-bearer is a little girl, she would dress the same as flower girl.

STYLE OF WEDDING	FORMAL Before 6 P.M.	FORMAL After 6 P.M.
BRIDE	Gown: Midi or floor length, not-too-elaborate fabric in any color; train (optional). Alternative choices: a formal dress with wide pants modified by a covering front panel, or a dressy mini. Headdress: Short, extremely full headpiece without veil, or fresh flowers arranged in hair, attached to ribbon streamers or comb. Accessories: Single flower, floral bouquet, or flowers and ribbons combined with prayer book; jewelry and gloves (both optional); shoes to match.	Gown: Midi or floor length, not-too-elaborate fabric in any color; train (optional). Alternative choices: a formal dress with wide pants modified by a covering front panel, or a dressy mini. Headdress: Short to medium-length veil that doubles as train (optional); short, extremely full veil or fresh flowers arranged in hair, attached to ribbon streamers or comb. Accessories: Single flower, floral bouquet, or flowers and ribbons combined with prayer book; jewelry and gloves (both optional); shoes to match.
BRIDESMAIDS (And maid/matron of honor)	Gowns: Mini, midi, floor length or pants (same as bride's), not-too-elaborate fabric in colors to blend with wedding colors; train shorter than bride's or not worn at all, depending upon bride. Headdresses: Cap or tiara-style headpiece without veil or trimmed with fresh flowers or ribbons. Accessories: Floral bouquet; jewelry and gloves (both optional); shoes to match. Note: Maid of honor's outfit can be more elaborate.	Gowns: Mini, midi, floor length or pants (same as bride's), not-too-elaborate fabric in colors to blend with wedding colors; train shorter than bride's or not worn at all, depending upon bride. Headdresses: Cap or tiara-style headpiece with veil shorter than bride's or not worn at all, depending upon bride, or trimmed with flowers or ribbons. Accessories: Floral bouquet; jewelry and gloves (both optional); shoes to match. Note: Maid of honor's outfit can be more elaborate.
GROOM (Best man and all other men in party)	Clothes: Oxford jacket with gray striped trousers. Accessories: Black shoes, black socks; tie to match; gray gloves; black homburg or derby hat (gloves and hats optional).	Clothes—Winter: Black or midnight blue dinner jacket with matching trousers; cummerbund (may match bridesmaids' gowns); dress shirt with white turned-down collar. White turtleneck may be substituted for dress shirt. Clothes—Summer: White dinner jacket, with black trousers; cummerbund (may match bridesmaids' gowns); dress shirt. Accessories: Black shoes (patent or kid), black socks; tie to match; gray gloves and black homburg hat (optional).
MOTHERS (Bride's and Groom's)	Gowns: Street length to floor length (not dependent on bride's gown), or wide pants modified by covering front panel; not-too-elaborate fabric in any color to blend with wedding colors; train shorter than bride's or not worn at all, depending upon bride's choice. Headdresses: Hat or headpiece, no veil. Accessories: Corsages; jewelry and gloves (both optional); shoes to match.	Gowns: Street length to floor length (not dependent on bride's gown), or wide pants modified by covering front panel; not-too-elaborate fabric in any color to blend with wedding colors; train shorter than bride's or not worn at all. Headdresses: Hat or headpiece with veil shorter than bride's or not worn at all. Accessories: Corsages; jewelry and gloves (both optional); shoes to match.
FLOWER GIRL	Gown: Midi, short, floor length or pants, to match bridesmaids or bride, not-too-elaborate fabric in color to match wedding colors; train (optional). Headdress: Cap or tiara-style; no veil. Accessories: Tiny bouquet or corsage, jewelry and gloves (optional).	Gown: Midi, short or floor length, not-too-elaborate fabric in color to match wedding colors; train (optional). Headdress: Cap or tiara-style headpiece with veil to match bridesmaids or bride. Accessories: Tiny bouquet or corsage, jewelry and gloves (optional).
RING and/or TRAIN-BEARERS	Clothes: Dark or light colored suit, blazer with light trousers, or to match men. Accessories: Black shoes and socks. Note: If ring-bearer is a little girl, she would dress the same as flower girl.	Clothes: Dark or light colored suit, or blazer with light trousers. Accessories: Black shoes and socks. Note: If ring-bearer is a little girl, she would dress the same as flower girl.

STYLE OF WEDDING	ULTRA-FORMAL Before 6 P.M.	ULTRA-FORMAL After 6 P.M.
BRIDE	Gown: Midi or floor length, not-too-elaborate fabric in any color; train (optional). Headdress: Short to medium-length veil that doubles as train (optional); short, extremely full veil or fresh flowers arranged in hair, attached to ribbon streamers or comb. Accessories: Single flower, floral bouquet, or flowers and ribbons combined with prayer book; jewelry and gloves (both optional); shoes to match.	Gown: Midi or floor length, elaborate fabric in any color; train (optional). Headdress: Floor-length veil that doubles as train; short, extremely full veil or fresh flowers arranged in hair, attached to ribbon streamers or comb. Accessories: Single flower, floral bouquet, or flowers and ribbons combined with prayer book; jewelry and gloves (both optional); shoes to match.
BRIDESMAIDS (And maid/matron of honor)	Gowns: Midi or floor length (same as bride's), not-too-elaborate fabric in colors to blend with wedding colors; train shorter than bride's or not worn at all, depending upon bride's choice. Headdresses: Cap or tiara-style headpiece with veil shorter than bride's or not worn at all, depending upon bride's choice, or trimmed with fresh flowers or ribbons. Accessories: Floral bouquet; jewelry and gloves (both optional); shoes to match. Note: Remember that all bridesmaid's outfits are identical with exception of maid of honor whose outfit can be more elaborate.	Gowns: Midi or floor length (but not longer than bride's), elaborate fabric in colors to blend with wedding colors; train (optional). Headdresses: Cap or tiara-style headpiece with short veil (optional) or trimmed with fresh flowers or ribbons. Accessories: Floral bouquet; jewelry and gloves (both optional); shoes to match. Note: Remember that all bridesmaid's are identical with exception of maid of honor whose outfit can be more elaborate.
GROOM (Best man and all other men in party)	Clothes: Cutaway coat with gray striped trousers, gray waistcoat; formal white shirt with wing collar. Accessories: Black calf shoes, black socks, tie to match, gray doeskin gloves and black silk top hat (gloves and hats optional).	Clothes: Black or midnight blue tailcoat with matching trousers, white waistcoat; stiff front shirt with wing collar. Accessories: Black patent pumps or oxfords; tie to match; black socks; white gloves and black silk top hat (gloves and hat optional).
MOTHERS (Bride's and Groom's)	Gowns: Floor length or shorter (not dependent on bride's gown); not-too-elaborate fabric in any color to blend with wedding colors; train shorter than bride's or not worn at all, depending upon bride's choice. Headdresses: Hat or headpiece with veil shorter than bride's or not worn at all, depending upon bride's choice. Accessories: Corsages; jewelry and gloves (both optional); shoes to match. Note: Mothers' outfits should have similar look.	Gowns: Floor length or shorter; elaborate fabric in any color to blend with wedding colors; train (optional). Headdresses: Hat or headpiece with short veil (optional). Accessories: Corsages; jewelry and gloves (both optional); shoes to match. Note: Mothers' outfits should have similar look.
FLOWER GIRL	Gown: Midi, short or floor length, not-too-elaborate fabric in color to match wedding colors; train (optional). Headdress: Cap or tiara-style headpiece with short veil (optional). Accessories: Tiny bouquet or corsage, jewelry and gloves (optional).	Gown: Midi or floor length, elaborate fabric in color to match wedding colors; train (optional). Headdress: Cap or tiara-style headpiece with short veil (optional).- Accessories: Tiny bouquet or corsage, jewelry and gloves (optional).
RING and/or TRAIN-BEARERS	Clothes: Dark or light colored suit, or blazer with light trousers. Accessories: Black shoes and socks. Note: If ring-bearer is a little girl, she would dress the same as flower girl.	Clothes: Dark or light colored suit, or blazer with light trousers. Accessories: Black shoes and socks. Note: If ring-bearer is a little girl, she would dress the same as flower girl.

17

Two Tickets to...

ARRANGEMENTS FOR YOUR HONEYMOON

YOUR HONEYMOON is one of the most important trips you will ever take——and certainly the most romantic. Because it's the groom's responsibility to pay for the honeymoon, *this* shopping trip might well be taken by the groom alone. You might suggest to your fiancé that "honeymoon shopping" is something he can do while you're looking for your gown; he can get brochures and information on various places of interest, and the two of you can meet, look through the brochures, and make the final decision. Have him look at this chapter with you first; the rest will be easy.

It's important to think of your honeymoon in terms of a vacation, a time to relax and be together completely alone. During the pre-wedding time you'll be experiencing happiness and lots of excitement. So try to choose a spot for your honeymoon that will be

A honeymoon is a vacation

Relaxation is important

Honeymoon budgeting

relaxing—a place where you can enjoy being with your new husband, where you can spend a restful time together before you settle down into married life.

Relaxation means different things to different people, and there is a honeymoon to fill each couple's needs. The type of honeymoon you choose will depend on the kind of people you are and what you like to do on vacations. Most of the newlyweds I've spoken to have the same comment: They wish they had kept it simple and not planned to do so much. Many feel that they took too long a wedding trip; by the end they were eager to get back and begin their life together in their new home. And don't feel that because you're on your honeymoon you much seclude yourself totally from all outside contacts. Some people need and want only each other, but if you're both gregarious and enjoy meeting new people, you should take this into account when choosing a honeymoon spot.

Of course you're going to have to consider how much money you can spend, and unfortunately, the practical must enter into this decision at this point. You should make up a small budget, listing the various expenses you will have for your honeymoon, such as the following:

1. Hotel

2. Transportation

3. Food (Include 15 percent to 20 percent for tipping.)

4. Sight-seeing (places of interest, side trips you may want to take)

5. A contingency fund (This is extra money which you allow for side trips, added expenses or that special little something you just have to buy; it should be 10 percent of your total honeymoon cost.)

If finances are a problem, remember that you don't have to go far to "get away from it all." A friend may be able to offer a summer house (and summer resorts can be charming and secluded in winter months).

Want to try something unusual? Investigate the contests for honeymooners in the bridal magazines. You might win one, and this would solve all your financial troubles. Sure, you'll find yourself on mailing lists, but it's still worth it to enter and maybe even win. Also investigate package tours, but check what they offer carefully. If a tour is traveling to many places that you don't want to see or offering entertainment and dining that would not be your choice, you may find you'd save more money in the long run by planning your own trip.

When planning your budget think of transportation, for it will probably be the major expense of your honeymoon. Traveling by car or bus is much less expensive than traveling by plane, but if your time is precious, getting there fast might be worth the extra cost. Traveling by boat is the leisurely, luxurious way to go, but you need both time and money for this kind of a honeymoon. (If you go by boat, be sure to take along seasick pills—just in case. Also be wary of sunburn. These things can cause you to be uncomfortable during your honeymoon.) If you travel by train, prices may be more moderate, but you'll have to plan your trip by the train's schedule; and train travel is time-consuming, too —though it's a nice way to see the countryside.

Travel cost, time

However and wherever you decide to go, make your travel arrangements and hotel reservations well in advance. A travel agent can do this as well as help in the planning of your honeymoon; but if you decide to make your own reservations, be sure to confirm them. Horror tales abound of honeymoon couples arriving for their wedding night to have desk clerks shrug not so politely at their plea for a room. Save yourself this headache and confirm your reservation in writing. A letter of confirmation might read:

Reserve in advance and confirm

Dear Sirs,

This is to confirm my reservation for the bridal suite in the new wing of the Hotel Southmore for Friday, June 12, 1970.

My check in the amount of $20 is enclosed as a deposit for this room.

My wife and I plan to arrive at approximately 3 p.m. on June 12, and we guarantee payment of the room for this evening.

Sincerely yours,
Frank Melrose

Notice that this letter specifies time of arrival and desired room and wing accommodations. You might even include the room number if you know it. This letter, or the standard confirmation form that some hotels send, and a copy of your cancelled check are your guarantee, so take both with you on your honeymoon.

Many couples decide to spend their wedding night in a hotel near the wedding site. This helps avoid arriving in the middle of the night, traveling while exhausted and adding nervous strain to an already exciting day. You can take your luggage to the hotel in advance, thus avoiding pranksters who tie your pajamas in knots or make off with your bags.

If you are married on a weekend, there is yet another benefit of spending your wedding night in town or close by. By beginning the major part of your travels

Spend your wedding night in town

202

on a Monday, you will find the going easier: Roads are less crowded, airlines less booked, and you might even realize a reduced rate by booking your fare during the week rather than on a weekend.

If you are going to stay at a nearby hotel, make sure reservations are confirmed here, too, as well as at your ultimate destination. Your fiancé can confirm in person and might also check the room assigned to you to make sure it's comfortable and nice, before giving a deposit.

Confirmations

It's wise not to spend your wedding night at the same hotel where either the ceremony or the reception took place. Go to a different spot. This will avoid confusion and will take you away from the site where all of the excitement occurred. You'll be more relaxed, just by putting that amount of distance between yourself and the wedding site.

If you're married in a hotel, by the way, the banquet manager will often give you a bottle of champagne as you leave. You might want to enjoy this with some wedding cake once you are off on your own. If you have champagne sent to your room, order splits. These are small bottles which serve two, and you can keep the other bottles cold while you're enjoying champagne from the first one. You can also have the fun of popping lots of corks, and you can keep any extra splits you don't finish for later.

There are several sources to help you select the kind of honeymoon you will most enjoy. Travel agents, of course, can give you brochures and guidebooks and offer their own ideas. If you work with a travel agent, don't hesitate to tell him that you are honeymooners. All kinds of unexpected "extras" can happen. When my husband and I went to Hawaii on our honeymoon, the travel agent planned surprises for us. The airline had made arrangements to serve a wedding cake; when none was available, they graciously gave us a large bottle of imported champagne with the compliments of

Choosing the spot

the captain and the crew signed on an improvised card —the menu! When we arrived at our hotel in Hawaii, we received yet another bottle of champagne—this time from the management—and neither thoughtful touch would have been possible had we not confided our status to the travel agent.

You can always plan your trip by yourselves if you prefer. Travel information is available by writing to the consulate of the country you are visiting or the Chamber of Commerce of the city you plan to see. The automobile clubs are international, too, and can offer you many colorful brochures and much helpful information. Brochures and booklets are great fun; collect lots to look through, and even if you don't decide to go to Bora Bora, you might find some suggestion in that brochure which you could apply to your honeymoon plans.

Ask friends and relatives for recommendations. You don't have to commit yourself to accepting their ideas, but ask them what places they've enjoyed or disliked, and why. You can learn from their experiences and mistakes.

Guide books and travel magazines like *Holiday* and *Venture* Magazine are full of suggestions, and the travel section of the Sunday New York *Times* is excellent—it has a calendar of events issued periodically that covers many areas of the United States as well as foreign countries. If you don't have much money to invest in gathering information, remember: Brochures are free and magazines and newspapers are available in most public libraries.

What are possible honeymoon spots? Everywhere and anywhere can become a honeymoon paradise, from biggest city to tiniest resort cabin. The basic consideration is whether you want to relax or whether you want to be on the go.

The big-city honeymoon is for couples who want lots to do. A honeymoon in New York would offer

Big-City honeymoons

theater, unusual restaurants and plenty of sight-seeing. If you enjoy hustle and bustle and don't mind paying for all the excitement, New York could be ideal for you. San Francisco is a quaint yet sophisticated spot, rather like a large European city. It has charm, great restaurants and marvelously different ethnic flavors. The big-city atmosphere carries throughout the spread-out Los Angeles area, which offers the mountains, the desert and Disneyland—all near by. New Orleans is a lovely city that boasts a warm gulf climate. French cuisine and Mardi Gras in January. Washington, D.C., rich in history, has much to see and do; and it is only a pleasant drive away from Williamsburg, Virginia, which is a totally restored colonial town and a relaxing and informative vacation spot.

If you decide on a big-city honeymoon, be sure to take your walking shoes and pace yourself. Don't try to do a week of sight-seeing in two days. Perhaps you could relax your first day, sight-see on the second or third, and take it easy again before leaving for home.

If you'd rather enjoy the sun and surf and yet have ever-present entertainment, consider taking a short cruise to the Caribbean or to Mexico. Florida and the Bahamas are scenic spots where you can spend most of your time sipping tropical rum drinks and relaxing on the beach. And Hawaii is a honeymooner's paradise—just as romantic as the films make it appear. If you take a cruise or plan to spend time aboard boats, be amply supplied with seasickness remedies—just in case.

The sporting honeymoon can be a joy for lovers of the out-of-doors. A trip to Colorado for skiing might be ideal for you, or a western-style honeymoon at a dude ranch or mountain climbing area might be a challenge. I wouldn't advise trying any new sports on your honeymoon, especially the more strenuous ones. And wherever you go, be careful of sunburn or windburn. Nothing should be allowed to interfere with your relaxation and happiness.

Sunny honeymoons

205

Foreign travel should be considered only by seasoned travelers. It's not only expensive, it also requires more planning and, generally, more time. There is more that can go wrong far from home—especially when you're dealing in a foreign language—so reflect seriously before making your honeymoon your first European holiday.

If you *do* want to travel abroad, Africa, Asia, and South America offer cities and resorts as charming and active as the better known European spots. For a long and leisurely cruise, you might fly to Europe and then cruise through the Mediterranean. This would offer a combination of relaxation and interesting sight-seeing, because the boats dock frequently in the various interesting ports.

Traveling out of the country means making many arrangements in advance. You'll have to get shots, passports, health certificates. Be sure any injections you need are taken long before the wedding day, so that your reactions to them can't spoil your fun. A good travel agent is essential when arranging a long or complicated trip out of the country. Try to avoid taking a strenuous tour of any sort as it's tiring and doesn't allow much privacy.

What to take

Once you have decided where you are going, you must begin thinking about what you'll take along. The bride can be responsible for this planning and help her fiancé as much as he likes. Men usually hate packing, and women are usually good at it. You'll be helping him in this and many ways in the future, so why not start now? Pack clothing which will be comfortable and appropriate to the climate and to the activities you've scheduled. You'll want to look attractive, so investigate drip-dry clothing and fabrics that don't wrinkle easily. Keep in mind that the darker colored fabrics and miracle fibers won't show wrinkles as much. A hint to those of you who don't want to be immediately spotted as newlyweds: Bring along some old clothes that don't look just-bought. Honeymooners are notorious for wearing spanking new articles daily.

Try to travel light. Don't make your husband carry tons of luggage on your first trip together. Go through your wardrobe, see what you have and write down what you'll need. List all items, including undergarments, toilet articles and special clothes for sports activities. You might want to pack a camera and some film, too.

Travel light

It's a good idea to take the electric rollers that heat up for a fast touch-up to your hair. This will keep you looking nice, and you won't want to spend all your time at a beauty salon (even if one is available) or in curlers in front of your husband. Think about investing in a hair piece or wig, too; these are wonderful, particularly if you'll be swimming or taking part in lots of sports.

Look nice

When you are listing items you already own, check carefully to make sure that each is in good repair and freshly laundered. Don't take too much, for wash and wear items can be easily laundered, and most hotels have cleaning facilities if you need them. Any items you won't be using right before the wedding can be packed in advance, and easily wrinkled clothing can be put in a special section of the closet for easy last-minute packing.

Once you've done your packing, try to help your fiancé. He will probably need sportswear, slacks and jackets, accessories and toilet articles, as well as a suit or dinner jacket if you're traveling to a resort or big city. Make sure all of his things are mended and ready to go.

Your fiancé's packing

Many articles of personal clothing that you buy to wear on your honeymoon and during your first year of marriage, are known as your personal trousseau. There's no set amount of things you must buy for a trousseau, and the articles needn't be all white. The amount of clothing you buy is entirely up to you. Include luscious nightgowns as a must on this list!

Personal trousseau

Going-away outfit   Most brides get a going-away outfit—a basic part of the trousseau—which is worn traditionally at the beginning of the honeymoon trip. Some girls buy a suit, although a dress is just as appropriate. In any event, it is usually a fairly dressy outfit, and is something that you should be able to wear for several years. It's wise to choose something that travels well and doesn't wrinkle, as well as fits in with your total wardrobe needs. A complete outfit is usually the best choice; therefore, as in choosing the wedding dress, proper undergarments and accessories should be kept in mind at time of purchase. You'll be wearing your going-away corsage with this too, so keep your flowers in mind when choosing.

Some couples choose going-away outfits which match in some way. You don't want to look like twins, of course, but suits chosen in harmonious, complementary colors and fabrics can be a good investment.

Take adequate luggage, either a matched set for you both or a flowered set for you and a less feminine bag for your husband. Many men prefer the hanging garment bag, which is lightweight and easy to handle. As you pack your suitcase, leave a little extra room for any souvenirs you may buy on your honeymoon. All travelers vow not to buy, but almost everybody does. And since this is a particularly meaningful trip for you, you'll surely want mementos to bring home.

With your luggage readied, your reservations made and your destination set, you can relax and dream about sharing a wonderful honeymoon together. This is the last of your shopping trips, and now it's time to move on to the planning of the ceremony and reception for your wedding day.

Part Four

PLANNING YOUR CEREMONY

18

A Lovely Setting

SELECTING A SITE FOR THE CEREMONY

ONCE YOU HAVE ESTABLISHED the date and time for your wedding, you must choose a location for the ceremony. Because the place and the person who will perform your ceremony are so closely related, Chapter 19 ought to be considered jointly with this chapter as you set out to begin your ceremony plans.

First, it is essential to plan your needs for the ceremony in terms of size, expense, decorations, music, and any special touches you might have in mind. Consider lighting, convenience and what assistance is available. If you plan a large wedding, an assistant at the site can help make things easier for you.

If your wedding is strictly a religious affair, you can simply select an appropriate church acceptable to both families. (See Chapter 22 if religions differ.) However, most girls will also want to consider personal

211

aesthetic preferences. Do you want an intimate chapel wedding? A large church affair? A modern civil ceremony? An unusual wedding of some kind? This is the first decision to make.

With your ideas firmly in mind, you can begin to look for a site for your ceremony. The following are brief descriptions of some of the most usual places in which to be married.

Some typical ceremony sites

Small intimate sites will lend a religious or spiritual aura to your ceremony. You would choose them if your ceremony will be a small one. Many large cathedrals and synagogues offer smaller chapels, often specifically designated as wedding chapels. These chapels vary in size: The chapel at the Washington Cathedral, in Washington D.C., for example, holds about 150 people comfortably; the chapel at St. John the Divine in New York can accommodate at least fifty more. If you and your fiancé attended the same college, a nice choice might be your school chapel; it is usually interdenominational and would permit all interfaith marriage ceremonies.

A wedding chapel

The rectory is the office of the clergyman attached to a large church. The surroundings are less formal than those of a chapel, and would be ideal for couples who prefer an informal religious ceremony.

A church rectory

If you are a member of a church, cathedral or synagogue and plan a large, formal wedding, you might want your wedding ceremony to take place in the church or synagogue you attend. Remember, however, that a small number of wedding guests could easily be dwarfed if the site is too huge.

Your place of worship

A wedding ceremony in one of the above-mentioned sites can provoke some questions. In religious ceremonies in general, you must find out the requirements of the particular religion involved. Must all the members of the wedding party be of the same religion? Is a wedding kiss permitted? Can a second marriage be performed? If you are having music, is the organ in

212

good condition, and is there an organist provided by the congregation whom you *must* use? If you want wedding bells, does this house of worship have them? Are the pews comfortable, perhaps provided with cushions? Can you decorate the site as you choose? Is there a wedding consultant to assist you?

For an informal, civil ceremony, consider being married in City Hall or in a judge's chambers. You might bring both sets of parents and a few close friends or relatives if you wish, but you need at least two people to witness the ceremony. A dressy dress or suit would be an appropriate bridal outfit. The same ceremony could also be performed in a judge's chambers, which is more private and less rushed than City Hall.

Ceremony site

Often community centers can be rented for weddings, for they have available adjoining rooms for reception facilities, and you can usually decorate them as you see fit. A rented hall often offers many benefits, minus any religious atmosphere. Weddings in such sites can be as formal or informal as desired and professional guidance may be available.

A rental site

If you consider one of the above sites, find out if there are other weddings scheduled right before or after yours. Will there be much noise nearby if any other events are scheduled? Is there musical accompaniment available? Are there lecterns and other furniture that must be moved? If so, who will handle this? What are the seating arrangements? Who will provide them? Is the lighting directly overhead? Is it attractive?

A room or suite of rooms is often available for wedding ceremonies in hotels or private clubs. The big consideration here is cost, which can sometimes be quite high if the place you choose is in great demand. They offer many advantages: professional assistance, particularly attractive settings and flexibility in sizes and shapes of rooms. Like the community center or hall, a conveniently adjacent spot is often available for the reception area. In such places, decoration and music is provided

Hotel or private club

by the bride, but hotels and clubs have their own caterers, florists, and arrangers to help you. Again though, it will cost. And, as with a rental site, you must check to make sure that conflicting parties will not disturb or rush your own wedding.

Are they accommodating?

Find out about how much of your own decorating you can do. Are there time restrictions on your stay in the hotel's or club's rooms? How attractive and comfortable is the area to be provided. Will the banquet manager or the person in charge give you plenty of leeway in using your own ideas and providing your own florist, organist?

A private home or garden

If you live in a country area, or reasonably near one, you might want to be married in your own home or in the home of someone close to you. You will be able to decorate as you please and insure a feeling of warmth and hospitality for your guests. When you plan a wedding on private property, determine if there is enough space, not only for the guests' seating and the wedding ceremony, but also for the kind of processional and recessional you have in mind. Though quite formal, a wedding in a private home is usually relaxed—especially an outdoor wedding which offers a garden atmosphere for ceremony and reception.

What if it rains?

A garden wedding provokes special questions: What if it rains? Have you an alternative plan to move people inside? Will you be able to handle all the necessary ceremony arrangements by yourself? Is the house in an area where neighbors might be disturbed in any way by the ceremony, or will be likely to disturb you? Is this home convenient for the majority of guests? Will the reception also be there? If not, is it near to the reception site?

...the other extras

In choosing any of these sites, find out if there is a convenient spot for the bride and the bridesmaids to meet and a place for the groom and his best man to wait before the ceremony. Think seriously about things like parking spaces and travel arrangements to the reception area, for all of these are extras for which you may be charged.

There are a number of unusual sites for wedding ceremonies, and you need only begin looking and asking to discover a spot that might be ideal for you.

There are many unique places that you might consider. For example, in southwest Missouri, near the city of Springfield, there is an area filled with caves. One particularly beautiful cave is known as The Bridal Cave, and you might want to join the many couples who have been married there. In California, on the Palos Verdes peninsula, you might be married at The Wayfarers Chapel, which is perched high on a hill and has floor-to-ceiling glass and a 360 degree view of the ocean and the surrounding hillside. In New York City, you might choose the small chapel at the United Nations for your ceremony site.

Unusual sites

Often, the unusual is closer to home. You could be married on a boat. Although ships' captains are no longer empowered to perform weddings, a clergyman or judge could be brought on board. Or a public park might allow an outdoor wedding, so that even if you live in a large city a "garden" ceremony would be possible. A recent bride had her ceremony in a lovely park near her home and then followed it with a reception that was like a grand picnic—nothing like the receptions most people think of as traditional. Restaurants, too, sometimes with outdoor patio areas, are often willing to rent their facilities for both wedding and reception. So if you are eager for something out-of-the-ordinary, start looking around right away. Something truly unique might be available.

Patio, park, or boat

After you have considered your various preferences, talk things over with your fiancé and both sets of parents, if possible. Then discuss your plans with the person who will officiate at the ceremony and reserve the time and date with him.

Talk things over

If everyone is agreed on these specifications,

215

Confirm your plans make a reservation verbally with whoever is in charge. Send a letter of confirmation soon after, just to make sure there is no confusion. The letter can be light and friendly, while including all the necessary information: date, hour and length of time reserved. Also, list carefully any unusual requirements you have for the ceremony, indicating any special permission required for such things as rearranging and decorating.

Because your plans and even your choice of site may be dependent upon the rules of your religion and/ or availability of the person officiating, glance through the following chapter before making final, final plans.

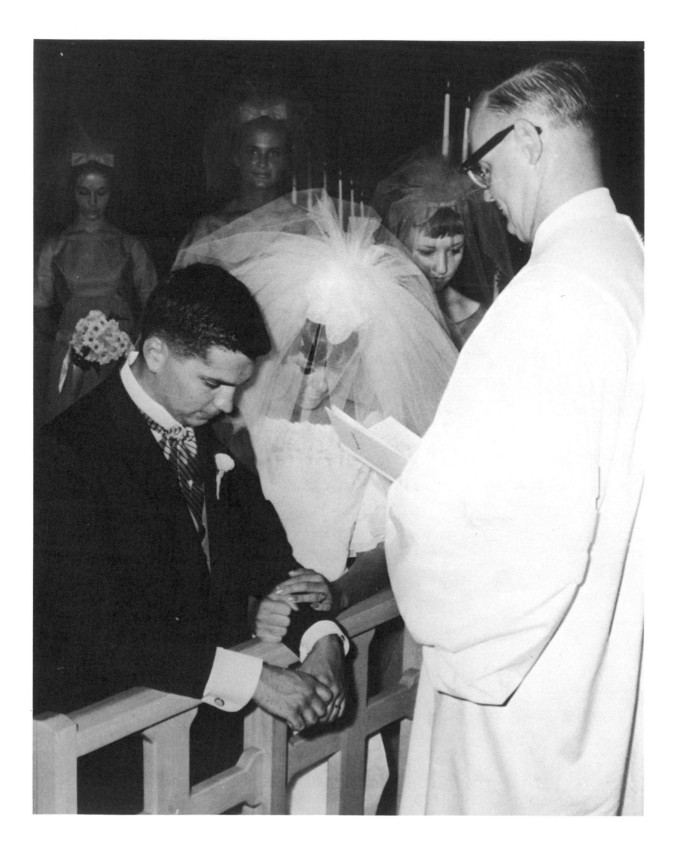

Who Will Officiate?

CHOOSING A JUDGE OR CLERGYMAN

IT'S WISE TO DECIDE who will perform your marriage ceremony well in advance of the wedding date, for he will be involved with much of your day and may need to advise you about religious rituals. Whether you are planning a church wedding or a ceremony at a non-religious site, your clergyman or judge will need to know where he is to stand and when he is needed; no doubt he will contribute suggestions and guidance.

If you plan a religious ceremony, be aware that within most religions there may exist different and sometimes conflicting attitudes about what is necessary and correct procedure for a wedding. In the Catholic religion, for example, there are both traditional and modernist priests; in the Jewish religion, Orthodox and Reform rabbis—all with individual ideas; and within the Protestant denominations young and old ministers can have differing viewpoints. When speaking to your clergyman, make it a point to gain a clear idea of what is required, and be certain that the rules of the religion are acceptable to both your family and that of your fiancé. Some couples approach their clergyman timidly, wondering: What will he expect of me? Since this is the most important ceremony of your life, it is only fair that you be married in a manner that pleases you.

Seek a clergyman who agrees with your approach, not one with whom you must agree. The ceremony he will perform is one of the most important ceremonies of your life. You are paying for his service and his time, so you should have a voice in what will be done and what can be done and how things will be handled.

This is not to say that whoever officiates would not have good ideas, but hold your own if you have something you particularly want to do. Don't let other people talk you into doing things that are not what you want. Helpful advice is one thing; being told that there is only one way to do something is another. So be cautious if you find this attitude cropping up when you're talking with the person who will be performing your ceremony. If you feel the attitude there, and you're concerned that it may grow more and more complicated, then I would advise you to go someplace else and look for another person to officiate at your ceremony.

If you belong to a congregation, you will doubtless have the leader of this congregation marry you, but if you must look around, proceed cautiously. Try someone recommended by friends or family, and go to him with your plans well formulated so there will be no misunderstandings. You will need to find someone who is available at the right times, of course, and also someone you like and trust. Try to choose someone who has performed many wedding ceremonies so that he will be experienced and able to help you.

Be sure to take him into your confidence and give

him complete information about yourself; be honest and straightforward. If you are divorced and remarrying you may want to ask if this will cause any problem. Also, be sure to mention if this is an interreligious marriage, and ask if he will still marry you under these circumstances.

If you plan a nonreligious ceremony, you might investigate the possibility of being married by a judge. If you don't know any judges who are willing to perform the wedding service, ask friends or the family lawyer to recommend someone. Another alternative is to call City Hall and ask them to refer you to a judge in your area. You will ask a judge the same kinds of questions you ask a clergyman, though often you'll find his requirements of a personal, rather than religious nature.

If a judge officiates

Once you and your fiancé have agreed on who will officiate at your ceremony, be honest and straightforward with him about your needs and worries. If you are marrying for the second time, find out what problems, if any, this fact causes. Check with him about all the details of the ceremony, and advise him of the religious backgrounds of all members of the wedding party in case this would cause him to have second thoughts about performing your ceremony.

Your pre-ceremony talk

Find out the restrictions, if any. Are there any songs that cannot be used? Does your clergyman permit the wedding kiss? Some do not, you know. How does he feel about having photographs taken during the ceremony? If you plan to tape-record the ceremony get an OK in advance. One friend of mine surprised a judge with a tape recorder, and when he realized he was being recorded his delivery suddenly became very slow and dramatic. She laughs about it now, but I assure you, it wasn't funny at the time. Check, as well, the legal requirements for the service itself, particularly if you and your groom are planning to write your own vows or adjustments to the standard.

Discussing details

Don't ask what the fee will be. It's not considered

polite. The amount varies from $10 to about $50, with the average being $20 to $25. The groom pays the fee—cash in an envelope—immediately following the actual ceremony, or he can have his best man handle this detail.

Confirm your plans

After you and your fiancé have made your choice, reserve that date verbally; later send a brief note to confirm the vital details. You might at this time make a date to discuss further plans with him as necessary, and arrange and confirm a convenient day and time for the wedding rehearsal.

Get your license

Next make a date with your fiancé for a trip to the Licensing Bureau or City Hall to buy your marriage license. Requirements for marriage licenses vary from state to state, but most states insist upon some sort of health and/or birth certificate and a blood test, and they are valid only for a given length of time. When to get your license is important, too. Your state may have a waiting period requiring you to get the license several weeks or months before the ceremony. You can also get the license *too soon*, as it generally has an expiration date. Remind your fiancé to take some cash to pay for the license (usually a nominal fee), gather all required data and set off.

Make an occasion of it. Why not take your camera with you and snap a picture of each other holding the license, perhaps in front of City Hall. Or have a picture of the two of you together taken by one of the photographers that are normally there. Then go out to dinner or brunch and celebrate.

Getting your license is really exciting because it's the first time you will see something tangible about your marriage. All the information is written down and your wedding is closer to becoming a reality. There it is: The Beginning.

20

Watch the Camera!

SELECTING A PHOTOGRAPHER

YOUR WEDDING PHOTOGRAPHS are extremely important, as they are, after all, the only tangible record of your wedding day. You'll enjoy looking at them again and again, and each time, I am sure, they will bring back special memories of your wedding day. These pictures will give you hours of pleasure and are sure to provide delight and amusement in the years to come—for your children and friends and relatives as well. So go about selecting your photographer with great and special care.

Don't be tempted to use a friend or relative as your photographer or permit your guests to take photographs while a professional photographer is working, as their interference could ruin his shots. If guests are eager to take pictures, suggest they take snapshots of you or the groom preparing for the wedding or at the reception. Even during these times their photographs should be taken only when the professional is not working.

Choosing your photographer

It may take you a good deal of time to find a really good photographer, but it's worth it. Shop around, and don't make this a place for cutting corners financially. Most girls spend at least half the price of their wedding gown on wedding photos, and it makes sense. After all, the gown is carefully stored away, but the pictures remain an active pleasure. If you choose your photographer carefully, your photos will always be a beloved memento.

How to judge him

A photographer who is reputable, experienced, reliable and personable and, of course, produces excellent work is the ideal choice. To judge the quality of a photographer's work, study very closely his sample albums, which will be available in the waiting room of his studio. Are the photos natural looking? Is the color good? If so, will you select color or black and white? Do the subjects look at ease? Has the photographer shown imagination or does he merely line people up and snap away? For an extra check, look at wedding photos the photographer has taken of friends; see if the quality is consistently good or falls short of his sample albums.

Questions to ask

Ask him the following specific questions as they apply. Will he stay only for the ceremony or throughout the entire reception? Specify the length of time you would like him to be there, and see if he is agreeable, or you may miss that final photograph of you and your husband leaving for your honeymoon. Has he ever taken pictures at your wedding site before? This kind of experience can be very helpful. How many proofs (the first pictures that you see made from the negatives from which you choose the final photographs) will he take? You choose the proofs you like best and have them made into photos for your album, so the larger the selection, the better for you. What are the costs involved? How much of a deposit is required? (More than 50 percent is unreasonable.) Is there an additional deposit required *before* the photographer develops the proofs and/or final photographs? (Such a deposit should *not* be required.) What is the rate schedule for the photographs? How much will it cost you or the members of the wedding party to have extra photos made up? What is the cost per photo, and how much can you save by ordering duplicate prints of an individual shot? There should be reduction for ordering in quantity.

Who will the *actual* photographer be? Will it be the owner of the studio or one of his assistants. Some large studios hire outside photographers to take your pictures with the result being poor-quality work. Will the studio send a photo assistant to help arrange formal shots? (She makes sure that the gowns fall properly, the flowers are well placed—in short, she handles all the minute details that make a picture perfect.) How will the photographer be dressed when he appears at your wedding? Will he wear a suit or will he show up "casual" in blue jeans and sneakers? Some do. He should be dressed appropriately for the occasion, in a suit and tie. Gather this information from many photographers and compare the services with the prices they charge. Examine the quality of their work and then make your final decision.

More questions

Once you have decided which photographer you will use, confirm all arrangements with him by letter. List the costs, deposits and time agreed upon for final payment. Make particular mention of any special rates or discounts he may have offered you verbally. Give him the date, hour and site of your wedding, and, if you wish, tell him how to get to the exact location and where he is to go when he arrives. If you want him to meet you and/or the wedding party at the site at a prearranged time, be sure to indicate this. Include the name of the

Confirm these details

specific photographer who is to do the work, how he should be dressed and how long he is expected to stay. Mention the approximate length of time the studio has given you to complete the proofs and the finished photos.

Candids or formals

On a separate sheet of paper list the photographs you particularly want taken, so the photographer can bring this information along with his equipment to the wedding, and keep a copy of this list for yourself. Your list might include either candids, which are unposed photos, or formals, which are posed by the photographer or a combination of the two. Generally the basic shots include: candids of the wedding party arriving and preparing for the wedding; formals of the wedding party before the ceremony; candids during and after the ceremony; formals after the ceremony; and candids and/or formals at the reception. Formal pictures are never posed during the ceremony, and can delay the reception if scheduled after the ceremony.

Possible photos

This list will lessen confusion on your wedding day and guarantee you the pictures you want. You needn't include all the shots indicated here; add and delete as you wish. Keep in mind that these are desired "proofs"; you needn't have all of them developed. Make a long list and then choose only the very best ones for your wedding album.

The following shots are customary:

Before your ceremony

* Before the ceremony: Guests and various members of the wedding party arriving. Flowers and decorations before anyone has arrived. You and/or your bridesmaids completing your final touches. You with your parents and the groom with his family.

Before your processional

* Before the processional: (These are best if candid.) You with your flower girl and/or train-bearers just before you walk down the aisle. Pictures of the bridesmaids as they wait. Your groom as he waits. Your mother and/or father.

* During the ceremony: (These pictures should be

taken only with the permission of the person performing your ceremony and the knowledge of the wedding party.) The processional, ceremony and recessional. You on your father's arm, as you start down the aisle to meet your groom. The wedding party taking part in the ceremony. The wedding kiss or the exchange of vows and/or rings—if it does not interrupt the ceremony. You and the groom as you leave the ceremony site.

*The reception line: You and your husband. The entire reception line. Individual special guests greeting the newly married couple.

*Don't forgets: Individual pictures of the person who has performed the ceremony—with his wife if she's present—and of the organist or the soloist, if either of them are personal friends.

*The reception and after: Pictures including various highlights of the reception. (They are explained in detail in Chapter 26, and complete the list.)

Along with your list of photos include the names of the wedding party and of anyone else whose photo you might especially want to have. Beside their name, explain their relationship to you, and provide a short description of the way they look or what you think they will be wearing, as necessary. Having someone to assist the photographer by pointing out the various people named would not only be helpful, but would also speed up his picture-taking—and provide you with interesting shots of everyone who is important to you.

With all arrangements for your ceremony photographer complete, you've reached the half-way point. Yes, half of your entire wedding ceremony is now planned. What's next? One of the most creative and feminine projects of all wedding planning—choosing your wedding colors, flowers and decorations.

During your ceremony

After your ceremony

Your VIP list

21

Flowers, Flowers, Flowers

ARRANGING FOR DECORATIONS

FLOWERS WILL ADD beauty, fragrance and distinction to your wedding ceremony. It will be a pleasure to select flowers to use for decoration, for bouquets and boutonnieres, for corsages—and if planned carefully these flowers will give your wedding a truly beautiful, harmonious look.

Begin by making a sketch of the ceremony site. There is a sample sketch in this chapter to give you an idea of things to note. You should include the size of the room, the layout of the various areas such as aisle, seating, altar area and the placement of the lighting fixtures, musical instruments, entrances and exits. List the color scheme of the ceremony site, too. Make note of the colors to be worn in your wedding, and indicate on your sketch where the floral decorations are to be placed: Eventually you'll be able to fill in their color,

231

Sketch the site

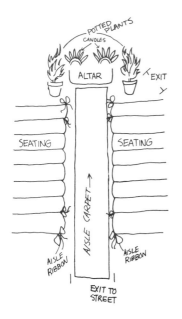

Shades of color

Complementary colors

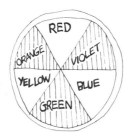

size and style, too. This decoration plan will help you to visualize what you will want and need and should be taken to the florist you ultimately choose to make his job easier.

Before you begin to decorate your wedding site, pick the color scheme to be used. A color wheel (see Chapter 13) will be invaluable for this. There are many different color schemes, of course, but some general rules and suggestions may help you in making your choice. Avoid using one shade of a color exclusively.

Finding all items in the exact same shade is an almost impossible task. For example, all cloth trim would have to be cut from the same bolt of material to insure sameness, including your gown, those of your bridesmaids, and all tablecloths used at the reception. Even if you choose to have an all-white wedding, in reality you are really going to be dealing with slightly different shades of white.

You can, however, use different shades of the same color for an interesting effect. This is called a monochromatic color scheme, and it can be very lovely if your shades are chosen carefully. For example, you might use varying shades of blue from pastel to royal, a scheme which would be particularly effective in a very light and airy church. Or you can combine two distinctly different colors. Think of white as a color and combine it with any other hue of your choosing, such green and white, violet and white or red and white.

You can also choose two complementary colors that are of equal intensity or shade. This type of color scheme works well if you can use an accent color (a third shade) in a dark hue of one or two of the colors. For example, if you choose the complementary colors red and green, you might accent them with a dark tone of green. Other complementary colors you will find on a color wheel are yellow and violet, blue and orange and of course varying shades of these tones. Any color that is positioned directly across from your chosen color and is of equal intensity is a complementary color. Using complementary colors is very effective for an evening wedding or a wedding at a dark site.

Try an analogous color scheme using colors that are side by side on the color wheel: red and orange, violet and blue, green and yellow. It is considered the most formal of color schemes, and works very well in a bright church or at a daytime wedding. *Analogous colors*

Three-color combinations work well for evening weddings or weddings at a site not brightly lit. This is a dramatic color scheme, but difficult to work with. You must be very careful or the results will be gaudy. Often, too, people think of white as a color and successfully combine it with two analogous or complementary colors.

A multicolor combination would be most effective in spring or fall, drawing color inspiration from the pastels of spring or the earth tones of autumn. Multicolored bouquets of spring flowers would blend with multicolored bridesmaids' gowns, giving a pleasant look, fresh from nature. *Multicolors*

Use natural colors, and avoid tints that are fluorescent or gaudy. Don't change the natural colors of your flowers, like dyeing carnations to match a dress. The flowers no longer look attractive when their color is forced, and you can't be sure that dyed flowers will have a uniform hue. Also avoid gold or silver-painted leaves, and if you use sheaves of wheat or greens, use them in their natural shades. To add color to a bouquet, try colored ribbons. *Natural colors*

Think of flower color as a means of focus to determine your color scheme. Consider the areas you want accented during your ceremony—like the altar. Don't fill it with a riot of color, but choose one color or combination of colors to decorate the spot. This is true of the wedding clothing, too. Choose flowers and bouquets that accent the total outfit and bring the eye to the floral focal point. And as you are the main focus *Focus attention* of the wedding, you should make your floral arrangement unusual in some way so that it will draw all the eyes to you.

Areas to be decorated

Floral decorations—potted plants or individual flower arrangements, perhaps combined with candles —usually appear in the altar area. If you plan a Jewish ceremony, you may want to have the *chupah* made of flowers as well as cloth. Or frame the altar with a floral arch. Such decorations will be visible to the guests even after the wedding party is assembled before it.

Aisle area

The aisle, too, is often decorated, with flower arrangements at the ends of the rows of seats, or pews. Ribbons sometimes are draped from pew to pew, serving as markers. You might use chains of sturdy flowers (like daisies) as an alternative to ribbons. You can place a pedestal at the end of each row with a flower arrangement on top, perhaps in a basket, but be sure it does not obstruct either vision or passage. If you are using an aisle carpet, the long white roll of material on which the wedding party walks, this will add to the decoration of the aisle area. Ribbons rather than flowers may be used to reduce expense if you have several aisles to decorate.

Entryway

The entrance to the aisle area or the foyer of the ceremony site can be beautified with flowers, ribbons, potted plants, et cetera. You may, if you are being married in a hotel, wish to decorate the lobby, the first area the guests see as they enter; a discreet sign directing your guests to the werding site is appropriate here.

If you are having your wedding in a spot with a staircase, use ribbons, streamers or garlands to decorate. The entrance to the wedding site, if equipped with a canopy, might also be festooned, as could a carpet leading up the steps to a church in which you are being married.

Automobiles

Your wedding car and the others used for the processional to the church can be decorated with streamers or garlands of flowers and/or ribbons (in such an instance, artificial flowers are perfectly acceptable). If you are featuring silvery, glittery accents, use small metallic ornaments with your flowers; if you are having a Christmas wedding include tiny ornaments in your arrangements, or have the greens be evergreen boughs. Clear all decorations with the clergyman or banquet manager in charge of the ceremony site, taking care not to overdo. You don't have to decorate every area listed. These are merely suggestions. (Decorations and other items for your reception are covered in Chapter 27.)

Now, begin to list the flowers that you want for the members of your wedding party. The traditional needs are bouquets for the bride and the bridesmaids; boutonnieres for the groom, the ushers, the best man, the judge and the fathers of the bride and groom; corsages for the bride's going-away outfit, the mothers, and for friends you wish to honor; plus a decorated basket for the flower girl.

The wedding party

Begin with the easiest choice—boutonnieres for the men. These are single blossoms, perhaps a carnation, rosebud or shaft of lilies of the valley, and are quite often white. The groom's boutonniere matches the bride's bouquet in the choice of flower if possible, or is at least different in some way from those of the ushers and fathers, whose boutonnieres should all match.

Boutonnieres

The flower girl carries a small basket, decorated with flowers or ribbons, which contain rose petals to scatter in the path of the bride. You might want to give the flower girl a small corsage of her own, made of one or two small flowers to match her mini size. She could wear a headdress of flowers as well, but this, too, should be small and blend with the colors of her outfit.

Flower girl

The corsages for both mothers should be elegant and chosen to blend with their outfits. A single large blossom is a good choice, perhaps a gardenia or an orchid. Ask both mothers what their favorite flower is,

Corsages

235

and be guided accordingly. Keep both corsages similar in size and cost, so that neither mother feels slighted. Next order a few extra white carnation corsages for last-minute gifts for a grandmother, relative or friend, perhaps someone who has been particularly kind.

Headdress

You may want a floral headdress for yourself and your bridesmaids. Austrian brides wear a wreath of fresh myrtle, a bloom they consider the symbol of love. You might also like to wear orange blossoms in your hair, or a combination of flowers and ribbons. Flowers can form a crown or tiara for the wedding veil itself. Whatever flowers you choose for a headdress can be delicate looking but must be sturdy to remain fresh and intact throughout the day.

Bridesmaids' bouquets

There is an infinite variety of flowers for your bridesmaids to carry which they can properly coordinate with or contrast to the color of their gowns. They might carry baskets of flowers, perhaps filled with multicolored spring arrangements or long-stemmed blossoms, attached and wired carefully so they can't slip out. A basket is best with a circular shaped handle for easy carrying. Specify that your florist bind the handles with white ribbon rather than green, as the green comes off on hands or gloves when handled. A helpful hint: If you plan to use large quantities of ribbons in your arrangements, it's wise to buy all the ribbon at one time to assure color consistency. And give your florist a supply of this cloth ribbon to be used in place of his paper ribbon.

Alternative suggestions

Nosegays, which are small bunches of flowers like miniature carnations, roses, lilies of the valley, babies breath or daisies, would make attractive bouquets for your attendants. Another possibility would be long-stemmed arrangements held in the arms, like a dozen or more long-stemmed roses or mums, tied prettily with a bow. In addition to all varieties of fresh-cut flowers, you can also use straw, dried or paper flowers, or fresh greens mixed with a few colorful buds.

236

Your bridesmaids might carry muffs fashioned from flowers or from fur with a flower accent. Remember, when choosing bouquets for your bridesmaids to select one for your maid of honor that is larger or more elaborate in design, as she should stand out from your other attendants.

Seasonal blooms

Give preference to those flowers which are available during your season; this ensures blossoms that are both fresh and less costly. Flowers grown under artificial conditions will look lovely, but the better specimens are those that are naturally in bloom at the time of year you plan to marry. This is also true of wild flowers, and some of following may be available in your locale:

Southwest: California golden poppies, Texas bluebonnet
Southwest and South Central: columbine
Great Plains and Northwest: syringa, goldenrod
Midwest: violet, carnation
Northeast: mayflower, red clover
Southeast: orange blossom, peony, rose, carnation

Your bridal bouquet

Your bridal bouquet is your most enjoyable decision. It can be elaborate, a formal cascade of flowers, or it can be a single lovely blossom. Choose it to blend with and accent your wedding gown. For example, if your gown has beautiful detail in the front panel, select a single flower or understated bouquet. If your gown is simple in line with more design detail at the back or on the train, you may prefer a large elaborate bouquet. When you discuss your bridal bouquet with your florist, give him all the information available about your gown, its style and color and the look you are trying to achieve. The same holds true for selecting the flowers for all members of your wedding party.

Some general ideas you might consider for your bridal bouquet are:

1. A cascade of pure white roses.

2. A single white orchid surrounded by cascading Stephanotis and pure white carnations.
3. A large nosegay of roses and carnations with streamers of velvet or satin bows. (Tiny blossoms could be added hit and miss on each ribbon, too.)
4. A large arm bouquet of long-stemmed flowers drawn together with a large, lush bow. (At least a dozen of most types of flowers would be required.)
5. A single tulip, daffodil, rose or carnation.
6. A delicate nosegay of baby rosebuds, lilies of the valley, or violets.
7. A single flower or small arrangement of flowers combined with a prayer book and ribbon streamers.

Going-away corsage

Next choose a corsage to wear especially with your going-away outfit. If your bridal bouquet is sizable, you might have the florist work your going-away corsage right into its center. The bouquet remains beautiful, to be treasured by the girl who catches it, and you have an actual part of your bridal bouquet as a corsage to wear and treasure.

As you prepare the list of flowers that you want, make note of who will pay for each. The groom traditionally pays for the bride's bouquet and her going-away corsage plus the boutonnieres for the ushers and best man. Sometimes he also offers to buy corsages for both mothers. This should be discussed in advance and indicated on your list. Then all flowers can be ordered from the same florist for economy and consistency.

Cutting costs

For your first trip to the florist you should be equipped with a sketch of your wedding site showing your decoration plans, and the list of flowers required for the wedding party. This list will enable the florist to give you an accurate estimate. You can compare estimates from several florists if you like and make sure you are getting the most for your money. Once you have an approximate estimate, it may be necessary to trim some items. If you need to save money, you might consider some of the following ideas.

Use flowers from your ceremony as decorations for your reception; you might even consider using flowers from other parties earlier in your wedding week if they are fresh enough. This idea works well with hardy cut flowers, potted plants, or dried flowers.

Using cut flowers carried in a basket rather than flowers requiring arrangement into bouquets can help you save, for you pay the florist a sizable amount for the labor involved in making up complicated bouquets and arrangements.

Or make the arrangements yourself. This is a particularly workable idea if your wedding is to be fairly small. Each bridesmaid might carry a single flower. A floral arrangement for the altar area or the aisles might be cut flowers arranged simply in decorative vases. However, attempt your own floral work only if you are confident and enjoy the challenge.

Prices vary with the flower, and less expensive flowers for your bouquets and arrangements can be beautiful, too. Don't be embarrassed to ask your florist the price of the flowers you are thinking of using or to request less expensive blooms in the same color. Your florist will naturally want to sell you his more expensive flowers, so make your questions about less expensive choices pleasant but firm.

If you have additional money to spend—happy thought!—and you would like to choose a more unusual or elaborate floral decoration scheme, consider the use of flower garlands to replace ribbons. The ceremony area could be more elaborately decorated as well, perhaps adding a floral arch or a special trellis.

Extra money

Bouquets for the maids can be used to form designs that will enhance the decoration of the altar area. Each girl's bouquet is threaded onto a wire frame, and when all the girls are assembled at the altar they join their bouquets together to form a semicircle of flowers

239

around you and your groom. If you think you might like to use such a floral pattern fashioned from bouquets, create the pattern ahead of time and have your florist design and construct the bouquets to fit.

Flowers for portrait

Also arrange for a bouquet of either fresh or artificial flowers to use for your bridal portrait. This is necessary only if your photographer won't have flowers available for you to use, and you might as well add this to the list and complete your business all in one session.

Choosing a florist

To be certain of quality, choose a reputable florist, one who has been in business for at least two years. He should be reliable, perhaps someone you have dealt with before or to whom you have been referred by a satisfied customer. He should by all means be someone who has handled decorations for weddings before, and, although you want him to be creative, he should not be temperamental or excitable.

See examples

It's wise to see examples of the florist's work. Many florists can describe in great detail the beautiful arrangements they'll make for you, but the reality may not live up to the talk. So ask to see photographs of other weddings the florist has designed, or, if at all possible, peek in on a wedding he is currently handling.

As with your photographer, you will have to make sure the florist is available on the day and hour you need him, that he doesn't have conflicting commitments which will make him rush delivery and arrangement of your order. You should determine if he will come himself, or if he will send a replacement. If you have a great many flowers to be arranged and placed, you might suggest that he bring an assistant to help him.

If the florist has worked at your site before, it will be very beneficial, for he will be aware of the lighting problems and the layout of the hotel or church. He will be able to complete his work more easily if he is familiar with your site, but if he is not, be sure he will see the site and check arrangements well in advance of your wedding.

If all details, including the price, are agreeable to you, confirm all arrangements with the florist in writing. Whether you write a confirming letter or use a copy of your total floral order, list all bouquets and decorations, specifying the types and quantities of flowers to be supplied, all floral decorations plus such items as aisle carpeting, additional ribbons, and any accessory pieces like arches or baskets which the florist must furnish.

Confirm details

The florist may require a deposit—customarily up to 50 percent. In no event should you pay the total amount before the day of your wedding; wait until after the flowers have been delivered, checked and properly arranged. In your letter of confirmation, note how final payment will be made and the precise amount due. Give the exact date, time and place of your wedding, and mention who will supervise preparations for the ceremony. I had a friend who ordered mixed spring flowers for her wedding, with arrangements containing yellow roses. On the day of the wedding the arrangements arrived with yellow daisies in place of roses—not only disappointing the bride but also causing her to be grossly overcharged. Don't let this happen to you!

Appoint someone to check that the flowers received on your wedding day are correct, delivered on time and arranged properly. This might be a close friend or relative, preferably a person not otherwise involved in the wedding. If you have someone outside your immediate family to handle these responsibilities, it will save your mother or father the overwhelming feeling that they are responsible for everything. For further information on who can help with last-minute details, see Chapter 34.

Chosen with care your flowers will provide your ceremony with an elegant and sweet-smelling background. They will lend color and highlights to the occasion, a contribution from nature that will add special beauty to the celebration of your day.

22

Words and Music By...

SETTING THE MOOD WITH SONG

THE WORDS AND MUSIC for your wedding ceremony should be chosen as much as possible by you and your fiancé. They are a meaningful and beautiful part of your ceremony, and as such, deserve your personal attention. You and he will want to discuss the details of your ceremony very carefully with whoever will perform your ceremony, as well as with both sets of parents.

First, let's consider music. Music is an integral part of the ceremony, no matter how much is played. You should select the music to be played and the instruments to be used, as well as deciding whether or not to have a soloist. Well-planned selections add a feeling of unity and blend your pre-wedding recital with the processional, ceremony and recessional.

The music for your ceremony may be played on any instrument you like. If you are to be married in a church, the logical choice is the church organ. Alternative or additional instruments might be the strings, a harpsichord, an orchestra of reasonable size, or a single piano or accordion.

Add a soloist if you like. He or she can sing before or during the ceremony. Meet with the soloist in advance, request the various songs you want and agree upon a fee as required. If your soloist is a friend, it's more personal to give a gift rather than money. It's not advisable for you or your fiancé to plan to sing at your own wedding. The ceremony is for you to take part in and to enjoy, so avoid putting yourselves under any unnecessary strain.

Ask your clergyman for help

You should work with your clergyman and organist, if you are using the church organist, in the selection of the music for your ceremony. They will have many good ideas, and will, hopefully, discuss the music in such a way that you will be able to make choices and decide upon the music which you particularly like. Even if you plan to have other musicians come to your ceremony site to perform the music, it is still courteous for you to get approval on your choice of music from your clergyman. In the case of the judge, it's polite to at least inform him of the type of music that you will be using. He may offer additional suggestions too.

If you are musically inclined and have composed your own wedding music, have it played for your clergyman or judge just to be sure. They can help you decide if it's really appropriate for your wedding.

The music for your wedding can be divided into four parts: pre-wedding or recital, processional, ceremony and recessional.

Pre-wedding or recital music

Pre-wedding or recital music is played for the enjoyment of your wedding guests as they wait for the beginning of the ceremony. This music sets the mood and tone for your wedding. If your ceremony is to be very solemn and religious, then you would want to choose music that would be of a similar nature. Lighter music would lend itself to a more informal ceremony, one that is shorter and less sedate. Recital music usually lasts about a half hour, but the musicians should be prepared to play for an hour or more in case there is some kind of delay. Your guests can then be entertained without having to listen to one or two songs repeated constantly.

There are many choices for pre-wedding recital music. You might like to consider some of the following: *Some music you may like*

"Chant d'Amour"	Gilette
"Evening Star"	Wagner
"On Wings of Song"	Mendelssohn
"Orange Blossoms"	Friml
"Romance"	Debussy
"Salut d'Amour"	Elgar
"Songs"	Brahms
"Swan"	Saint-Saens
"Choral Preludes"	Bach
"Airs"	Handel

Selections for your processional, the march of all the members of your wedding party as they move to the ceremony area, might be: "The Bridal Chorus" from *Lohengrin*; Purcell's Trumpet Voluntary in D; Mendelssohn's "Wedding March" from *A Midsummer Night's Dream*.

Processional music

Ceremony music can feature one or two vocal solos. Usually it's nice to have one solo sung as a special wedding prayer right before you take your vows. This will vary according to your religious beliefs and preferences. Also keep in mind that the more solos sung at this time, the longer your ceremony will be. If there is disagreement over the songs to be sung, I would suggest

Solos, if you choose

that you have the alternate songs performed at your reception. One or two additional solos can be sung during the pre-wedding recital. Choose from the following:

"I Love You Truly"   Bond
"At Dawning"   Cadman
"Because"   d'Harddotl
"O Promise Me"   DeKoven

Recessional music

Music for the recessional, the march from the altar, is usually Mendelssohn's traditional "Wedding March" or "The Bridal Chorus" from *Lohengrin*. But you can also include wedding or church bells in your recessional if they are available. They will add a festive and joyous note to your recessional.

Cost of music can vary

The cost of providing music for your ceremony will, of course, depend upon the number of musicians you engage. If you have your wedding in a church which employs an organist, the organist should receive her fee even if a friend plays for you instead. This fee is usually from $15 to $20, and covers a twenty to thirty minute recital before the ceremony, accompaniment for the soloist and music for the wedding rehearsal. A less formal wedding without a rehearsal might require a fee of $10. Be sure to ask your clergyman's advice about organists' fees. If you are hiring professional musicians other than the church organist for your wedding, check Chapter 29 for the procedure for contracting professional musicians.

If your budget is low and you want to keep music costs low, use fewer musicians or make use of recorded or taped music. This can be very effective, particularly for a smaller or less formal ceremony held at home.

Try to listen to your musicians perform before you engage them. You might attend a church ceremony and hear the organist play, noting not only the performance but also the quality of the organ. And if you plan to use the bells, ask to hear them rung, too.

Your music all selected, you can now consider another important and meaningful part of your wedding—the words. The words and/or vows that are spoken during your ceremony will usually be those provided by the traditions of your religion or the legal words provided by a judge. But they can also be words that express your own special love and individual thoughts. For a religious ceremony, ask your clergyman what the vows will be, and have him explain them to you. Afterwards you might ask if any changes or additions can be made—incorporating a special prayer or poem that you have composed, or something that is particularly meaningful to you. If you or your fiancé are of different faiths and you want to take religious vows, consider a ceremony performed by clergymen from both faiths. Check whether your religions permit such arrangements and remember that a religious ceremony can be altered only with the approval of the clergyman involved. If you intend to have a civil ceremony with a judge officiating, he will most likely have a copy of the ceremony and vows to be exchanged. You can ask to read this ceremony in advance and find out if it is permissible to make changes or additions.

Now to consider words

One couple I know wrote their entire wedding ceremony. It was a combination of vows, prayers and thoughts that had personal meaning for both. You might want to write your ceremony, adapting ideas from religious or civil ceremonies, or composing one completely original in content. If you do this, be sure to have the approval of the person who will perform the ceremony. Also ask him to look over the ceremony which you have prepared to be certain it meets the religious and/or legal requirements of a wedding ceremony. If you like, carry this a step further and write a special program for the wedding. This might list the members of the wedding party and contain a copy of the actual ceremony and vows. These programs are mementos for you and your guests; if you are artistic you could also design them.

Write your own ceremony

A brief letter outlining any changes or unusual

procedures planned for the ceremony can be sent at this time. This kind of confirmation will be much appreciated and will be an extra help for the clergyman, judge, banquet manager or whoever will be concerned with the ceremony coordination. For example, if you want to tape-record your ceremony, mention it at this time. Such a recording can be a beautiful keepsake—or an utter disappointment, depending upon how it's handled. Whoever takes care of taping the ceremony must be knowledgeable about tape recorders and capable of managing things competently and quietly. Enclose a copy of the ceremony with your additions and changes noted, and list any special arrangements you are requesting. To be super efficient, include some carbon copies of the ceremony, so those involved can easily follow along.

With the all-important words and music of your ceremony in order, you are ready to combine these choices with your processional, recessional and ceremony to create a complete and harmonious wedding that will be uniquely your own.

23

Who Goes First?

PROCESSIONALS, RECESSIONALS AND RECEPTION LINES

THE WEDDING PARTY forms a line called a processional when approaching the altar for the wedding ceremony; maintains prearranged groupings as the ceremony is performed; then turns to leave the area, forming a recessional line which ends happily in a reception line. These lines and groupings can be lovely to watch; their patterns are pleasing and meaningful additions to all wedding ceremonies.

If your ceremony is to be a religious one, your clergyman will advise you of the processional, recessional and reception line to be used. If not, you may want to choose your own style for each formation by combining parts of the procedures explained here with your own ideas.

There is a general processional and recessional which is used not only for most Christian services but

251

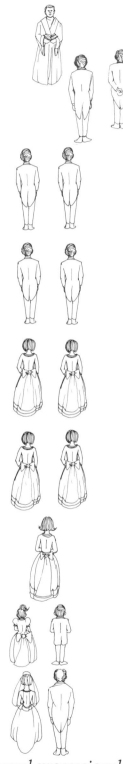

also for many civil ceremonies. The drawings in this chapter will show you the exact placement of all members of the wedding party, but briefly the procedure is as follows: The groom, best man and clergyman or judge take their places at the altar. The ushers are first to come down the aisle, in pairs or one by one, followed by your bridesmaids, maid of honor, flower girl and finally the bride on her father's arm. If you have both a maid and a matron of honor, they can walk together, or the one who will assist you most during the ceremony can follow behind the first. Next would follow your flower girl, either alone or paired with the ring-bearer, if you have one. If you have train-bearers, they would, of course, follow you, holding your train. When you reach the altar, you will stand to the left of your groom, with your maid of honor to your left and the best man to the groom's right. Your bridesmaids would be on the left side in a line forming a semicircle, facing the ceremony area. Your ushers would be on the right side in the same formation. If you prefer, you can have the bridesmaids and ushers standing in pairs facing the altar.

The flower girl and train-bearers are usually seated after they have completed their part in the processional. The ring-bearers would take their place beside the best man and/or beside the maid of honor. Once their portion of the ceremony is completed, they could also be seated.

In this type of processional, your father would escort you to the altar area and stand behind you until he answers the question, "Who giveth this woman in marriage?" Your father would say, "I do," and then take his seat next to your mother. This procedure is called "giving the bride away."

The recessional follows the ceremony and is led by the bride and groom, followed by the attendants in pairs: flower girl and ring-bearer, maid of honor and best man, bridesmaids and ushers. The children may be excluded from the recessional, if you like, and the best man may also stay behind to pay the clergyman or judge and make sure everyone exits from the ceremony site comfortably.

Special note: Having an odd number of attendants is not a serious problem regardless of when it occurs. An extra maid can be escorted by two ushers. An extra usher can be placed in the center of two maids and/or lines of attendants. At the altar the attendants can form a triangular arrangement rather than a semi-circle, and your guests will be none the wiser. If other unusual problems arise, don't panic. Adjust your plans calmly instead. There is always a solution. For the general processional, the ceremony seating area is usually divided, with the groom's relatives and friends seated on the right and the bride's on the left. The groom's father and mother are seated in the right front row, and the bride's parents on the left front row.

The Catholic processional, placement at altar and recessional are similar to that described above with three possible exceptions. One is that two to four choristers may precede the ushers in the processional and recessional. Another is that placement at the altar might include an acolyte to assist the priest. The third is that your father will not "give you away" during this ceremony, but rather kiss you, present you to your groom as you reach the ceremony area, then take his seat next to your mother.

A double wedding requires some changes in the procedure, as illustrated in this chapter. If the brides are sisters, their father walks between them. One wedding party forms to the right as the girls reach the altar, the other to the left; if the brides are not related, the bride whose party will be to the right goes down the aisle with her father, followed by the bride, also with her father, who will go to the left. There would be no division in the seating; friends and relatives of either bride could be seated on either side of the ceremony

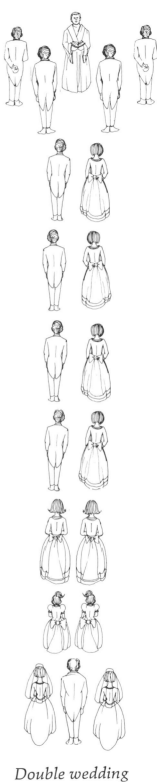

Double wedding   253

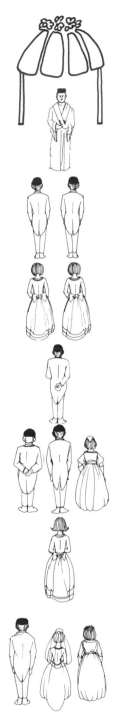

Jewish processional

area. A recessional would be led by the bride and groom from the left of the altar area, followed by bride and groom from the right.

An Orthodox or Conservative Jewish wedding begins with the ushers entering in pairs, followed by the bridesmaids in pairs. After them is the ring-bearer, followed by the best man. The groom then enters with his father on his left and his mother on his right. The maid of honor walks alone and is followed by a flower girl. The bride enters last, with her father on her left and her mother on her right. The rabbi may lead the processional if the ceremony takes place at a site other than a synagogue. Depending upon the individual congregation, the left or the right side may be designated to seat the bride's guests and the opposite for the groom. Male guests and members of the wedding party wear head coverings; sometimes *yarmulkes* are provided as the guests enter. At the altar area, the rabbi, bride, groom and honor attendants stand under the *chupah*, or decorated canopy, for the service. Space permitting, both sets of parents are included under the *chupah*; if not, only the fathers. In Jewish ceremonies, the bride stands to the groom's right rather than to his left, with her maid of honor next to her. The recessional is led by the bride and groom, the bride's parents following, and the groom's parents after them. The other wedding attendants follow in pairs.

The Reform Jewish ceremony is somewhat different from that described above. The *chupah* can be optional, and the processional has the groom escorted by his best man rather than by his parents. The bride enters with her father alone. In a Reform ceremony, the left side is reserved for the bride's guests, and the right side for the groom's guests. The bride might receive her guests or her groom in the anteroom of the temple before the ceremony. The placement at the ceremony area and the recessional are the same as in the Orthodox ceremony.

For a wedding in a private home, the general processional might be combined with the use of a staircase if one is available. This can be very beautiful to watch, but only if the stairs are easy to navigate and there is adequate opportunity for your guests to see you as you descend the stairs. You can omit the recessional altogether for a home wedding, and you and your husband can merely turn to greet your guests once the ceremony is concluded.

If you are having your wedding in an area that is small or unusual in shape, you may need to modify the processional and recessional. Should your ceremony site have two side aisles rather than one central aisle, you could have your wedding party enter by one and leave by the other, or use one aisle only as a central aisle and not even seat guests in the other portion of the site. For a large wedding party, both aisles could be utilized simultaneously for processional and recessional.

A military wedding makes use of the general style already explained, but the bride consistently stands to the groom's *right* rather than to his *left*—during the ceremony and in the reception line.

All of the procedures outlined above are very general, and you should ask your clergyman or judge for suggestions or religious variations. When pacing the processional, guide your attendants by suggesting that they leave the space of two pews or rows of seats between the person in front of them and themselves. The bride and her father would leave twice this amount of space, or four rows. When two people walk together, they should be in step, but there's no reason for the entire wedding party to be self-consciously worried about the way they move. If they can keep an easy, natural rhythm, they need not be in time with the music being played to achieve the desired effect. Certainly they will look more graceful than if they minced along in a desperate attempt to keep exactly in step with the person in front of them. Though the recessional is usually more brisk than the processional, an interesting variation would be to have a slow and stately recessional, with the bride and groom greeting their guests with their eyes and smiles as they return up the aisle.

The Protestant ceremony officially begins when you reach the altar area and let go of your father's arm, transfer your bouquet from your right to your left hand, and join your right arm with that of the groom. The service may begin with the clergyman asking, "Who gives this woman in holy matrimony?" Your father, having replied "I do,"—or "We do" to include your mother—will then leave the altar area to join your mother in the first pew. You then approach the altar and hand your bouquet to your maid of honor. After vows are exchanged, the best man produces the wedding ring to give to the minister or the groom; the maid of honor does the same with the groom's ring, if a double-ring ceremony. If a wedding kiss is included in your ceremony, your maid of honor lifts back your veil before you turn to your husband. She then returns your bouquet, you turn and take your husband's right arm, and the recessional begins.

The Jewish ceremony is basically the same for all three branches. The ceremony begins once you are under the *chupah*. The rabbi blesses two goblets of wine and hands one to your groom, who sips from it and then shares it with you. The best man then produces the ring and gives it to the rabbi. At a Reform ceremony, the groom will place the ring on the ring finger of the left hand; at an Orthodox or Conservative ceremony, the ring might be placed on the index finger of the right hand. An Orthodox or Conservative ceremony may be recited in Hebrew, with the marriage covenant given in Aramic and possibly translated into English afterward. At a Reform ceremony, most of the words are in English. The rabbi usually gives a short talk on the seriousness of marriage, and a second glass of wine is prepared and shared by bride and groom. The groom then steps

Protestant ceremony

Jewish ceremony

on the wedding glass, previously wrapped in a cloth and placed beneath his shoe, breaking the glass to symbolize your joyful union. You then turn to face your guests, kiss your groom, and take his left arm and begin the recessional.

A Catholic wedding may include a Nuptial Mass. This is determined by the priest, who will give full instructions concerning what you and each member of your wedding party must do. This includes sharing Holy Communion as part of the ceremony. The ceremony itself is similar to the Protestant, except that the priest first blesses the ring before it is placed on the bride's finger. The father of the bride does not "give away" his daughter in a Catholic ceremony. He lifts her veil as they reach the first pew, kisses her gently, then presents her to her groom, afterwards taking his seat.

Catholic ceremony

If it is possible to make additions to the wedding ceremony you will have, you might want to consider the lovely custom of candle lighting for your ceremony. Two candles are placed in the altar area, already lighted. A third candle stands between them, and after you have been pronounced man and wife, you each take a lighted candle and light the third candle with both flames. Blowing out the first two candles symbolizes the joining of your lives together.

Wedding candles

If you will be having a civil ceremony with a judge officiating, you could use any combination of the processionals, recessionals and reception lines described here. You may want to use aspects of the various ceremony styles as well; there would be no religious vows exchanged, but you might add some of your own thoughts or a special poem or prayer to the basic civil ceremony.

The reception line is the same for most types of ceremonies, with any variations that you or your clergyman might add. The purpose of the reception line is to formally introduce to all the guests the new couple as

Reception lines

husband and wife. It's your guests' chance to wish you well, and your chance to see that your groom is introduced to everyone attending and vice versa.

The reception line usually begins with your mother, followed by your bridesmaids or your maid of honor. You are next, and on your left is the groom. The last person in line might well be another bridesmaid—a good idea because this person can function as a "greeter" or hostess and direct guests to the refreshment area. It speeds guests along to refreshments and avoids the feeling that the line has just "fizzled out." Optional additions to the reception line are your husband's father, who would stand next to your mother with his wife to his left, and your father, who would be next to your mother-in-law. It is sometimes best if your father acts as host and makes sure all the guests are enjoying themselves and meeting one another. The best man is usually not in the reception line, but if your groom's father is his best man, it would be a nice gesture to include him.

For a military wedding, the bride stands on the groom's left rather than on his right in the reception line.

Although some people choose to dispense with the reception line, preferring to enter immediately into the festivities of the reception itself, it seems to me that the reception line not only provides a transition from the solemnity of the ceremony to the gaiety of the reception, but also permits guests to voice their congratulations at a moment when they can have the bride's complete attention. They will not leave after the ceremony is ended with the frustration of never really having the chance to meet the young couple and wish them well. If a reception line seems to you to be too formal an idea, look at the suggested modified reception line in this chapter. This shorter version is less formal and moves quickly yet cordially on to the reception festivities.

Appoint a "greeter"

The processional, recessional and reception lines form the graceful patterns that frame your wedding ceremony, making it a beautiful and lingering memory for all those who attend.

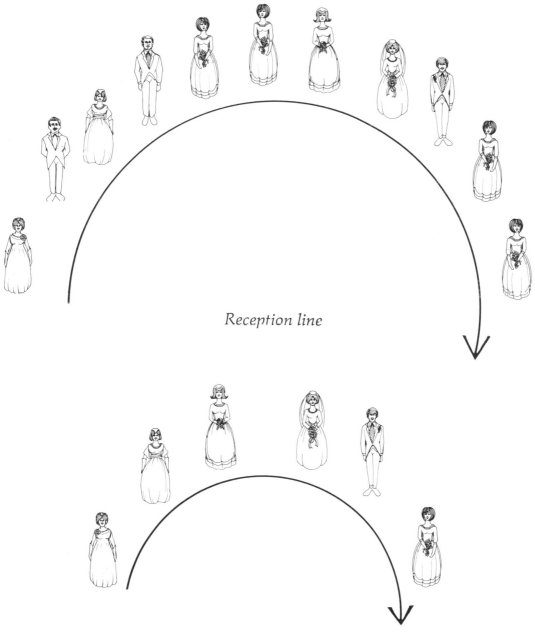

Reception line

Alternate reception line

24

Get Me to the Church on Time

PROCESSION TO THE CEREMONY SITE

IT'S A GOOD IDEA at this point to give some thought to how you will reach your ceremony site. Whether it is a long trip to your church, synagogue, hotel, or club, or merely down the stairs to the spot designated for your ceremony in your own home, the assembling and procession of your wedding party must be planned in advance.

If you plan to have a formal or informal procession of cars to your ceremony site, you and your family would dress and prepare for the wedding ceremony at home. Before getting ready your father should check that the cars which will be used for the procession are decorated and ready to go, and your mother should attend to the last-minute details necessary to the ceremony or reception.

261

You might invite your attendants to come to your home and join in the procession to the ceremony site. Your maid of honor and your bridesmaids can help you dress for your wedding, or at least be on hand to admire your gown and help with any last-minute details of dressing. You can make this an occasion by serving a light breakfast or brunch to the girls. Ask them to come informally dressed, bringing their gowns, and they could then dress at your home after you have shared your brunch together. This type of party would be a little extra work and expense, but it can be a lot of fun. If you're the type who doesn't like others around when you're nervous or excited, arrange to meet them later, dressed and ready to take part in the procession.

When the girls arrive at your home, give them their bouquets or corsages and perhaps a prepared list of the day's procedure. Your father might take some candid photos at this time—and perhaps offer a champagne toast especially for you. All your attendants will doubtless tell you what a beautiful bride you are, and I'm sure you *will* look lovely. But remember that everyone in the wedding party will be trying to look her best, too, so tell the girls how nice they look and take this occasion to thank them for all the wonderful help they've given you during the past months.

Your fiancé can do the same

While the bridesmaids are gathering at your home, your fiancé can have his best man and ushers meet at his home. They might also share a brunch or a toast, and your groom may have a list of information— names of important people who will attend the wedding and what will happen when—for them. Next he can pass out their boutonnières and present his mother with her corsage.

Both groups of attendants are now ready to leave for the ceremony site. You can provide transportation for them if you like. Family cars, perhaps decorated with streamers or flowers, or rented limousines, if your budget allows, can make the procession distinctive. If chauffeurs are too expensive, friends and relatives can help drive the wedding party to the site. Horse-drawn carriages would lend a feeling of romance to your procession, and these might be available for a country wedding or in New York near Central Park. Add decorations or flowers in your wedding colors for a festive touch.

It's nice to arrange to pick up relatives, friends or elderly guests who are without transportation. These people need not take part in the procession itself, but you could show your consideration by making some kind of transportation available to them. Have a supply of maps available for everyone driving to your wedding, especially if your site is in an out-of-the-way spot or a long distance from most guests' homes. And if a large number of guests will attend your ceremony, plan to have someone direct traffic at the site—a policeman in a public area or a friend assigned to the job. And it would also be helpful to have someone responsible for parking cars.

Transportation considerations

The order of the cars in the procession would begin with your mother, some bridesmaids and the flower girl and her mother in the first car. The remaining bridesmaids and the maid of honor in the second car, and you and your father in the last car. This final car is usually the one used for the honeymoon— either the groom's own car or a family car you are using for the occasion. If you're concerned about keeping your gown clean, take a bed sheet along to cover the car seat. To avoid delay, allow plenty of time for traffic and other problems. Other last-minute catastrophes can be planned for in advance if your maid of honor brings extra needles, thread and safety pins along just in case.

Order of procession

Your groom, his parents, the best man and ushers generally make their own way to the ceremony site. The ushers should arrive first, as they have last-minute details before the ceremony and must be on hand to begin seating wedding guests. The groom and best man arrive next and wait with the clergyman or judge for the arrival of all the others—and you. Once the entire wedding party has arrived, they can take their places for the ceremony and you'll be ready to begin.

You can meet at ceremony site

Sometimes it's easier for the members of the wedding party to meet at the ceremony site. If so, there's no need to plan a procession. Everyone can dress at home and arrive completely ready for the service. You can dress at the ceremony site if you like, but you would be the only one to do so.

Quite often there are two waiting rooms available at the ceremony site to accommodate the wedding party—one for the women and one for the men. You can plan to dress in this room and meet your bridesmaids there, giving them their bouquets and special wedding jewelry at this time. The same could be true for the men in the wedding party. The groom and the best man, in any event, should have a room in which to wait for the beginning of the ceremony. The best man will assist the groom by checking his appearance and making any arrangements for the day such as paying the clergyman or double-checking that the guests are being seated properly. You might want photographs taken of the wedding party and both sets of parents while they wait for the ceremony to begin. If you're not superstitious about seeing your groom before the ceremony, you could even pose for formal pictures featuring the two of you and the whole wedding party. These pictures can be taken as much as two hours before the ceremony begins to allow the ushers enough time to seat even the earliest guests.

Your ceremony planning is finished—down to the last detail of your wedding procession. Now you can begin to plan the greatest party you'll ever attend—your wedding reception.

Part Five

PLANNING YOUR RECEPTION

25

Pick the Place

RECEPTION SITES, USUAL AND UNUSUAL

YOUR WEDDING RECEPTION should be the greatest party ever, for you are celebrating the most important event in your life—your marriage. If you choose the site early and carefully, your reception is bound to be a delight.

You can use the same site for your ceremony and reception if all your guests are invited to both and the facilities at the ceremony site are adequate, or you can choose an entirely different locale. A budget-minded alternative is to have a "delayed" reception—held several weeks after the ceremony—which helps to space out the cost of the entire wedding; and many couples find it to be a more relaxing way to celebrate their marriage. But no matter when your reception occurs, you'll have to pick the place and plan all the details well in advance.

Places for wedding receptions are similar to those you might choose for the ceremony. A hotel, club or rented hall, a restaurant, private home or garden site will all serve equally well. Some places of worship have adjoining party or reception rooms that can be used for wedding receptions, so be sure to ask about this possibility.

Unusual sites

And there are unusual sites, too. A park, a boat or a penthouse room of a tall building can provide a unique backdrop for a reception. A park or an area surrounding a farmhouse would serve for a picnic-style party—a particularly lovely idea for an informal type of reception. A reception on board a large boat could end with the guests watching from the pier as the bride and groom sail off to begin their wedding trip. A penthouse suite could be decorated with outdoor lights, candles and other appointments to emphasize a main feature of the reception—the view of the city.

Questions to ask

Whatever sites you consider, there are various questions you should ask about the facilities and arrangements to be sure this spot is suitable for your reception. Use the following as a checklist at each site.

1. Is the site available when you want it? (Some popular hotels have a year's waiting list!)
2. Is it attractive, comfortable?
3. Is it large enough, with room for food and beverages to be served easily, either at a buffet or at each table?
4. Is there room for a reception line, preferably an area where guests can come in one door and move easily through the line and into the refreshment area?
5. Is there a place for coats and wraps?
6. Are there adequate rest-room facilities?
7. Is it convenient to your ceremony site?
8. Are there adequate parking facilities?
9. What are the costs involved, whether you use their services or provide some of your own food and drink?
10. Will you be charged extra for the room(s) or is this included in the total cost?

11. Is the lighting good?
12. Is the seating as comfortable as you desire and can afford?
13. Is there a banquet manager or someone to coordinate the reception?
14. Does he have an adequate staff to help with serving and cleaning up?
15. Can you decorate as you please?

Are you having a hotel reception? Ask if they offer a complimentary wedding cake or a free bridal suite as an enticement for your business. Don't be afraid to ask if these extras are customary. Make sure they have handled wedding receptions before, as this is a crucial consideration. Deal only with people who are experienced with the unique and special problems of a wedding reception to guarantee that yours will be well organized and supervised. Ask whether there are other receptions scheduled in the same building on the same day, as this can create noise and/or traffic problems for you.

Hotel reception

If you plan to have your reception in a private home, perhaps out-of-doors, make sure that there is enough space and that the neighbors will neither resent nor create noise. For an outdoor reception, it's a good precaution to provide a marquee (tent) or an alternate indoor site in case of bad weather.

Home reception

Often in the planning of a wedding, the women of a family take over, plunging in with joy to make choices of flowers, clothes and foods. Keep in mind that your father can be of tremendous help to you in the business matters you'll be negotiating. He should be made to feel a part of all the bustle and excitement of preparing for this wedding; but beyond that, he may also be an excellent advisor in the all-important matters having to do with financial arrangements.

Ask your dad

Once you have seen and compared the various sites, you will be able to choose the one that best meets your requirements and makes you, your parents and

Confirm details

your fiancé happy. Confirm the details by a letter of agreement. (If you are beginning to plan a home reception and will handle all details yourself, you'll most likely make all necessary arrangements with a caterer —now.) In your letter, state the day, date, hour and length of time for which you are reserving the site. Mention all financial arrangements, including any deposits you have given. (A reminder: Make all deposits by check so you can have a receipt.) You or the banquet manager will list the cost of each item, so you can see how much is spent for food as opposed to champagne, room rental and other costs. Be sure to address this letter to the person who will coordinate all your arrangements at the site, and include the exact functions he will handle for you.

Your site chosen and confirmed—the basic plan begun—you can now begin to deal with all the necessary and fun details that will make your reception even more beautiful.

26

To Remember Always

ARRANGING FOR THE WEDDING PHOTO ALBUM

WHETHER YOUR RECEPTION is large or small, it's nice to have photographs of it to combine with your ceremony pictures in your wedding album. Even if you don't plan to have pictures taken at the ceremony, you may still want photos of the reception as a record of your happy day.

As you will recall from Chapter 20, there are two kinds of photographs to consider; candids, or informal pictures, and formals, or posed shots. Candids are best for receptions because stopping to pose for photographs can hold up the flow of the event and make the wedding party miss out on the fun. You can have either black and white or color photographs; black and white are more dramatic and less expensive, but color photos result in a more faithful representation of the day.

A friend or relative may take the photographs

during the reception, but select only one person for this rather than allowing anyone and everyone to get in on the act, perhaps ruining the chances of any really good work being done. This will save money, of course, and if you know a real camera buff whose work you like, it might be an excellent solution to any financial problems about hiring a photographer. The merriment and flurry of a reception show up well in movies, and again, a friend might be asked to take these films. You can have photographs made from the individual frames of film, too.

If you decide to have a professional photograph the reception, you can use the same photographer who will take the ceremony shots. This is the usual choice and makes for uniform photos for your album. If for any reason you want to use a different photographer on this occasion, look again at Chapter 20 and apply the same criteria to your selection of this photographer.

Give the photographer of your choice a list of the photographs you particularly want taken, as well as the names of any and all persons to be especially included in these shots. There are four types of photographs you might want to have taken during the wedding reception, and they run the gamut from the traditional "highlights" as they occur to a variety of candids of the guests as they move about and enjoy themselves. Feel free to add your own ideas to the list, too.

Arrival and pre-reception shots might begin with a photograph of the reception site itself before anyone has arrived. This could be followed by the arrival of the bride and groom, plus a few shots of the guests as they sign the guest book.

If the reception line is formed at the reception site rather than at the ceremony site, you could plan for formal pictures of the line and of special guests as they greet the bride and groom.

There are any number of possibilities for pictures taken during the reception. Photographs can be taken

Amateur photographers

The photographer

A list of pictures

Type of photos

of the guests as they help themselves to food from a buffet and/or of guests seated at their tables. You'll want pictures of the wedding party at the head table and of any special toasts which are made. Special events which take place during the reception will be a must. Traditional photos include the bride and groom sharing their first dance as Mr. and Mrs., and other special dances such as those of the bride and her father and the best man and maid of honor. The bride and groom cutting their wedding cake and sharing the first piece is also a must shot (often the bride feeds the groom with her fingers, but using a fork is much less messy!). You might want a photo of the band and/or any soloists you are using, as well as pictures of the bride tossing her bouquet to the next lucky single girl or the groom throwing the bride's garter to the single men. It's also nice to have candids of the bride and groom mingling about and chatting with the various guests.

You might like to have some pictures taken of you and your groom in your going-away outfits as you leave the reception— perhaps a photo of the two of you kissing your parents good-bye, or one of the guests and/or parents throwing rice at you as you leave, or one of you and your groom entering and leaving your car. If any of these pictures are missing, keep in mind that you can come back after your honeymoon and have a picture taken in your going-away outfit. This is cheating, in a way, but it does make a nice final picture to complete your wedding album.

Just to be sure you have all the photos you would like, send your photographer a list of those you want taken during your reception. You can combine this with the list of ceremony photos and you will be giving the photographer a helpful guide and also ensuring that you don't forget important pictures. Some photographers will have a list prepared—all you will have to do is check the ones you want. If your list is fairly long, you can be sure of a good variety of shots from which

Keep a copy of your list

to order your album.

When your proofs are ready

You won't be ordering your photos right away, but your photographer should have your proofs ready for you shortly after you return from your honeymoon. The proofs will look like actual photos, but they are different in two ways. First of all, they are not lasting —the colors will fade. Then, too, they are not retouched or corrected in any way. Such things as blending out lines in the face or removing hair that is out of place will not be corrected until the actual photographs are finished. When you look at proofs, you should always bear in mind that you are not judging the finished product.

Most photographers will request that you come in person to pick up your proofs, which is perfectly all right, of course, but *do not* order your wedding photographs on the first day you see them. Take them home and study them. Make your choices in the privacy of your home, and don't allow yourself to be pressured by the salesman at the photographer's studio or by your own emotions. It's hard to be money-conscious when you first look at your wedding pictures—you're going to want to buy them all. Take your time with this decision and you'll be happy that you did.

You choose first

When you get the proofs home, you and your husband should look them over carefully and choose the ones you want. Then show or send them to your parents, to members of the wedding party and finally to relatives and friends who might like to order some. Proofs are usually numbered, and it's wise to note the numbers you personally want to order before you send them off. This is a good precaution because if they are lost, you won't have the expense of having new proofs made up before you can place your order.

The wedding album

Your wedding album should cover all the highlights of your wedding day—the moments you'll most want to remember in the years to come. If you have pictures taken throughout the wedding and reception,

276

it's nice to have the photographs "tell the story." You would probably want to select a picture from any or all of the following moments:

1. Getting ready (bride and/or maids, groom, and others)
2. Pre-processional
3. During the ceremony
4. Recessional
5. Reception line
6. During the reception
7. Departure from the reception of bride and groom

And if you had a bridal portrait taken, you can include this as one of your selections for the album, too.

Ask the price of the various albums your photographer has to offer; you may find you can buy a less expensive or more attractive one from a stationer and insert the photos yourself. There are many styles of albums. It isn't mandatory to buy the traditional album with its white padded cover and gold stamping. Lovely albums come in multi-colored raw silk, for example. Or you might choose an album in the colors you used for your wedding. Some albums even feature a cut-out heart over each photograph so that each picture is seen outlined by a heart. This can be used for each picture in the album or just for the first photograph. Look at a variety of albums before choosing the one you plan to use.

Choosing the album

Photos are available in many sizes. It's not necessary to select only 8 by 10 inch photographs. A 5 by 7 inch is a nice size, and so are smaller shots. Don't let the photographer talk you into giant-sized pictures you don't want or can't afford. Study the price list carefully, for some photographers charge the same for an 8 by 10 inch as they do for a 5 by 7 inch.

Friends and relatives should pay for photographs they order unless you choose to give them as gifts. This is a nice thing to do, particularly for members of the

Photos for friends and relatives

277

wedding party. You might consider giving each person a small mounted photograph instead of an album, as the latter could become very costly indeed.

When you place your order, combine it with those of your family and friends so that the order is large. Duplicates of a particular shot should cost less. Combining all orders makes it easier for the photographer and cheaper for you, and you will probably receive better service because of the size of the combined order.

Place your order   It's best to figure the cost of your order in advance so that you won't be shocked by the amount when you arrive at the photographer's studio. Add the cost of photos and albums together, and then add any sales tax. When you know this amount beforehand, you will be less susceptible to ordering "just a few more" at the last minute.

The photographs of your reception will complete your wedding story. And as soon as they are added to your wedding album, the memories of your wedding day—all the joy and fun—will be yours forever.

27

More Flowers, and Other Ideas

RECEPTION DECORATIONS

DECORATING for your wedding reception can be even more fun than decorating for your ceremony. This is true because you're not limited to the exclusive use of flowers and you can include many unusual items that will become lovely mementos for you and your guests. Also you can be more creative with reception decorations. You are free to use flowers, garlands, ribbons, crepe paper—all these things—to decorate to your heart's content.

Just as you made a decoration plan for your ceremony, it's wise to make one for the reception. This will help you to visualize your decoration ideas, and it will later be useful to your florist. If your reception is to be held in a room at a club or hotel, the banquet manager might be able to supply you with a floor plan of the room. If not, make your own sketch, just as you did for the ceremony. Include all exits, existing pillars, lighting fixtures and the available outlets, and draw them on your plan to scale, so you have a clear idea of how much space you have to work with. Begin by generally indicating large areas for such things as dining and dancing and then work out the specifics of the site.

Next note on your plan the existing colors of the site. Fortunately most public rooms are decorated in colors that will harmonize well with any color scheme. But if you're having your reception in a private home, the existing colors may limit your choices. Basically, you can use the same colors as those used in the wedding ceremony and reuse many of your floral decorations; or extend the color scheme for the reception by adding to the ceremony colors. If, for example, you used blue and white for the ceremony, add green to lend a bit more contrast and variety to the reception.

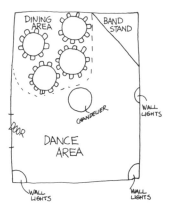

You will be decorating in two ways: First, you will be highlighting specific areas of the reception site; and second, you will be decorating the tables used for eating, serving or special displays.

Special areas

Decorated areas can include the entrance to the reception site, which might have a canopy or a runner carpet from the sidewalk to the entrance; the reception line area, which might be set off by a backdrop of flowers, greens or decorated mantel, or by a trellis or arbor, and the band or entertainment area, including the dance floor, which could be lined sparingly with garlands or potted plants so as not to crowd these areas. At outdoor weddings, you can add to the natural beauty of shrubs and trees by decorating them with flowers. And you can even float real or artificial flowers in a swimming pool.

Buffet table

Plan to serve buffet style? Then you will want to decorate your buffet table. The floral decorations or greenery used here should enhance the food being served and make it look even more appetizing. (See Chapter 28 for more details.) A table to be used for the wedding cake or champagne punch and its service can be decorated also. A bar can match either of the other tables in decoration or have a different look.

Like your decorations, your table size should be chosen for mood and look. If you plan to have your guests eat at individual tables, it's better to use a number of small tables than a few large ones. Small tables create a more intimate atmosphere and are conducive to relaxed conversations. You can use any shape tables and decorate them in a wide variety of ways. The following are suggestions for some usual and unusual methods of table decoration, which may perhaps give you some ideas of your own.

You'll probably want your tables covered with decorative cloths and set off with some kind of floral arrangement or centerpiece. The shape of the centerpieces should correspond to the shape of the table—round with round, square with square—and they should be low enough so your guests can see over them comfortably. Lower centerpieces are preferable, as they avoid the problem of a guest's shifting from side to side to carry on a conversation. Although centerpieces are quite often placed in the center of the table, a variety of interesting effects can be achieved by placing an arrangement to one side of a longer table or by using individual decorations at each place setting. Or try a single large flower in a vase with ribbons or streamers cascading from the center—each decorated with tiny flowers. This will create an interesting and delicate effect.

Tablecloths, too, can be decorative in their own right, and can be made, borrowed or rented. If you are working with a caterer or a banquet manager, he will most likely be furnishing cloths, but you may be able to specify your choice of color or pattern. If you make or bring your own tablecloth, the possibilities are unlimited.

For example, a square or rectangular table covered with a solid color cloth can be accented with a long, thin runner cloth going down the center of the table or

Tablecloths and centerpieces

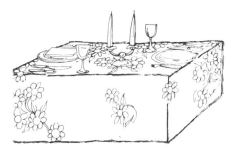

283

by ribbons or streamers forming a pattern. A round table covered with a plain cloth can be decorated in several ways. It can be covered by a sheer organdy or lace material, or by another type of solid color cloth, which has been cut in a pattern. You might make a cloth with sections in alternating colors—pie-shaped sections divided by ribbons or streamers.

The bar table could be decorated by draped material or flower garlands along the front and accented with napkins and accessories in contrasting tones. A cake or punch table could have two cloths, with the top —a lightweight material draped to expose the bottom cloth—caught back with flowers or ribbons like a curtain. The top of this table could be decorated with flowers, petals or fragile fern leaves. A pure white wedding cake would look perfect on a daintily flowered cloth, as would a clear crystal or silver punch bowl and its accessories.

Centerpieces

The centerpieces for your tables, and in fact many of your floral arrangements, may be determined by the types of containers you choose to use. Baskets, in a natural wheat color, painted a color or pure white, make marvelous flower containers. They can hold flowers for a centerpiece, or they can be hung, full of cascading flowers and ferns, in an entryway covering an entire section of the ceiling. Small berry baskets could be decorated and trimmed with ribbons, filled with paper or dried flowers and used attractively.

Trays

Trays can be used as containers for flowers and can also hold candles. A silver tray or a tray covered with paper to match your color scheme could be filled with many candles in different sizes to double as a centerpiece and a source of light. Or you might try flowers floating on water in a deep rectangular shaped tray for a unique table decoration.

Glasses and bowls

Glasses, goblets and crystal bowls make handsome containers, particularly if you decide upon individual arrangements for each place setting. A glass could hold a single floating flower or accommodate a tiny candle, floating in colored water for a particularly lovely effect. Another unique arrangement would be a glass, filled with aquarium pebbles that could be color-keyed to your decorating scheme, which holds a small candle in its center.

Potted plants are useful decorations, both as backgrounds to fresh flowers and as the main attraction. Covering the pots with the same color paper will give them a matching look. Pots of ferns and cut greens, like evergreen, boxwood, boston fern or baby's tears can be used to decorate tables and to combine with flowers. Greens add freshness to your decorations and are less expensive than flowers. Use them liberally; they will add a lush and beautiful touch to your reception.

Potted plants

Other decorative items are streamers of paper, garlands of real or artificial flowers and ribbons. These can be used to frame areas, decorate tables and stairways or to give attractive touches to items you want to decorate. A bow at the neck of a champagne bottle is a good example of this.

Other decorations

Someone once said that weddings are for looking back on—to remember tenderly. Both you and your husband and your guests should have something to remember this wedding by, some memento or souvenir that will bring your reception once again to mind.

Mementos

There are many lovely traditions that you might want to include as part of your wedding reception which would give you items to treasure and perhaps use again, or even things to hand down to other girls in your family—maybe one day to your own daughter.

One of these is a special wedding candle. It is usually a very thick, tall candle which is decorated with flowers to match the flowers which you will carry that day or with other symbols of your wedding day. You could use your wedding candle and have it burning at your reception, and then keep it to relight and enjoy on your future wedding anniversaries.

You might also want to consider engraving items that would be used during your wedding reception. You can engrave a special cake knife, which might have your name and your groom's name on it, decorate it in ribbons the color of your wedding color scheme, and use it to cut your first piece of cake. This is a nice memento.

Or you might buy, or someone may give you, two champagne glasses for your first toast as Mr. and Mrs. These glasses could be made of glass or silver and could be engraved with your name on one and the name of your groom on the other; they could also be decorated with tiny flowers and ribbons around the base of the glass. Or you might consider something like the French *coupe de mariage*. This is a two-sided cup from which the bride and the groom can drink simultaneously. There is a large bowl at one end for the groom and a tiny, more dainty bowl on the other end for the bride; these bowls are affixed to a piece of metal in such a way that they will turn, so that you can both drink from the cup simultaneously. The cup may be made of silver or another metal and could be engraved with your name, a special poem, one or two sentences which would be meaningful to you and your groom or simply the wedding date.

You, as the bride, will particularly enjoy collecting as many tangible memories of your wedding as possible. Most girls keep a wedding scrapbook or at least a box of special keepsakes. The "something old, something new, something borrowed, something blue" items might be things you want to save.

You might like to buy a bridal garter, or perhaps someone will buy one for you as a gift. Many bridal garters are blue or have blue ribbon on them, so you could wear this "as something blue." If you want to keep a bridal garter as a souvenir and your groom wants to throw one to the group of young eligible men, consider buying two garters—one to throw and one to keep.

You will also probably want to keep the ornament that decorates the top of your wedding cake. Most brides like to keep the ornament and at least one piece of wedding cake, which they would freeze and enjoy a year later on their first wedding anniversary. In addition, you may choose to save such items as matches, coasters or napkins which are engraved with your name and the date. Your mother or a friend can collect the things you'll want and keep them for your return from the honeymoon.

The wedding cake you provide for the guests to take home, and any individual mementos at their tables like flowers or place cards serve beautifully as souvenirs. The floral decorations at the reception might be given to guests, or a split of champagne might appear before each place setting. If your wedding has a particular style to it, gifts for your guests might be in that style: a fan for the women if there is an Oriental flavor to the day, or a lei if Hawaiian. If you have sent your guests a map of how to reach the reception site, this will serve as a memento, too, so design such a map with this in mind.

When you have settled on the ideal decorations for your reception, compile a list for your florist, combining all your needs for both ceremony and reception. You may find that you have gone beyond your budget in your planning; if so, money-saving ideas follow. Begin by asking your florist for a discount if you order all your flowers and decorations from him, or consider a few of the following ideas.

Potted plants can be used instead of fresh flowers in many cases, and you can often borrow such plants from friends. You can change your plans to have an outdoor reception if it's a time of year when Nature could do the decorating. You can also make your own decorations, using paper flowers or artificial ones.

To save on renting tables, use card tables covered with long matching cloths. Tablecloths can be made from interesting fabrics or sheets, and candles are often a lovely substitute for extravagant floral centerpieces.

Money-saving suggestions

287

Use masses of bows—everywhere you might want to use a single flower, place a bow instead. Collected from your wedding and shower gifts, the bows won't cost a cent. You can cover styrofoam shapes by attaching bows with pins to fashion a unique centerpiece. And a simple cluster of Christmas ornaments and evergreens for a winter wedding could form a perfect holiday theme arrangement.

If there's extra money

If you are fortunate enough to find that you have extra money to spend, here are some extras you might like to consider. Fountain-style punch bowls can be bought or rented. Often these feature colored lights and are quite stunning. If you use one, avoid filling it with fresh fruit punches because the fruit will clog the fountain tubing. Lovebirds perched in a corner of the room or nestled in flowers are an elegant touch. And, of course, you can always add more flowers if you like. But don't decorate every single available space. This would be overdoing it.

Getting help

Your florist will probably be responsible for a great deal of your reception decorations, so check Chapter 21 for helpful information about dealing with him. Or you may have a caterer or a banquet manager working with you to handle decorations. If so, give him specific details of your needs and desires both in conversation and letter. If you allow a banquet manager to place the order for flowers and other decorations, you may be paying an additional amount to cover the commission he receives for referring your business to certain suppliers. To save—find your own suppliers.

Your family and friends

You or your mother will most likely be ordering your decorations, but members of the bridal party can help in other ways. You may have a friend or relative take the names of your guests down in a guest book as they arrive for the reception, and another friend to help you gather your souvenirs. The others may be more than happy to help you make or choose the decorations for the reception. (See Chapter 34 for more hints on what your bridal party and your friends can help you with, here and throughout your wedding.)

With your decorating ideas completed and your mementos chosen for your special day, all that remains is to combine them with luscious food and drink and mood music of your choosing, and your wedding reception will be truly a grand and gala party.

28

Eat, Drink and Be Married

PLANNING THE MENU AND REFRESHMENTS

YOUR WEDDING RECEPTION is like any other gala party—only the occasion and the accompanying traditions are special and different. And, as at any party, the refreshments can suit your whimsy and desires. The food and drink for your wedding reception can be wedding cake with coffee or tea or a complete dinner served with wines. But whatever your choice, it's bound to make this party in your honor even more delicious.

Your wedding refreshments can cost a tremendous amount if you're not careful, so study these menus closely before you make any choices. There are four basic menus to consider for a reception. The first three are similar to the meals we eat every day, and the fourth is a simple reception menu that can be used at any time of the day or evening.

291

Brunch, served after a morning wedding, might have a menu which includes:

> Juice or fruit
> Meat or egg dishes
> Rolls and butter
> Coffee, milk or tea
> Wedding cake and fruit or sherbet

For a luncheon, you might serve:

> Fruit or appetizer
> Meat dish and vegetable
> Relishes or salad
> Rolls and butter
> Coffee, milk or tea
> Wedding cake and fruit, sherbet or ice cream

A dinner reception could include:

> Fruit or sea food appetizer
> Meat dish with one or two vegetables
> Salad or fruit salad
> Rolls and butter
> Coffee, milk or tea
> Wedding cake and fruit, sherbet or ice cream

A simple all-purpose menu which can be served at any hour might feature:

> Champagne, punch or mixed drinks
> Hot and/or cold hors d'oeuvres and relishes
> Wedding cake and fruit, sherbet or ice cream
> Coffee or tea

Groom's cake—a special dark fruit cake—can be served with any of the above menus, as can any liquor you think appropriate. An extremely elaborate dinner might also include soup, wines with each course, after-dinner liqueurs and demitasse.

These are general menus, of course; your actual choices will be far more interesting. As you select the food you will serve, pick items you can be sure will be enjoyed by the majority of your guests. Avoid experimenting with new or unusual foods. When in doubt, stick to beef and poultry. It's best, for example, not to have sea food for your main course. If you want to use sea food, have it as an appetizer, as fish is less popular than meats and fowl.

Your first decision

Your first decision will be whether to serve a buffet or a sit-down meal. This is a major choice and, once made, will help you decide what to serve and how much the reception will cost. A buffet is usually less expensive, and you must consider the amount of space you have and the help you'll need to serve the meal. You may find one kind of meal too formal or too informal. Be assured that both a buffet and a sit-down dinner can be nicely done, and both are appropriate for any kind of wedding reception.

Buffet dinners

A buffet meal means the guests select food from a buffet table and then return to their tables. Usually help must be provided for serving cake and coffee and for clearing away the tables. For a reception with only cake and liquid refreshments, seating need not be provided at formally arranged tables, though your bridal party would doubtless be grateful if a table was provided for them. Seating for everyone involves having a head table for the members of the wedding party and the bride and groom.

Your liquor bill

The liquor bill for your reception often accounts for as much as two-thirds of the total cost. As such an expensive portion of your planning, it needs careful attention. A champagne toast is featured at some receptions, and a case of twelve bottles of champagne will serve approximately twenty-five guests. You'll want to provide an ample supply of ginger ale for this toast, for children and nondrinkers. A fruit punch made with wine can be served instead of regular champagne, and in these mixtures, domestic champagne or a white wine can be substituted for the more expensive imported labels you might otherwise use. The number of guests your punch will serve depends upon your recipe and the size of glass to be used.

You can have an open bar with a bartender to

mix drinks to your guests' specifications. This is a costly, if hospitable, addition to the wedding reception and is really only necessary if you plan a lengthy cocktail period between the reception line and the serving of a full meal. If you decide to have a bar for your guests, you may be asked whether you want an open-host or an open-cash bar. With an open-host bar, you pay for *all* the liquor served, probably getting a discount for using the standard brands the hotel has on hand. The price for a single drink of one of these standard brands is usually $.95, but if a guest requests a special brand by name it might cost you as much as $1.05 or up. This is known as a "call brand." An open-cash bar is provided by you, but each guest pays for his own drinks. The cost per drink is higher than with open-host, for the bartender works with money in addition to mixing drinks. A standard brand will cost your guest about $1.00, and a call brand might cost $1.10 and up, depending on the brand requested.

If you plan to provide champagne or wine for your guests, the banquet manager will give you a price per bottle for the hotel's liquor. This can be $6 and up per bottle of champagne and $4 and up per bottle of wine. Some establishments allow you to bring in your own champagne or wine to serve. This can be less expensive, but even if the cost is the same, it's likely you're getting better wine for your money. If you do this, you'll probably be charged for "corkage,"—a fee for opening and serving your wine. This is usually from $1 and up per bottle. You can serve a champagne punch for about $20 a gallon, and a fruit punch for as little as $5 a gallon.

If some of your guests are nondrinkers who are very much opposed to liquor, you might arrange your reception in such a way that there would be one area for serving alcoholic beverages and another for nonalcoholic fruit punches or soft drinks. Then your guests can seek out the type of refreshment they personally

Open or closed bar

Liquor costs per bottle

For nondrinkers

enjoy.

The approach you take for handling food and drink will be geared to the reception site. If your reception is to be held at a club, hotel or restaurant, the maître d' or banquet manager will coordinate the refreshments, helping you to choose them and supervising their preparation. If your reception will be taken care of for you, there will be less work for you, of course. There are some disadvantages, however. You may have less choice of the type of food or drink being served, and costs will be higher than if you plan and handle your reception yourself.

For a reception held in a private home or at another site where you are responsible for details, you might want to hire a caterer to handle the arrangements for your food and drink. This would have the same advantages and disadvantages as working with a maître d' or banquet manager, and could result in a less hectic reception while still giving you some control over details. Another possibility would be to handle all the arrangements yourself, or combine your efforts with a caterer. If you handle these details, completely or in part, there will be more work and responsibility for you, but also more flexibility and lower costs.

If you will be dealing with a caterer, try to find one who is reputable and experienced with wedding receptions. You usually get what you pay for in a caterer, so don't be tempted to use someone solely because his prices are below those of the others you've contacted. The quality of his work and what he furnishes will be lower as a result. Ask friends and relatives for recommendations, and find out what they like most about the caterer's work.

Whether you use a caterer who comes highly recommended or you find one in the yellow pages, you will discuss your plans and requirements with him in great detail. Your first meeting should take place at his establishment where you're looking to see the kind of

Who handles arrangements?

Try a caterer

How to judge a caterer

work he is capable of doing. Your second meeting, after you have decided to hire him, should take place in your home, and this conversation would include all arrangements for food, drink and services you want for your reception. If at all possible, ask for several menu and liquor suggestions and choose the one that's best for you and your budget. But do it at home; don't be pressured into making decisions in the caterer's office during your first conversation.

Choose type of service

You should discuss with the caterer whether you want a buffet or a served meal, and explain all the placement of food and drink. The placement and seating for the head table and the physical arrangements for the reception site should be given him. As you work with the caterer, sketch your reception site, and mark and allow space for dancing, for decorations and for comfortable movement of your guests through these various areas. Find out if the caterer will provide such items as tables, chairs, plates, silverware, napkins, serving pieces, for otherwise you must rent or borrow these items yourself. Give him the approximate number of guests you plan to serve; this number will be changing as the time for the reception draws closer, and he should be kept informed up to the minute. Will the caterer provide for the serving of the meal? How many workers will be there to serve food and function as bartenders? How many hours will each person work, and what is the regular rate per hour and overtime charge? Be sure your estimate covers *all* items and services provided by the caterer.

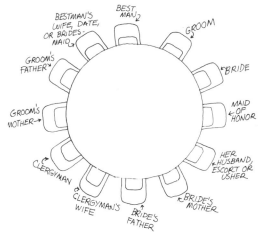

Confirm your plans

If everything is as you want it, you'll confirm all the above details either by signing a contract or writing your now familiar letter of agreement. In the letter, list the financial information item by item if you can. Indicate the amount of deposit paid, and give the caterer the date, the time and the name of the person he should work with—whether you, your parents or a friend. The best man or maid of honor might handle this responsibility for you.

If a maître d' or a banquet manager will be coordinating your reception, you will be discussing your plans with him. You will probably be given various menus from which to choose your food, and these menus should include the cost per person. Don't allow yourself to be pressured into ordering many expensive hors d'oeuvres before the meal if you will be serving a full luncheon or supper. If the meal is to have an appetizer, additional hors d'oeuvres are not necessary and will only serve to raise your total cost considerably.

Maître d' or banquet manager

A hidden cost can be a cake charge. If you provide the cake, and the banquet manager has someone to cut and serve it, he may charge as much as $.35 per person for this. Many establishments do, and you would have to add this to your costs. There is no extra charge if the banquet manager provides the cake—only if you bring it in from your own bakery.

What's a cake charge?

Will your reception be hors d'ocuvres, cake and coffee? Then you'll have to ask if there's a coffee charge. Some hotels might charge a price like $30 per one hundred guests to serve coffee "only."

Your conversation with a banquet manager should cover the same questions listed in the section dealing with a caterer—the number of people to be served, what he supplies, as well as what extra charges there might be. Ask for an estimate of the total cost—preferably broken down item by item. And confirm all details by contract or letter of agreement. Indicate in such a letter the name of any person authorized by you to spend additional amounts of money for liquor, food or special services which might be needed at the last minute.

Costs or size can make it desirable for you to cater your own reception. If you or your mother have had experience entertaining large groups of people, you may decide to handle your entire reception yourself. This is quite an undertaking, but when well done can

Do your own reception

result in a party in which you take a particular personal pride—because you made the arrangements and coordinated everything by yourself.

You can make up your menu, of course, and prepare your own food. Many restaurants will make up special orders of food and drink to take out, too. Buffet style is the best choice if you are arranging your own reception, using hired help as necessary. If you plan to serve liquor and mixed drinks, you should hire one bartender for every one hundred guests; for a party with punch or champagne cocktails, one bartender for every two hundred fifty guests should be enough. A bartender might need the help of a waitress to serve and clean up. The number of waitresses you hire will depend upon your serving style. Plan on one waitress for every fifty guests for a buffet—these women would serve food at the buffet tables, clean up after the meal and serve coffee and cake—plus one additional person to serve punch and help out where needed.

List your equipment

It's helpful to list all the equipment you will need to serve your guests, including items like casseroles, trays, punch bowl, chairs, tables. See what you have or can borrow to fill these needs, and rent everything else from a party rental company.

Sketches and checklists

It's a good idea to draw sketches and make check lists well in advance of the arrival of any help you'll have on the day of the reception. You can sketch your head table, showing where each item from silverware to centerpiece is to be placed. When the day arrives, you won't have to personally supervise everything, but merely check the finished table against your list. The reception procedure might be listed in the kitchen so that anyone helping you will know what must be done —and when.

Select main dish first

When you are planning your meal, it's best to begin by selecting the main dish. Large roasts are nice for receptions—turkey, lamb, beef or ham are good choices. They can be served precarved or a waitress can carve them for guests as they go through the buffet line. To use less meat, serve a stew or casserole which combines small portions of meat, cheese or sea food with rice or noodles. If this is to be your main course, and will be eaten by standing guests, avoid foods that are difficult to eat, like spaghetti.

Hot or cold hors d'oeuvres are usually served to guests as they have their first drink or champagne toast. Any type of hors d'oeuvres is acceptable. The hors d'oeuvres, the salads, the vegetables and the garnishes should all harmonize with the main course you serve, as at any party. Most important, particularly in the case of buffet, the food should be served so that it looks as attractive as it tastes.

Hors d'oeuvres

Punch needn't be pink and watery; use your imagination. It it's fall, serve mulled cider in decorative mugs, or use skewered fruits to decorate the drink. You might freeze some fruit into the ice cubes or in a ring mold, then float them for a color accent in the punch. Add sherbet or ice cream to the punch bowl to make it foamy and appetizing. Punch can be attractive, delicious and economical.

Salads or fruit dishes can be attractive additions to your buffet table. Arrange melon or pineapple in unusual pyramids and decorate them with tiny flowers or greens for an Hawaiian touch. Berries can be placed on toothpicks and attached to a styrofoam form, making little strawberry or cherry trees for tables or for the buffet. Green garnishes like ferns, mint or watercress can add a decorative note to various salads and jello molds. Carrots and tomatoes can be cut into shapes to decorate a plate, as can lemon and orange peels to border salads or other foods. Even mashed potatoes can add a decorative note if they are placed in a pastry tube and used as borders around other foods.

A pretty buffet table

Use goblets and glasses to hold small balls of butter or colorful napkins and place them at each person's place. Paper lace doilies are inexpensive and add

Unusual touches

299

a delicate look to trays or tables. Warm foods served in steaming casseroles and cold foods on beds of ice enhance the buffet table and make the food look more appetizing.

Your dessert will most likely be your wedding cake, but if you want to add extras, you might put a fortune cookie, with a good fortune or message at each guest's plate. A novel way to serve ice cream with your wedding cake is to shape the ice cream into balls and roll them in white or pastel flaked coconut. Place these snowballs in the freezer, wrapped in freezer paper, till you plan to use them. You can serve them with your cake or insert little birthday candles in them and put them on a tray. Dim the lights and light the candles for a special effect.

If you plan to have the dark fruit "groom's cake" for your guests to take home, you can bake it in a bundt pan so it will be round with a hole in the center. Drizzle thin white frosting on top, decorate with pieces of candied fruit and you have a decorative cake for your buffet table. If you want a groom's cake but haven't the time to cut up a cake into slices, make your fruitcake in individual cupcake tins. Each *cupcake* can then be easily wrapped in a square of saran wrap and tied prettily with a bow.

To save money, consider having a cake/champagne/coffee reception instead of a complete meal. Cut down on the cost of liquor by serving punch instead of mixed drinks, or limit the amount of liquor served. At home, buy only a certain amount of liquor and when it runs out, close the bar. If you're working with a caterer or a banquet manager, give specific instructions to close the bar at a certain hour or to limit the number of bottles to be opened.

A grand and glorious party—with food and drink fit for a new Mr. and Mrs.—is possible on any budget. And on such an occasion what bride would want less?

Your wedding cake

29

Music's a Must

FOR MOOD, DANCING AND ENTERTAINMENT

MUSIC WILL LEND a lovely touch to your wedding reception. It's really a must! It doesn't matter if you have a strolling violinist, recorded music, or two whole orchestras providing continuous music. What does matter is that you have well chosen and performed music that will set a happy mood and provide entertainment for both you and your guests to enjoy.

Music can serve many purposes for your reception. It can be used for background or for dancing. It entertains, it sets a mood; and sometimes you may want to point up special events which take place during your reception. You can select appropriate tunes to happily speed along your reception line, to highlight the cutting of the wedding cake or the throwing of the bridal bouquet or garter. You might even want to dedicate songs to special guests or pick the music for specific dances.

The "emcee," or Master of Ceremonies

A single musician

Band

Unusual music

Should you plan on having many of these dedications or musical highlights, you might want the bandleader to function as an emcee. Check on bandleaders who do emcee work carefully, however, and find out what kinds of things they are in the habit of talking about at wedding receptions. An emcee should behave with dignity and not tell off-color jokes or extended anecdotes. Be explicit with anyone you hire to perform this function, outlining exactly what you expect of him.

Choose music to suit the mood you want for your wedding reception—and music that comes within your budget. The amount of space that you designate for the musicians may also determine the size of the group you can have. You will probably want music that is much lighter and more informal than the music for your ceremony. Songs that were alternate choices for the ceremony, ones not used because of conflict, can be played at the reception, as can any and all of your favorite tunes.

Any number of musicians is appropriate for a reception. The single musician is chosen by the instrument he plays; if you are limited to one performer, consider a violinist, an accordionist, an organist or a pianist. It's best to select an instrument which can create a variety of sounds, as all of these can.

If your budget allows, hire a group of musicians. A string quartet, a two-or three-man dance combo, or even a full band or orchestra is possible. If you want lots of music and you have the money to spend, you might use two groups—featuring different styles of music and used in rotation for continuous music during your reception.

Want unusual music? Bossa nova specialists, a mariachi band, Hawaiian performers or country western groups are all possibilities. A romantic note could be added to your reception by using a group that features a harpsichord or a recorder. These instruments would add a special Renaissance flavor.

To keep costs down, use recorded music. It's suitable and can be very nice. You should have someone who will be responsible for making the music continuous. Records, tapes or even a radio tuned to an FM station with no commercials would provide pleasing music throughout your reception.

You should talk to as many musicians and groups as possible, and compare what they offer, what they charge and what their experience is before settling on a final choice. You can call bands listed in the yellow pages if you live in a large city, or friends and relatives may have recommendations. Your banquet manager could probably recommend a group to you if you're being married in a hotel, but if you use his group he will probably receive a percentage of their fee for referral.

Where to find musicians

Sometimes musicians who perform at religious ceremonies are available for receptions, so you might look into this. And you can always contact the local branch of the musicians' union. In larger cities the union often provides a hall for auditions, and you can listen to various bands perform before you make your final choice. It is always wise, no matter what the circumstances, to hear a group play before hiring them.

Once you've chosen the musicians for your reception, you should either sign a contract with them or confirm your arrangements by letter. You can write information and/or requirements into a standard contract, by the way, so this serves as a complete agreement.

Your contract

The following should be included in any contract or letter you sign:

Place: Give the day, date and time of your reception, the address of the site and the name of the person the band leader is to contact in case of questions. The banquet manager in a hotel can coordinate the musicians, or your mother or someone who represents you can handle follow-up details.

List place

*Names: List who is to come. If you contract a specific bandleader and you want him to function as emcee, be sure you specifically mention his name, and state: "Mr. Smith, will *himself* appear at the wedding reception." Some leaders organize several groups that may be booked to perform on the same night; if you want the man whose name the group carries, write that into the contract or letter, so you are assured he will lead the group at your reception.

Dress: Write out exactly what you want the musicians to wear. If you are having a formal wedding and your musicians are to be in view of the guests, they should be properly dressed. Most musicians wear either suits or evening dress which is appropriate for a wedding reception, but there are exceptions. Don't let the way the musicians dress detract from the look of your wedding reception.

Duties: Write out what the musicians are expected to provide: the number of instruments and their type, the number of hours they are to play, how long and frequent their breaks will be and any specifications for the soloist they may provide. Mention the name of any emcee you are having and what his duties will be.

Cost: The information about the rate charged by the musicians should be spelled out very clearly. You should know what the total cost will be; what their rate is for the amount of time for which you have commissioned them; what their overtime rate per hour is—in case you wish to keep them later than the original time contracted for; the amount of the deposit required. Name the person authorized to request overtime, so that there will be no confusion. If a guest dances by and says, "Oh play one more," the musicians may charge you overtime if no one is taking notice of how long they have been playing. And overtime can be very costly. Also, you should have information about the amount of the final payment—less deposit—and whether you must pay by credit card, personal check or cash. It's best

Names

Dress

Duties

to pay by check so you have a receipt, and to make final payment to the musicians after they have performed rather than paying them in advance. This will assure you that the musicians will arrive promptly and will perform properly. If they do not you can withhold payment; otherwise your complaints will be of little value.

Give the bandleader a list of "Who's Who" in your wedding party and any special friends or relatives that he should know about. He will then be aware of the people who are most important to you at your wedding reception, and can more easily handle announcements and song dedications.

List Who's Who

Also give him a list of general music, including your favorites, to be played throughout the evening. You could choose a variety of easy listening, musical comedy, light classical or current popular songs.

On this same list star* the songs that are special requests or dedications. If you plan for the bandleader to act as emcee and dedicate songs to particular guests, he should have their names and the songs to be dedicated long before the wedding reception, so he can have the appropriate music.

Your special songs

Dedications can be anything you wish. Your list of songs could include the "Anniversary Waltz" or "your song" for your first dance as Mr. and Mrs., and special songs dedicated to other members of the wedding party or perhaps your parents. For example, you might have "Moonglow" played for your parents to dance to because it is their song, or a song like "Linda" might be dedicated to a bridesmaid named Linda. But if she happens to be single, arrange in advance, with one of the ushers, to invite Linda to dance so that she can enjoy her song. Special dedications are a nice touch and help start the dancing and keep it flowing.

It will be helpful to give the bandleader an outline of the procedure you'll be following during the reception. This includes information about the reception line, where it will be and what type of music you would like played. Music to be played during the meal, music for dancing, special tunes as background when the cake is cut—all these would be information the bandleader will appreciate having in advance.

A room for the musicians

Also, it's courteous to let your musicians know what accommodations you have arranged for them. It's most important to provide them with a room for their instrument cases or any extra articles they may bring with them—a room where they can take their break, have a cup of coffee or enjoy a piece of wedding cake. They should have a place they can call their own for the evening where they can be as comfortable as possible.

Once the arrangements are completed for your wedding reception music, be sure to inform everyone concerned. The caterer, banquet manager or anyone involved with the reception planning should know so he can make whatever plans are necessary. This done, you'll know that on the wedding day you'll need only to sit back and enjoy the beautiful music that's being played especially for you.

30

A Tasty Tradition

SHOPPING FOR YOUR WEDDING CAKE

WHETHER A BEAUTIFUL addition to your buffet table or proudly displayed on a cake table all its own, your wedding cake is the crowning touch of beauty for your wedding reception. It's a tasty tradition you'll not want to break.

What most people call the wedding cake is really the bride's cake. This is the special, highly decorated cake that is served at the reception—the cake that you and your groom share. In addition to the bride's cake, you may want to have what is called the groom's cake. The groom's cake is the *real* wedding cake, as tradition would have it. It's made of a dark fruit cake and is not eaten at the wedding reception; rather it is cut into individual portions and given to the guests to take home with them. If they believe in the superstition, they'll put it underneath their pillows to dream that night of the person they will marry. Whether the cake is put under someone's pillow or not, the groom's cake is usually provided for your guest's enjoyment after the wedding festivities are ended. You may choose to provide both a bride's cake and a groom's cake, or perhaps only the former. In any event, it's nice to make arrangements for guests to take some cake home.

You can place the cake in small boxes, designed especially for this purpose, next to the door or beside each place setting on the tables if you're serving a sit-down meal. (This would add to the decoration and would be a very nice way of making sure that everyone knows he is invited to take home a piece of wedding cake.) The boxes can be decorated in the colors of your wedding or in white with colored bows. These boxes may be filled with cake by your baker if you prefer to handle this in advance, or you can have someone present at your wedding cut a small piece of cake for each guest. Waxed envelopes are available for packing cake, and you can usually have anything you like printed on the outside of the box, such as "wedding cake" or "Pat and Alan's wedding."

Throughout this chapter, the bride's cake is called the wedding cake. A groom's cake is always a fruitcake (this preserves the best), so you needn't make decisions other than the size you'll need. Wedding cakes, however, come in a variety of sizes and shapes, and can be decorated in many delicious ways.

Decorations for your cake

The decorations on your wedding cake should blend with your reception decoration plan in color and style. You need to choose the color for the basic icing and the colors to be used for decoration, which can be the same as the icing or a contrasting color. The cake or buffet table on which the cake is placed should accent the colors you use for the cake.

Use natural colors

Avoid using vibrant colors to decorate your cake. Pastels are much better; they are the most appetizing, while darker colors (particularly in combination

312

with white) tend to look artificial and unappetizing. The watchword for cake decoration is naturalness. Avoid using colors that are not in keeping with the natural colors of items you simulate: Rosebuds should be pink or yellow, not green; leaves should be green, not orange. A traditional choice and a very beautiful one is the wedding cake in all white, icing and decoration.

The design of your wedding cake can be as ornate or simple as you wish. Flowers are often used as decorations, and they may be fresh or fashioned from icing. Whichever you choose, the flowers should match either your bouquet or the floral decorations of the reception. Romantic symbols like swans, bells, hearts, cupids, and wedding rings are frequently used to decorate cakes. Don't put writing of any sort on your cake. It's not appropriate for this occasion.

Cake design

You can also design your wedding cake around a special effect. I once saw a cake in which the two bottom tiers were separated and a small, self-contained fountain placed in the separation. With electrically operated pumps and lights and the use of colored water, an unusual and colorful effect was achieved, making the cake a real center of attention at the reception. Another speciality is a cake fashioned entirely from spun sugar. Both of these are beautiful but expensive effects.

Unusual effects

Whether your cake is small or multi-tiered, you'll want to choose an ornament to place at the top —preferably one that you can keep as a memento. A single symbol like those listed above or a combination of two or more can be used effectively. Another choice would be the traditional small figures of a bride and groom. Have whatever ornament you use made of plastic or fabric—so you can keep it forever. (You might also freeze carefully a piece or section of your wedding cake, to share with your husband on your first wedding anniversary.)

Top ornaments

313

Fresh flowers can also be used as the top ornament on your wedding cake. A small nosegay in a vial or bowl of water can be placed into a specially-planned-for indentation at the top of the cake, which will keep the flowers fresh all through the reception. Later, the flowers can be pressed and saved as well.

Cake flavors

Besides choosing the various colors and decorations for your wedding cake, you also get to pick the flavors to be used. It's nice to have cake and icing that are favorites of yours and your fiancé's, so find out what his favorite kind of cake is before placing your order. Any kind of cake is acceptable—especially pure white, chocolate, lemon, sponge or marble. If you're going to have a cake with a filling between the layers, you might want to use chocolate, butterscotch or a fruit filling you particularly like. Jam is very tasty, too.

Icings

The icing that you choose for your cake should, of course, match the type of cake and filling you have. If you want a white icing, by the way, but you like chocolate flavor, see if your baker can accommodate you. There is a candy which is white but which tastes like chocolate. Why not carry it a step farther and have "white chocolate" icing?

Shapes of cakes

Any shape is acceptable for a wedding cake, and you are not limited to a tiered structure. You can have a square, round or heart-shaped cake, and if you do want tiers, they can be in graduated sizes of the same or alternating shapes (a round layer, a heart-shaped layer, and another layer). You can also have the bottom tier made of real cake and the top layers of a synthetic. A skillful baker will make it impossible to tell the difference, and you are saving money. And the topmost layers become a souvenir.

Bake your own cake

Wedding cakes don't have to be bought. Your cake may be a gift from a friend or relative, or you may want to make it yourself. Naturally you or the donor of such a gift would have to be skillful to make a cake as beautiful as you want. Some caterers or banquet managers will give you your wedding cake as a gift for using their services.

But if you buy your cake, be aware that a highly decorated and ornate creation can cost as much as $100. Naturally, cost is determined by the number of people you need to serve, and an elegant but tiny cake will be less costly than a cake for one hundred and fifty people.

You can have your wedding cake and groom's cake made up in various places. If you allow a caterer or a banquet manager to arrange the order for your cake, be sure to get a price from him and see pictures or samples of his baker's work before he places the order. If he will not provide as beautiful a cake as would your own baker, don't accept this kind offer of help.

Where to order your cake

Choosing a baker is like choosing a jeweler or a photographer. If you haven't one you know and trust, shop around carefully and compare quality and price before settling on the baker to do the job. Try to find a man experienced specifically in baking wedding cakes, for these are more difficult and elaborate than ordinary cakes. See and taste samples if you can, and make sure that the baker can do the job in ample time for your reception. If you decide to bypass the baker, be sure you leave enough time so you can make the cake in advance and have one less last-minute detail to worry about.

Once you have selected a baker and placed your order, it's wise to note all details and specifications in a letter. Generally a bakery will have an order form which includes all the necessary information, and you receive a copy of the order. If not, send a letter and keep a carbon copy. The letter or form should list the design, giving a complete description of all parts. Also included should be the delivery date and time, the address of the reception site, the name of the person who will receive the cake and your name and phone number in case of any questions. Give the total cost of

Have a copy of your order

the cake and any terms of payment, as well as the amount of the deposit you have given.

Your wedding cake is a highlight of your reception, and a lasting reminder of your wedding day. Now that the last and sweetest detail for your reception is completed, you can take a few minutes to breathe a sigh of relief and begin to enjoy the fact that, finally, you are really "getting close."

Part Six

YOU'RE GETTING CLOSE

Beauty That Lasts

YOUR OFFICIAL BRIDAL PORTRAIT

AS YOU GET CLOSER to your wedding day, you'll probably begin to feel a little nervous; I know I did. The best way to combat a case of nerves is to keep busy. Keep looking forward to the wedding, but get lots of things accomplished. Forge ahead and begin planning for that most important photograph—your bridal portrait.

Your bridal portrait is a picture of you in your complete bridal outfit: gown, veil and all the accessories that you will wear on your wedding day. It is generally in black and white, but can be in color, too. This picture is usually of the bride alone, though some girls like to bring their fiancé to the sitting and include him in some of the pictures. You can do this if you like, of course, but keep in mind that when announcing marriages, most newspapers want a black and white photograph of the

319

bride alone.

How will you use it? You can use your bridal portrait for the newspaper announcement of your wedding, or you may want it solely as a keepsake or as special gifts for your family and friends. You could have it framed, or mounted on a special thank-you card to send to members of the wedding party. It's a very special picture, taken once in a lifetime—you will want it to be as nice as possible.

When to take it Plan to have your bridal portrait taken one or two months before your wedding (as soon as your gown is ready) so you will have one less thing to worry about in the pre-wedding rush. However, some brides have their bridal portrait taken *after* the ceremony and honeymoon have taken place. You might want to do this if you don't plan to announce your wedding in the papers, and it can be an excellent idea. After your wedding you may be even more relaxed and the result will be a better picture.

Where Your bridal portrait can be taken in various places—the bridal salon during your last fitting, in the photographer's studio or at another site of your choosing such as a garden or home. The studio is the best spot, in spite of the fact that you will have to bring all of your things there. The photographer's lighting is already set up to complement his background, and he works best in his home area. A bridal salon may cause lighting problems, and it may be hectic and noisy. If your photographer has never worked at this site before, he may not want to take chances on the outcome of his work. An alternate site, such as your home, could make things more relaxing for you, but again, the photographer may be unwilling to bring all his equipment to a spot where lights and backgrounds are out of his control. You would probably be best advised to use your photographer's studio, but this will of course depend upon the man and the studio in question.

The photographer who takes your portrait shots

320

may be the same one you used for your engagement photographs and/or all the other pictures of your wedding, or you may seek out someone who specializes in bridal portraits. Sometimes, if you use the same photographer for all your pictures, you may get a special rate for the bridal portrait. But using a different photographer for these shots will give your wedding album an interesting variety.

Who will take it?

If you do decide to use a photographer who specializes in bridal portraits, find him and question him in the same manner described in Chapter 20. But keep in mind, however, that there are a few extra things to consider.

When you go into a studio, more than likely the photographer will have books of portraits that he has taken. Check these over carefully to see whether the portraits look interesting, the girls relaxed and natural and the lighting flattering and attractive. Keep in mind that the sample books show his best work, so to judge the quality of his general work, subtract about 10 percent from the quality of the samples. Remember that his samples are his *very* best work; the pictures he takes of you may not be.

How to judge photographers

Check to see if the studio is comfortable—air-conditioned or heated as the season dictates. Are there dressing room facilities for you? Will you need to bring your own mirror or provide your own makeup lighting?

It's reasonable at this time to ask to see some of the backgrounds he might be using for your portrait. You will want to know the length of the photo session (an hour to an hour and a half is the average) and how many shots he will take (usually around twenty). Ask how long he takes to make up proofs and inquire if he does the entire developing and printing process himself. Will he take your pictures, or will an assistant do the work? Does the studio provide a girl on the day of the photo session to help you dress and to arrange your dress for the best possible photographs? (If your photographer does have someone like this, talk with her a bit to see if she is helpful, calm and competent.) Your photographer may be supplying you with a bouquet of artificial flowers for the picture; if this is the case, ask to see them to make sure they are similar to the flowers you plan to carry and are in good condition.

Costs

Price is another important consideration. Costs of portrait sittings vary, but they generally range from $25 to $55. You will probably be asked to give a deposit; but more than 50 percent is not reasonable, since you are essentially paying for something you have no guarantee will be to your liking.

Once you've gathered all the necessary information, you can begin to compare photographers. Don't spend much time with any one unless you are seriously considering using him. Just tell him you'll call back if you are interested, and leave; then go on to another photographer with whom you might prefer to deal.

When you have compared photographers, you are ready to decide. Don't be guided here purely by price. Your first concern for this all-important photo is the quality you'll get for your money.

Before making an appointment

Before you set up an appointment, there are certain arrangements to be made. Pick up your gown a few days before you want your photo session to take place; if you wait till the last minute, needed alterations may not be done. Even if you use a sample of the gown that is still on order for you, make sure that all necessary alterations are done on it so it will look good on you.

The beauty shop

You'll want to make an appointment with your hairdresser. Be sure your hair is styled as you plan to wear it for the wedding (and you might make the appointment for your wedding day at this time, too.) A manicure is a good idea, particularly if you want some shots of your hands—showing your ring, or bridal bouquet. Use a light polish, as it gives your hands a more natural look. Too dark a polish provides an unpleasant contrast.

If your photographer is not supplying you with flowers for the sitting, arrange for an artificial bouquet from your florist. Make a note to gather all your accessories in advance of the portrait session, and remember to include undergarments, prayer book, shoes, veil.

The florist

Once you have made these arrangements, you'll be ready to make and confirm an appointment with your photographer. Make your appointment for the time of day which is best for *you*, and don't be swayed by suggestions that the morning—or afternoon—is the best time; the best time is when you feel you look your best. Only you know when you will be most rested and relaxed and ready to have this picture taken. Try not to make an appointment for the morning following a bridal shower or a pre-wedding party; if you're tired the day you have your portrait taken, it will show up in the pictures.

The day of the sitting

It's a good idea to make a list of the bridal portraits you want taken during the session, and take a carbon of this with you when you go to select your prints. List first the photographs you want for yourself and for gifts to friends. I would advise selecting additional pictures later, so you can compare them with the shots taken during the ceremony and the reception; you may like some of the latter pictures better, and you can save duplications and money.

List the shots you want

One nice pose to have is a long shot, where the bride is seen full-length. You can have a front, rear or profile shot of yourself taken at enough of a distance so that your entire outfit is shown in full. Close-ups of your face, in profile and/or full view, or a picture of you reflected in a mirror might be nice to have. You might also like special shots which point up the features of your gown. If your dress has a lovely standaway collar or embroidery on the bodice, you might want a picture that features these details. If you have a beautiful train, a picture of you looking over your shoulder into the

Possible shots

camera would allow the photographer to focus on this feature. Consider having photos taken against different backgrounds, but avoid any that are too busy and detract from you or your outfit. You might also consider a shot of your hands, resting on your prayer book or holding your bouquet. If you choose to emphasize your engagement ring, be sure that you tell the photographer —particularly if the ring is unusual.

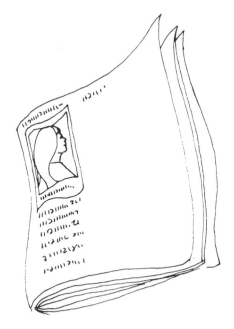

Newspaper announcements

Are you going to use your wedding portrait for a newspaper announcement? You'll need to check on the requirements for this. Some newspapers have certain regulations about photographs, but generally they ask for an 8 by 10 inch black and white glossy—a head-and-shoulder shot, perhaps including your flowers. Check requirements with the society editor of your paper; if you want your announcement in more than one paper, select several different poses. Many newspapers prefer to run a picture that is different from their competitors'. These photographs are usually full face, profile, or three-quarter shots.

When you call to check on photograph requirements, find out about the kind of copy that is acceptable. Some papers provide you with a form to fill out, but if yours does not, write up your wedding along the lines of the other announcements you find in their pages. This description of your wedding can be as lengthy as you like; the newspaper will do any cutting that is necessary. Check Chapter 1 for hints about sending information to the newspapers.

Your copy will include such things as the names of the bride and groom, both families and the wedding party. You will want to include what you and your bridesmaids wore, the type of ceremony you had (double-ring, military), the decorations, the education and background of the bride and groom, the honeymoon destination and the future plans of the bride and groom. This should all be neatly typed, and you'll want to include a cover letter which gives the name of your mother or someone else who can reliably amplify or add information if needed. Indicate in this letter the date that you would like your announcement to appear. Newspapers generally run announcements when they choose, but it can't hurt to give a preference. If you decide not to have a bridal portrait taken, by the way, feel free to send the newspapers the written announcement of your marriage anyway.

The actual photo session should be a very relaxed and relaxing occasion. Before you go, get a good night's sleep. Eat something immediately before the appointment to ensure peak energy and a healthy look. Try to make the events of this entire day as calm and as organized as possible. Don't squeeze in your session amidst feverish plans for parties or whatever. Arrive at the photographer's studio—in full makeup—well in advance, up to an hour early. This will give you ample opportunity to add finishing touches to your makeup, hair and gown.

Arriving for the sitting

Your makeup should be heavier than the street makeup you normally wear so that it will photograph naturally. False eyelashes are good in pictures, but of course you should know how to wear them by the time the sitting comes around. Don't get lashes that are too thick; make sure they are natural looking. (See Chapter 35 for more makeup hints.) Bring Q-tips along with your makeup; these are excellent for correcting your makeup if a bit of mascara has gotten on your cheek or your eye shadow is not properly blended or your lipstick needs to be straightened a bit. Q-tips are used by makeup men in the Hollywood studios because they don't smear like a kleenex or a piece of cloth would. They will correct an error, yet leave your "face" intact. Make sure you have extra powder and/or blusher for touch-ups in case your face becomes shiny under the photographer's lights. Go easy on white highlights above the eyes, for these sometimes catch glare under the lights. And remember: If you start a tan for your

Makeup hints

photographs, you may start peeling by the time your wedding comes around.

Take all your clothes and accessories—including hair spray, your own mirror and any jewelry you'll be wearing on your wedding day—to the studio and dress there. Pack everything carefully in garment bags, and if you need someone to help you with your gown or makeup, have a girl friend or your mother go along. Be sure that whomever you take with you is a calm person —someone you would want to have around. Don't take your best friend, even though you love her dearly, if she's the kind of person who will panic when called upon to help out. Wear something that is easy to remove so that your hair and makeup won't be disturbed too much.

After you've had your pictures taken, you should make arrangements with the photographer or the receptionist to pick up the proofs. Find out when they'll be definitely ready, pay your deposit if necessary (by check so you have the receipt), thank the photographer and be on your way.

I'm sure that your photography session will be successful for you and that your bridal portrait will be a picture you will cherish always, for it will capture that very special look you'll have as you slip into your gown —the radiant look of the bride you will soon be.

32

So All Goes Well

THE WEDDING REHEARSAL AND REHEARSAL DINNER

EVERYONE IN YOUR WEDDING PARTY including you and your fiancé will be concerned about his part in the wedding ceremony. What will the processional and recessional be like? Who will stand in the reception line —and where will it be? These and other questions are sure to be asked. The best way to answer them and to make sure everything runs smoothly is to have a wedding rehearsal—perhaps followed by a gala rehearsal dinner party for all.

You should schedule your wedding rehearsal for a day or two before your wedding. The rehearsal should take place at the ceremony site with the person who will be officiating, whether he be a clergyman or a judge, present to take part in and/or direct the rehearsal. If your wedding site is a hotel or restaurant, the maître d' or the banquet manager might also help with the rehearsal.

329

Pick the time

If possible, schedule the rehearsal for the same hour that the wedding will take place so that people will only have to remember one time for two separate days. This will help avoid confusion. Be sure to invite everyone concerned and let them know if there will be a dinner following the rehearsal so that they can dress appropriately and set aside the entire evening.

Rehearse to music

It's best to have music available, even if it's only a recording. Music enables the members of the wedding party to walk with the rhythm they'll use on your wedding day. Don't try to have them march in a prescribed step; rather have them walk slowly and naturally, as though they were walking down the street. This will help avoid problems and tension. The important thing is that couples, if your wedding party will be grouped in couples, should walk down the aisle in step with each other, taking medium-sized steps. Short steps make a person look as if he is swaying from side to side. Ask someone, perhaps your mother, to watch how each person walks and to suggest a change in the length of step if necessary.

The wedding party walks through the processional to the ceremony area and is informed about what will take place during the ceremony itself. Each member of the wedding party will learn what he is expected to do, where he should stand and when he should perform his assigned tasks. You should take your place and walk through the processional, too. The superstition that the bride should not take part in her own rehearsal is far less important than knowing what goes on on your own wedding day. If you are sure about what to do, you will have a more relaxed wedding day.

Ribbon bouquets

It's fun to take along ribbon bouquets for you and your bridesmaids to carry during the rehearsal. These can be made from the bows which tie wedding or shower gifts. Simply cut a hole in a paper plate and pull the ribbon from each unwrapped package through the hole. When the hole is filled, the top of the plate is covered with multicolored bows—giving you a colorful bouquet, complete with cascading streamers. You can make these yourself or ask someone at your shower to make them for you.

In addition to rehearsing the processional and the ceremony itself, the bridal party should also rehearse *Procedure list* the recessional. When this is completed, tell the members of the wedding party exactly where they are to stand in the reception line, and give them a list of the procedure to be followed on your wedding day. The list will be tailored to fit your wedding, but a sample list is at the end of this chapter as a guideline for you.

In addition to this list, you might want each person to have the names and telephone numbers of all the other members of the wedding party, plus a map with the address and phone number of the reception site.

Children in your wedding party may not understand everything you require of them, so it's wise *Children* to give the mother or guardian of each child the same information that you give the other members of the wedding party. And if you're concerned about the children remembering where to stand during the ceremony itself, request permission to place a small "X" of masking tape on the floor to designate where the child will stand.

If your wedding is large or complicated, you may want to ask someone to help you oversee your *Ask for help* rehearsal and be on hand on your wedding day to see that things progress according to plan. Some large churches have a wedding consultant who would be present during the rehearsal and wedding day to make sure all runs smoothly. If not, you can ask someone to do this for you, an aunt or a cousin, perhaps, but definitely someone who is well-organized and pleasant and not a member of the wedding party. (This would exclude your mother also, as she will either be taking part in the processional and recessional or she will already be seated by the time the processional starts.) She could make suggestions during the rehearsal, helping you decide, for example, how to place your attendants at the altar area so that the guests will have a clear view of the ceremony. She would be responsible for checking all or some of the following items:

1. Make certain the ceremony area is tidy and ready for the guests to arrive.
2. See whether the flowers have arrived on time and are arranged properly.
3. Check that the photographer is present and ready to take the wedding pictures.
4. Make sure the wedding party has arrived and are properly dressed.
5. As each person is about to begin the processional, give him the signal to start down the aisle and whisper softly to him to smile (some bridesmaids may be so excited about the wedding that they actually forget).
6. After the ceremony, direct the wedding party to the reception line area and see that they're lined up in correct order and are ready to greet the wedding guests.

Rehearsal dinner

A dinner following your wedding rehearsal is optional, but it's a very nice custom and one that you might consider observing. The rehearsal dinner may be sponsored by the groom's family or your own, or perhaps by a close friend; and it can be a formal or informal party—held in a home or a restaurant. You would invite all of the members of the wedding party, of course, including both sets of parents; and you might also ask out-of-town guests, your clergyman or judge and his wife, the soloist or organist who will perform at the ceremony and any additional friends or relatives you'd like to have there.

Your evening might be arranged so that you would have two separate parties, perhaps one for parents and relatives and the other for the younger members of the wedding party. Or you may prefer one party at which you separate the groups by seating them at different tables.

If you're entertaining at home, the easiest way to serve a group is a buffet. This can be casual, yet elegant, and requires much less planning and work than a sit-down meal. If you plan the rehearsal dinner at a restaurant, order the menu at the time you reserve the restaurant. The restaurant can serve you faster, and you will also know the total cost in advance. Arrange to have a friend take pictures, if you like. They'll be an added touch for your scrapbook.

Try a buffet

No matter where you have your rehearsal dinner, it's fun to have the traditional toast to the bride and groom. The toast can be made with champagne or whatever beverage you like, and may be given by the father of the bride or the best man; you may even have several toasts by various members of the wedding party. The rehearsal dinner is a good opportunity for you and the groom to give your gifts to your attendants, perhaps at the end of the evening. (For additional times and occasions to give out the attendants' gifts, see Chapter 33.)

Don't let the rehearsal dinner last very late, particularly if it takes place the night before your wedding. You'll want to get a good night's sleep, and you may have last-minute things to do that night, so give yourself plenty of time to relax. The best way to prevent the party from running too late in a restaurant is to arrange ahead of time for the check to be brought at a certain hour. This is the traditional signal for the evening to end. If your party is held at your home or in a friend's house, the hostess can say that it's time for the bride to get a good night's sleep as she has a busy day tomorrow. And when the bride leaves—the party ends.

The rehearsal dinner is only one of the many parties to be given in celebration of your wedding. It and the rehearsal itself make up another happy occasion that brings you closer to your wedding day.

❧ WEDDING DAY PROCEDURE ❧
FOR A FIVE O'CLOCK WEDDING

PRE-WEDDING

2:00 Bride's parents dressed and ready.

2:30 Bride begins dressing at home.

3:00 Maid of honor, bridesmaids, flower girl and her mother, ring-bearer, train-bearers and their mothers meet at bride's home, dressed and ready. They receive their flowers. Home photos taken.
Groom and his parents begin dressing at their home.

3:15 Bride and wedding party leave for ceremony site.

3:45 Ushers, organist, soloist meet the clergyman at ceremony site. Ushers are ready to receive boutonnieres, soloist her corsage. All prepare site for ceremony.

4:00 Groom and best man arrive dressed and ready. Receive their boutonnieres and complete final details for ceremony.

4:10 Head usher gathers all other ushers and advises them to take their places for the seating of the guests.

4:15 Organist and soloist take their places and the pre-wedding recital begins. Wedding guests arrive and are seated.

4:30 Bride and wedding party (including groom's parents) arrive at site.

4:45 Members of wedding party take their places for processional. Groom's parents and bride's mother have taken their seats.

THE CEREMONY

5:00   The processional begins. Vows are taken. Ceremony is concluded.

5:30   Recessional.
Your "greeter" leaves to be on hand at the reception site to greet the first guests.

5:45   All members of the wedding party gather in front of the site to pose for formal pictures.
The wedding guests leave the site and make their way to the reception.

6:00   Members of wedding party leave for reception.

THE RECEPTION

6:30   Guests begin to arrive at reception. "Greeter" hosts and offers refreshments.

6:45   Wedding party arrives at reception and forms reception line. Guests are directed to the line by a friend.

7:15   Reception begins.
Best man offers toast to bride and groom and reads telegrams.

8:00   Bride and groom share first dance.
Others join in.

9:00   Bride and groom cut the wedding cake, and it is served to guests.
Bride and groom leave to change into going-away outfits.
Bride and groom return to reception.
Single girls gather; bride throws her bouquet.
Single men gather; groom throws bride's garter.

10:00   Bride and groom leave for honeymoon.

33

A Week of Festivity

WEDDING WEEK PARTIES AND OTHER ENTERTAINING

THE WHOLE OCCASION of getting married is ideal for parties and celebrations of all kinds—many of which will take place a week or two before your wedding. The most popular kinds of parties, in addition to your engagement party and rehearsal dinner, are bridal showers, the bridesmaids' luncheon and the bachelor dinner.

A bridal shower is a party given for you by a close friend, perhaps one of your bridesmaids, the maid of honor or a close relative. The party brings together a group of your girl friends to have a good time and to give you gifts, usually practical items you will be able to use in your new home. In other words, they "shower" you with presents. The gifts you receive at your shower might be considered the modern equivalent of the bridal dowry.

337

Kind of shower

It's up to you to decide what kind of a shower you would like (what type of gifts you want to receive) and who is to be invited—unless, of course, the shower is a surprise. It's wise to choose a kind of shower which will provide you with items you really need and have not yet received as wedding gifts. You might consider a kitchen shower, a linen shower, or a miscellaneous shower, or you might even have a lingerie shower, at which you'd receive personal gifts. If you plan a shower to which both men and women will be invited, you might have a bar shower or a general household shower, or perhaps something unusual like a hobby shower. The girls might buy you gifts and the men might buy gifts for your fiancé.

Shower details

After someone has offered to give you a shower (usually in her home, a restaurant or a hotel), you and your hostess will select a date that is convenient for you as well as for everyone you'd like to invite and then make up a list of guests. It's best to limit the number to around fifteen, which is a reasonable group to expect someone to entertain and which will avoid the gift duplications that cause hurt feelings. You can also give your hostess a list of the gifts you would most like to receive, selecting a wide price range of items in the colors and materials of your choice. Many of those invited will call her for suggestions, so she should have this list on hand.

Whom to invite

Try to limit the number of showers given for you. Two or three can be managed easily, without strain for hostess or guests. In choosing the guest list for each shower, try to invite groups that are compatible and have things in common. You might have one shower for your office friends, another for personal friends your own age, and a third for relatives and older women. It's not necessary to invite every woman who is invited to your wedding, nor it is always necessary to invite only those who will be attending your nuptials. A friend who cannot be invited to your wedding for reasons of size or cost can be invited if you like; she'll understand, and will enjoy the opportunity to help you celebrate.

Wear the same kind of clothing you would wear to any party given in your honor. What you wear will of course depend upon the type of party planned and the time of day that it is given. As the center of attention, you will naturally want to look as nice as possible. If you can afford to and want to, you can get a new outfit for each occasion, but a simple basic dress that you can accent with different accessories is a good choice, too.

What to wear

Try to be considerate and help your hostess all you can, offering assistance ahead of time and arriving about half an hour early to help with last-minute preparations and to introduce the guests to one another if need be. Go along with anything the hostess plans for your party in the way of refreshments or entertainment. If she likes party games and you don't, cheerfully take part in them anyway. Keep the conversation flowing and help everyone enjoy the party as much as you can.

How you can help

The high point of any shower is the opening of your gifts. As you open each present, make some appreciative comment, but avoid comparisons. One bride I know thanked her guest for a metal cake decorator set, saying she much preferred it to the paper or canvas-bag variety. Although her statement pleased the giver, it embarrassed a second guest whose yet unopened gift was, unfortunately, a cake decorator set with a canvas bag. So don't compare gifts: You never know what the next one will be. Merely thank each person for her gift as it is opened, and comment only on that particular gift. Be enthusiastic about the gifts you receive, and don't speak of returning or exchanging them. If you receive two copper jello molds, be as delighted with the second as you were with the first. Should you want to exchange the gift later, do so quietly without mentioning it to the donor. Or if you need information in order to make the exchange, ask the girl privately to

Opening your gifts

help you with this. But don't talk about it at the shower. In this way, you will help to make your shower the fun occasion it should be.

Bridesmaids' luncheon

The bridesmaids' luncheon is a party for your maid of honor and your bridesmaids, given by you in their honor. It can be an informal luncheon or a formal afternoon tea, depending upon what you like. Try to schedule the luncheon on a day in the wedding week when you're not too busy, so that everyone can enjoy the party and be relaxed. You should include both your mother and your fiancé's mother, and perhaps your flower girl and her mother, at this party if you like, but no men. This means that you can serve the tiny tea sandwiches and demitasses that so frustrate men!

You could give your attendants their special gifts on this occasion. Even if you have already given the girls their gowns as gifts, you might want to give them a tiny remembrance at this time, perhaps a small perfume sachet or a delicate handkerchief embroidered with their initials.

The bridesmaids' luncheon doesn't have to be a fancy affair, but it can be frivolous, fun and feminine; and you can decorate away if you have the time and the money, possibly using your "second choice" wedding color scheme. You can make a special centerpiece for the table, perhaps in a tree or plant shape, and attach the small gifts that you have bought for each girl to the various parts of the centerpiece.

Be sure to let your bridesmaids know in advance if you're going to sponsor such a luncheon, or they may surprise you with one. Often this party is a surprise planned jointly by your attendants, who might present you with a gift at this time. But no matter who sponsors the bridesmaids' luncheon, it can be a lovely party and will no doubt make all of you feel closer to one another.

And bachelor dinner

The male counterpart of the bridesmaids' luncheon is the bachelor dinner. This party can be sponsored by the groom or given for him by his best man or all the ushers. It can be an informal cocktail party or a complete dinner, depending on what the host wishes to arrange.

If the groom sponsors the party, he would invite all of his ushers, his best man and both fathers; and he, too, might take this opportunity to give them their gifts. The traditional toast to the bride is the starter, and the rest of the evening is like any stag party and includes refreshments, decorations and entertainment provided by the host. The bachelor dinner, when given by the groom's best man and ushers, might be their occasion to present him with a gift they have purchased together.

You might want to schedule both the bridesmaids' and bachelor parties for the same day and have the two groups join afterward, or at least join your fiancé for a nightcap to discuss how much fun both of the parties were.

In addition to showers, the bridesmaids' luncheon and the bachelor party, there might be other parties given for you or sponsored by you in honor of your wedding. It's possible that your parents or your fiancé's parents may give a party for you to introduce you to your new relatives or to friends of your fiancé's family, and other members of the wedding party may give a cocktail party or a tea in your honor. On your part, you may want to give a party for the children in the wedding party if a number of them will be taking part. It's not really much fun for flower girls or ring-bearers to attend bridesmaids' or bachelor parties, so you could have a special make-your-own-ice-cream-sundae party just for them and their parents. It's a novel idea, and guests of any age are sure to enjoy ice cream and sweets.

If you will be hostessing parties in the days before your wedding, try to invite your guests early; don't forget anyone, and plan as enjoyable a party as possible. When you attend parties in your honor, be gracious and thank your host or hostess; later send a personal note or a small gift. Parties can be wonderful

Other special parties

341

fun, and you'll be going to lots of them in the days before your wedding. Enjoy them thoroughly, but don't forget the little kindnesses that make parties worth giving and attending.

Out-of-town guests

If many of your guests will be traveling quite a distance to attend your wedding, you will want to include them in the festivities and make the time they spend with you and your family as pleasant and enjoyable as possible. They have, after all, given of their time and money to come, and you'll want them to know how much you appreciate their love and interest. They must consider your wedding very important, or they would not travel a distance to spend this very special time with you.

It isn't your responsibility, nor is it the groom's, to pay for the accommodations of out-of-town guests, but it's both helpful and kind to help them obtain hotel rooms in your city. This is a particularly nice gesture if these friends and relatives are not familiar with your area. Some of the guests, close friends or relatives, might be invited to stay in your home if you have adequate space and facilities for them; or you can arrange for some guests to stay with your groom or other members of your wedding party.

Help entertain them

It would be impossible for you or your fiancé to be constantly entertaining your out-of-town guests, but there are some ways you can make them feel not only welcome, but also an important part of the festivities. You can make a special point of inviting them to your pre-wedding parties, your rehearsal dinner or any showers or bachelor dinners if appropriate. To help share the responsibility for entertaining these guests, you might arrange with your family to sponsor a small, informal party in their honor. Your fiancé's family or a member of your wedding party might plan this if your family cannot. A pool party or a picnic would be nice, or a special brunch the day of your wedding—well before the ceremony. Your parents and your new in-laws might wish to sponsor an intimate party following the wedding reception, perhaps enjoying another piece of wedding cake and coffee. This will provide your guests with relaxed and informal entertainment and will give your parents and your new in-laws a chance to get to know each other better—and it will fill the time gap for friends and relatives as they wait for their flights home.

In addition to including your guests in your wedding festivities and perhaps having special parties for them, you might want to give them some suggestions for things they can do on their own at their leisure. Let them know what the various points of interest around your town are, including special sight-seeing musts, or give them the names of some good restaurants to try. Your guests will then not only be attending your wedding but enjoying a small vacation at the same time.

Other ideas

The extra time you take planning and sponsoring social events for your out-of-town guests can keep them from feeling that perhaps they wasted their time and money coming to your wedding. It will leave them, instead, with the feeling that they were welcome and that their presence made your wedding even more special for you.

Your week of festivities highlights the excitement and joy of the wedding day to come. Handled with thoughtfulness and consideration, it can be a time to remember—for the out-of-towners and the bridal party as well as yourself.

34

Your Friends in Need

HOW WILL IT BE POSSIBLE to have everything done in time for the wedding? How can I be sure that things will run smoothly? These are very real concerns, of course, whether your wedding will be small or large. You will want things to be as beautiful as you've always imagined, so you've got to ask for help.

The logical people to ask for help are the members of your bridal party and your family. Don't be afraid to ask them to help you do things; they'll be willing and helpful because they want your wedding to be as beautiful and memorable as you do.

The members of your bridal party have no doubt been helping you in many ways throughout the planning stages of your wedding. There are general duties that the bridal party usually performs as well as some extra tasks that you might ask them to do. Be sure to tell them how they can help; even if they have been in weddings before, you cannot expect them to anticipate all your needs. Be specific, and be nice, and you will find the help you need.

Your maid of honor can help

Your maid of honor can be of great help to you before the wedding as well as on your wedding day. During the preparation and shopping periods before your wedding, she might do some or all of the following:

1. Address invitations and/or announcements.
2. Help you list wedding gifts.
3. Help you shop for your gown and the gowns for the bridesmaids.
4. Help you shop for your new home, and for crystal, china and silver.
5. Help you move articles into your new home.
6. Be a general morale booster.

...before the wedding

She might also help you with the planning and entertaining that will be done:

1. Attend pre-wedding parties, including the rehearsal dinner, showers, the engagement party and bridesmaids' luncheon.
2. Sponsor a shower, an engagement party or a bridesmaids' luncheon.
3. Help entertain out-of-town guests.
4. Run errands and make phone calls.
5. Help you plan the ceremony and reception.

...during the ceremony

There are many things your maid of honor can help you with for the ceremony:

1. Help you dress.
2. See that the bridesmaids and flower girl are ready and dressed properly.
3. Supervise the children in the wedding party.
4. Have emergency items like needle and thread, extra bobby pins, combs, et cetera.
5. Keep and carry the groom's ring (if a double ring ceremony).
6. Assist you with your gloves, your bridal bou-

quet, your veil and/or train during the wedding ceremony.

7. Witness and sign your marriage license.
8. Take your going-away outfit to the reception site.

There are also things that you might want your maid of honor to help you with during the reception:

...during the reception

1. Help you change into your going-away outfit.
2. Help you pack in preparation for your honeymoon.
3. Make sure that you have all articles needed for your honeymoon.
4. Find your parents and bring them to you for good-byes before you leave for your honeymoon.
5. Gather all the bridesmaids and other single girls for the throwing of the bridal bouquet.
6. Care for your wedding gown, veil and accessories after you leave for your honeymoon, returning them to your home, or taking them to the cleaners to be heirloomed.
7. Gather and keep mementos of the ceremony and reception, such as the wedding cake ornament, a piece or layer of your cake (frozen until your return), matches, napkins, your guest book, any ribbons or flowers that you might want.
8. Mail your wedding announcements on your wedding day.
9. Mail your photograph and announcement to the newspaper on your wedding day.

In addition to the above duties, your maid of honor may help you in other ways during both the ceremony and reception. General duties that may need to be performed are listed toward the end of this chapter, and you might assign some of them to your maid of honor.

...and in other ways

The best man is your groom's honor attendant and he has many duties which are similar to those of

Your best man can help

...before the wedding

the maid of honor. He will assist your groom in every way possible.

During the planning, preparation and entertainment period before the wedding, the best man might do any or all of the following:

1. Attend pre-wedding parties, such as the rehearsal dinner, the bachelor dinner (which he may sponsor for the groom) and parties for any out-of-town guests.
2. Shop with your groom when he is buying the ring and perhaps when buying the bride's gift.
3. Help the groom make the arrangements for the honeymoon.
4. Coordinate the rental of the outfits to be worn by the ushers, the best man, the groom and both fathers.
5. Be a general morale booster.
6. Run errands and place phone calls as necessary.
7. Help your groom move his personal articles into your new home.

...during the ceremony

There are many things that the best man might be required to do before and during the actual wedding ceremony:

1. Help your groom dress and get ready for the ceremony.
2. Check that the ushers are ready and dressed properly.
3. Supervise the ring and/or train-bearers.
4. Have extra gloves, studs, collar buttons, comb.
5. Carry the bride's wedding ring and produce it to give to the clergyman or the groom at the proper time.
6. Assist the groom with his gloves or any other accessories during the actual wedding ceremony.
7. Witness and sign the marriage license. Carry the marriage license or advise the groom and/ or clergyman where the license is, making sure

that it is available at the proper time.

8. Pay the clergyman or judge his fee, preferably before the ceremony (in cash or check).
9. Escort the maid of honor (or provide for her being escorted) to the reception site.

The best man can help both you and your groom during the reception:

. . . during the reception

1. Offer a toast to the bride and groom (perhaps writing out the toast on a 3 by 5 inch card so as not to forget).
2. Read aloud the telegrams you receive on your wedding day during the reception.
3. Dance with you during the wedding reception, perhaps cutting in after the first dance with your husband.
4. Mingle with all guests and dance with the maid of honor, the bridesmaids and other women, keeping the dancing continuous and making sure that everyone dances.
5. Help your husband change into his going-away outfit, complete the final packing for the honeymoon trip and take complete care of all luggage for you and your husband.
6. Call your husband's parents in so that both of you can say good-bye before you leave for your honeymoon.
7. Gather the ushers and other single men for the throwing of the bridal garter.
8. Protect you and your husband from any pranksters that might bother you before your wedding, during the reception, or as you leave.
9. See you and your husband off, clearing the way for you, carrying your luggage to the car, and opening the door as you leave.
10. Send champagne, wine, flowers or a special note to you and your husband in care of the bridal suite where you plan to spend your wedding night.
11. Take care of your husband's wedding outfit, returning it to his home, the rental office, or

349

taking it to the cleaners.

In addition to the many duties listed above, you might want to ask the best man to handle the financial coordination for the reception.

Your bridesmaids can help

Your bridesmaids can also help you during the planning and entertainment period before your wedding. They, like the maid of honor, would do some of the following:

1. Attend pre-wedding parties, such as the rehearsal dinner, the engagement party, bridesmaids' luncheon and bridal showers.
2. Individually or as a group sponsor a bridal shower for you.
3. Help entertain out-of-town guests.
4. Run errands and place phone calls.

They can also help during the wedding:

1. Assist the maid of honor in any way they can during the ceremony and reception.
2. Assist during the reception in any of the ways listed in the general duties section.

Your ushers, as chosen by your groom, also have specific duties for your wedding:

1. Attend the wedding rehearsal and practice their parts in the wedding ceremony.
2. Attend pre-wedding parties, such as the rehearsal dinner, bachelor dinner and engagement party.
3. Entertain out-of-town guests.

Your "head usher" can help

Your groom and/or best man might want to appoint one of the ushers as a "head usher." He would have more responsibility than the others and should be more mature, or perhaps a closer relative of the bride or groom than the others.

He might be responsible for some of the following duties:

...with the ceremony

1. Assist the best man as needed throughout the ceremony.
2. Be in charge of distributing the boutonnieres

to all of the men in the wedding party.

3. Deliver messages from the bride's family to the groom's family before the wedding ceremony.

4. Seat the bride's mother and the groom's mother and father if they are not to take part in the wedding processional.

5. Be responsible for coordinating the rental of the wedding outfits for all of the male members of the wedding party.

6. Supervise the other ushers, advising them of special seating for friends and relatives of the bride and groom and checking that the seating is balanced, with an equal number of guests seated on each side of the ceremony area.

In addition to the above duties, the head usher would supervise the other ushers as they perform all or part of the following duties:

...supervise others

1. Prepare the site for the ceremony, including lighting candles, turning on lights, placing the aisle carpet, ribbons, *chupah*, flowers and standards in preparation for the ceremony.

2. Seat guests as they arrive.

3. Roll out the aisle carpet and/or aisle ribbons at the appropriate point during the ceremony.

4. Help honored or elderly guests and/or relatives of the bride and groom leave the area after the ceremony.

5. Dismantle and care for the various items used during the ceremony, such as the aisle carpet, ribbons, standards, or *chupah*.

During the reception, the head usher and all of the other ushers should do the following:

1. Dance with the various bridesmaids and other women guests so that each one is invited to dance at least once at some point during the reception.

2. Assist the best man as needed throughout the wedding reception.

3. Mingle with all of the wedding guests, making appropriate introductions and conversation.

Children should not have special duties

The children, if any, in your wedding party should not have any duties to perform other than their part in the actual ceremony. They should, however, be included in all pre-wedding parties where appropriate. For example, you might want to invite the flower girl, ring-bearer and train-bearer to the wedding rehearsal dinner but not to the bridal showers or the bachelor dinner.

Ask others to take charge

It would be helpful to assign one person to co-ordinate your ceremony and one to coordinate your wedding reception on the wedding day, though your mother and/or father may decide to manage these occasions.

If they would rather not, you might ask a relative or a close friend to assist you; or a bridal or wedding consultant could handle the ceremony and a banquet manager or maitre d' the reception.

The two members of your wedding party who can assist you the most are your best man and maid of honor. Your maid of honor might be in charge of the actual wedding ceremony and your best man the reception.

You may select one person to perform these duties or divide the duties among a group of people. You, as the bride, should not attempt to coordinate the ceremony or the reception on your wedding day—that's too much to ask. Have someone else take care of this for you.

Ceremony checklist

Whoever you choose to coordinate your wedding ceremony should use the following as a checklist to make sure everything takes place as planned for your ceremony.

PRE-CEREMONY

1. Decorations, candles and flowers arrive and are checked, paid for if necessary, and properly placed for the ceremony.
2. The clergyman or judge arrives and begins preparing for the ceremony. (If it is a home wedding, advise the clergyman where he might change into his robes and escort him to the ceremony area.)
3. The musicians arrive, take their places, and prepare for pre-wedding recital.
4. The photographer arrives and sets up his equipment.
5. The bridal party arrives and are directed to the rooms they will occupy until the processional begins.
6. The guests arrive and are seated by the ushers. (The guests might be greeted by the maid of honor or the bride's mother at a home wedding.)

DURING CEREMONY

1. Check that everyone is properly dressed, ready and in position for the processional.
2. Cue the processional to begin (this could be the seating of the bride's mother).
3. Begin the processional, and instruct each person when to start walking down the aisle, suggesting quietly that each one smile.

AFTER CEREMONY

1. Guide the bridal party in forming the reception line.
2. When the reception line is formed, advise the photographer to take pictures.
3. After the last guest has gone through the reception line, advise the bridal party to begin making their way to the reception area.

The person who is coordinating your wedding reception should use the following checklist to make sure that all runs smoothly. The list will vary, of course, according to the type of reception.

RECEPTION CHECKLIST

Reception checklist

1. Check whether the photographer has arrived and begun taking pictures.
2. Check whether the flowers and decorations have arrived and are properly arranged.
3. Check whether the musicians have arrived, set up and started the proper music.
4. Greet guests and direct them to the refreshment area.
5. Invite guests to sign the guest book.
6. Advise guests where they may check wraps.
7. Receive wedding gifts, note them, and arrange for them to be taken to the bride's new home.
8. Introduce guests to the various members of the wedding party and to the other wedding guests.
9. Supervise the buffet table and the serving.
10. Advise the members of the bridal party when to begin the dancing—starting with the bride and groom's first dance.
11. Remind the bride and groom when to cut the cake and see that it is served to all guests. Advise bride when to throw the bouquet and groom, the bridal garter.
12. Supervise financial arrangements for food, flowers, drink and music, paying for all items by check and/or awarding tips as well as authorizing the musicians to play overtime if desired.
13. Supervise passing out rice or rose petals to throw at the bride and groom.
14. Supervise the cleaning up of the reception site and return of all rented or borrowed items.

With the help of these "friends in need," your day will be well managed and you will be blissfully free to really enjoy your own wedding.

Part Seven

THE BIG DAY AT LAST

35

The Look of Love

DRESSING AND MAKING-UP

TODAY OF ALL DAYS you want to look especially beautiful, your very prettiest—for yourself and for your husband-to-be. This is the first time you'll be wearing your wedding gown for its real purpose—your wedding ceremony and reception—and for the pictures that you will have taken to capture this moment in time for you and your husband to treasure.

You'll want your total look today to be perfect—your gown, your makeup and hairdo all complemented by and enhancing your look of love.

Makeup comes first. Brides should look fresh and natural, but you can achieve this naturalness by wearing a little more makeup just as well as not wearing any. The secret is to apply it carefully. The following are suggestions for a makeup that will show you at your

357

loveliest without making you look like a department-store mannequin. Do, however, try them out before your wedding day. If you're a dash-of-lipstick–dash-of-liner type and think you might like to try some of these methods, you will need to begin practicing well in advance of the wedding so you can achieve a pretty look no matter how excited or nervous you may be on your wedding day.

Try your makeup first

Slip into an old housecoat or wear some kind of protection so that you won't get yourself and your undergarments soiled. Then begin with your makeup base. The cream bases that are available in tubes and come in a variety of colors are the best to use. Gently dot small amounts of base all over your face and neck and slightly below the neckline of your dress. Don't forget your ears and the little spaces behind the ears. Use a shade of base that matches your skin tones well (if you are accustomed to wearing base, use your normal color or perhaps a slightly darker shade for an evening wedding), and apply a little more than the amount you would use for street wear. You'll be in the spotlight today, both literally and figuratively, and there are pictures to be taken. Once you have dotted your face with the makeup base, smooth it out and blend it in with the pads of your fingers, using a very light touch. Then pat the makeup into your skin gently, to give yourself a finished look.

Brides quite often don't get a good night's sleep the night before their wedding because they are so excited about the day to come. So to take away color that you don't want, such as darkness or "shadows" underneath your eyes, stroke on some erase, then gently pat it in.

Base

When your base is completed, apply the various colors that add life to your face. I would advise using more blusher or rouge than you would ordinarily because on your wedding day you're very likely to be a little pale. You'll be experiencing a great deal of emotion and happiness, and it's very natural to be nervous and elated. Quite often when this happens, the blood rushes from the face, and you become pale. If you use a little extra blusher today, you'll be able to compensate for this paleness.

Your eye makeup should not differ drastically from what you'd normally wear for a formal occasion. Try eye shadow and shading in subtle colors to match your gown. If you wear a blue gown, wear blue eye shadow, or select a shade to match the color of your eyes or the flowers you plan to carry. Either approach can be very beautiful.

Eye makeup

False eyelashes are very good to wear, for they will make your pictures much more attractive because they define your eyes quite nicely. But try them on and wear them for awhile to make sure you like them and feel comfortable with them—before your wedding day.

False eye lashes

Waterproof mascara is an excellent idea, too. Many people think that it is the mother of the bride who cries at her daughter's wedding, but many times it is the bride herself. You won't cry because you're unhappy, but because it is a very special day. The decision to marry is very important, and it's only normal to be emotional when you experience all the beauty, excitement and joy of your own wedding day.

Lipstick is the last color to add—directly from the tube or with a lipstick brush if you prefer. I would suggest using a relatively light shade, as it will show up in your pictures better. A kissproof brand is good because, not only will you give your husband a wedding kiss, but you will be kissing others and they you, and they can end up with very pink cheeks if your lipstick isn't kissproof.

After all your basic makeup is applied, you might want to try a trick which many actresses use to ensure their makeup staying fresh during performances under hot lights. Buy some "translucent" powder—powder which, while it has a shade to it, is relatively pure of

A special trick

artificial colorings. Puff it liberally all over your face and then carefully splash lukewarm water over your face and all makeup areas, except the eyes. You will notice that the water will bead if you have applied enough powder. This is a good sign—it means that your makeup is setting properly. Pat your face dry gently with a soft towel. If you use this technique, you will wind up with an almost indestructible matte finish on your face—and your makeup won't rub off on your gown, your guests or your groom. You may want to touch up your mascara or eyeliner a bit, but translucent powder adds no color of its own, so it won't dim the colors you've already applied—it will merely enhance them. If you are going to use another kind of powder, it's best to keep your eyes protected when you puff it on, and if it's a pink-toned powder, go easier on the blusher and/or rouge.

If you wear glasses   A special cosmetic consideration for many girls is glasses. If you normally wear glasses and simply cannot see well enough to put them aside during the ceremony and reception, consider some of the following suggestions. (By the way, this is not only a cosmetic problem; glasses can catch and reflect light in the wedding photographs.) If you want to invest in contact lenses, try them out a few months before you're to be married so that you wear them naturally and comfortably by the time your wedding comes around. If not, buy glasses that are especially suited to your wedding gown, in a style and color that blends well with your outfit. If either of these suggestions is too costly to consider, at least plan to set aside your glasses when photographs are taken; or check with your photographer to see if he has done work with other girls who wear glasses, and if possible have a look at the results of these photos. Explain your situation. He may have some additional suggestions.

Although you won't be applying makeup to your hands, you are going to want to consider their condition for your wedding day. They'll be getting a lot of attention, as people will want to see your ring and photographs will be taken. Soften your hands with hand cream several weeks in advance of the wedding, and have a professional manicure or a good do-it-yourself one a few days before the wedding. Keep your nails relatively short to help avoid last-minute breakage, and wear a light or clear polish. If you do break a nail, wear false nails for your wedding—no one will be the wiser.

Check your hands

Your hairdo comes next. Many brides make the mistake of changing their hairstyles drastically for their wedding. For example, a girl who normally wears her hair loose and flowing decides that for her wedding day she will wear it piled high on her head—arranged in an artful and fancy manner. She does so, and as she comes down the aisle her groom turns to look at her, sees her new hairdo, and for a moment doesn't even recognize her. This can be a very jolting experience for him. To avoid it, don't make a drastic change in your hairstyle. A natural hairstyle will be better for you too. For one thing, the more ornate your hairdo the more likely you are to be constantly worried that pins will come out or the set will droop while you dance at the reception. Save yourself the headache: Wear your hair arranged in the usual manner.

Choose your hairstyle

Hairpieces are really a great invention, and I'm all in favor of them. If you own one that looks attractive and natural on you and pleases your fiancé, then by all means wear it on your wedding day. If not, I would strongly advise you against experimenting with hairpieces for this occasion. Stick to the tried-and-true style that you know you like.

Also, be cautious about having a haircut, permanent or touch-up scheduled too close to the wedding day. If something goes wrong, there may not be enough time to correct it. It's best to invest some time and money in finding a good hairdresser several months before the wedding if you don't already have one. And

Time haircuts carefully

experiment with the style of your choice well in advance —not the week before the wedding.

When choosing your hairstyle for your wedding, take your bridal veil and headdress along with you to the beauty salon. In this way you can match your hairstyle to your headdress so that you can be comfortable as well as attractive on your wedding day.

Need help?

If you think you might need help with your hairdo on your wedding day, ask your hairdresser if he would be willing to come over to comb out your hair. You'll have to pay for his service, of course, but it will be worth it if you'll feel more attractive and relaxed because of the special attention. But remember that if your stylist is a man or woman of "temperament," you might be better off doing without; you don't need to surround yourself with high-strung or nervous people on your wedding day. You could also ask a friend who is handy with hairdos to help you, or get one of the new ten-minute heat-up curler sets—particularly if you're worried about high humidity or other weather problems that might cause a freshly styled hairdo to flop.

After you've applied your makeup and checked your manicure, cover your hairdo and put on your wedding gown. Your hair is then ready for its final combing. Your maid of honor or whoever is helping you dress can check your shoulders to make sure your final combing has left no debris on your gown.

Before you begin to make yourself beautiful for your wedding, it's best to have everything you'll need assembled—to take with you if you'll be changing at the site of the ceremony or just to lay out the night before if you'll be dressing at home. Use the following checklist, reviewing it carefully the night before your wedding.

A quick checklist

1. Gown, veil and all accessories for your wedding outfit. (Ready a garment bag if you need to travel with these items.)

2. Going-away outfit and accessories (also in a garment bag).
3. Deodorant, dress shields, perfume or cologne.
4. Makeup.
5. Nail repair items, polish, Kleenex, towels, cotton, Q-tips or any other makeup accessories.
6. Combs, brushes, hairpieces, pins, spray, electric or regular curlers for touch-ups, hair accessories such as ribbons or flowers.

All of these suggestions are for you to use as you want. I know they work, and I know they are of value. If you're trying any new ideas as far as your makeup or hairdo are concerned, be sure to try them out well in advance of your wedding day so you know what the results will be.

Now that you are fully dressed in your bridal gown and veil—your makeup, hairdo and headdress in place—and you look exactly as you always dreamed you would look, it's time for you to walk down the aisle to meet your groom.

36

Down the Aisle

YOUR DREAMS COME TRUE

AS YOU GET INTO THE CAR next to your father, your eyes are on the cars ahead, which hold your mother and your bridesmaids. Your thoughts, too, are on the hours ahead, when you will become a bride. As the car draws closer to the ceremony site, excitement mounts.

A little nervous, you step from the car and enter the church to join your attendants. The ushers are seating the wedding guests, and you join the processional forming at the rear of the church. In the distance you may glimpse your groom and his best man waiting with the clergyman at the altar. The lights are low, and with all the decorations in place it's hard to believe that this is the same spot where the rehearsal was held. Your father comes to your side and places your hand through his arm, and suddenly the music begins: Your ushers and bridesmaids begin down the aisle, and the eyes of your guests are turned, awaiting you. As you approach the altar, you see your groom more clearly. It's a serious moment, but there's a smile in his eyes only for you, and suddenly you're not quite so nervous anymore.

The ceremony seems to move quickly. The vows and rings are exchanged before you know it, and then your maid of honor is lifting back your veil so you can receive your first kiss as a married woman. With the striking up of the recessional music, suddenly your mood catches the tune and you walk back up the aisle with a broad smile and tears of happiness in your eyes. As you approach the vestibule of the church, the ushers begin escorting the guests in the front rows out of the ceremony area.

As you ride from the ceremony to the reception site, you look at the man sitting beside you; neither of you can really believe that you're married! But the shine in your eyes and the flush on his cheek are the proof that it's true.

"There's hardly time to talk or think..."

There's hardly time to talk or think once you arrive at the reception site. The reception line must be formed quickly, with barely a few seconds to hug your attendants and have them congratulate you. Then the first guests arrive and, while the photographer snaps pictures, everyone begins going through the receiving line. The women are exuberant, some crying happy tears. Much hugging and kissing, with the men somehow at a loss for words but full of warm congratulations for you and your groom. They move on to your "greeter," who directs them to the refreshment area, where all is in readiness—decorations, flowers, music.

Your first dance as "Mr. and Mrs."

Once the reception line is ended, you move with your new husband to the refreshment area, accepting more informal congratulations and talking with your guests. Then to the main reception area, where you are seated at the head table with the other members of the wedding party. The best man rises to propose the toast, and you and your groom remain seated as all the guests drink to your good health and happy future. There are telegrams from those friends and relatives who could not come to the wedding. After he glances through these messages to make sure you want each one read aloud, the best man reads these good wishes, and the dancing begins. You and your husband share the first dance to your special song or to the "Anniversary Waltz"; then your father cuts in, dancing with you while your groom goes to find his mother. The groom's father then cuts in on you, and your father goes to your mother while the groom dances with his own mother. All partners then switch again, so that by the end of the number you and your husband and both sets of parents are all waltzing around the floor. The wedding party and guests join in, and soon the dance floor is filled with happy people. The celebration has begun.

The food is delicious, and the head table is full of happy chatter. After you've finished eating, the dancing begins again. You and your husband move about the room, chatting with guests, dancing, and seeing to it that everyone else dances. Your wedding cake is brought in, and, to a fanfare, you and your groom cut the first piece. Amid the applause and picture taking that follows this moment, the cake is cut by the caterer's helpers and served to your guests. You even remember to set aside the ornament for yourself and an extra piece of the cake for a cousin who couldn't attend.

You give your garter to your groom, remove some flowers from the center of your bridal bouquet to save for your scrapbook, and now give your maid of honor and best man the signal to gather the single men and women. The girls cluster around you and you turn slightly, throwing the bouquet over your shoulder. Your husband throws your bridal garter to the bachelors in the crowd, and now there are promises of two future weddings.

Now you and your groom leave to change into your going-away outfits while the music continues and the guests keep on dancing. Your maid of honor finds your parents, who join you after you're dressed for final kisses and good-byes. The best man calls your husband's parents, too, so that you can share this intimate, happy-sad moment alone with all those dearest to you.

All the guests know you are about to leave, so as you rush with your luggage to the waiting car, showers of rice and rose petals follow you, along with the cries of fond farewell. The photographer is there, too, snapping a last picture as you get into the car and leave for your honeymoon.

As the center of attention throughout your wedding day, you'll be expected to be charming, warm and receptive to all comments and expressions of happiness and good wishes. Particularly in the reception line and during the reception itself, people will be approaching you constantly with exuberant comments and excited reactions to the day. You might find it difficult to constantly summon up the expected responses: After all, you're excited and in an emotional state yourself.

In the reception line keep conversations brief. A simple thank you, a compliment about the guest's appearance, and a gracious introduction to your husband are sufficient. Don't strain yourself by attempting to remember the wedding gift given by each guest standing before you. It's not worth it to put yourself under the pressure that remembering each gift would require.

Later, during the reception itself, do all you can to be a gracious hostess. Try to drink less than you might normally, for the excitement of the occasion might cause the liquor to go quickly to your head, preventing you from enjoying the day and causing you to behave in a way you would not like. Although you as the bride would not offer any toasts, you can always

Some last good-byes

A simple thank you

suggest special ones to your groom. Your response to toasts in your honor should be gracious, but long speeches are not necessary. A smile and happy "thank you" to the person making the toast is sufficient. It's not necessary that you dance with every man at the wedding, but do try to dance with your best man and ushers, your male relatives and your father and father-in-law at least once, perhaps reserving the last dance for your own father.

As you circulate to speak with specific guests, you needn't be at a loss for words. Simply thank them for attending, tell them you hope they're having a good time, and say that you look forward to seeing them after you return from your honeymoon. Keep your comments general; don't promise to entertain them on a specific date in the future, for you shouldn't feel pressured to organize your new home in a hurry. Naturally, intimate friends and relatives will be people you'll have no trouble conversing with during this period, but don't huddle with friends now. This is a day when all guests should get equal time.

Talk to all your guests

If you're distributing the reception decorations to your guests, or if you're having them donated to a charity, you might want the emcee to announce this sometime during the reception. Often each guest at a table chooses a number from one to ten (or whatever number of people are seated at the table) and the emcee announces that whoever has picked number six "wins" the centerpiece to take home.

Guests can "win" a centerpiece

You can make the change into your going-away outfits early in the reception if the day is warm or you are uncomfortable in your bridal gown for some reason. There's no reason why you can't go back and continue to enjoy the reception after you've made this change, and it will give the photographer an opportunity to take some good pictures of you in your going-away outfits.

You and your groom should try to find time to

369

Some special thank you's

thank your best man and maid of honor, as well as your other attendants, during the course of the reception. A quiet moment when you could take them aside is all that's needed; it's of first importance to have some time alone with your respective parents, but your attendants also deserve a moment of personal attention and thanks.

Your glorious day will speed by, and soon you and your husband will be alone together. But while your wedding day lasts, enjoy it thoroughly. This once-in-a-lifetime ceremony and party is for your enjoyment and is entirely in your honor. May it be beautiful enough to make *all* your dreams come true.

37

Alone at Last

THE HONEYMOON BEGINS

AS YOU DRIVE AWAY from your reception and breathe a sigh of relief that everything went beautifully and just as you always wanted it to, you'll begin to really relax, and all of a sudden, it will hit you—here beside you is your actual legal husband. You're a Mrs. now, no longer a Miss, and heading for the most romantic vacation of your life.

If it's fairly early when the reception ends, a quiet dinner before leaving on the honeymoon can be lovely; or you might want to meet your best man and maid of honor for a drink and a talk. If it is late in the day, you will probably head straight for the spot you've chosen for your wedding night and perhaps share coffee or champagne and that "last slice of wedding cake" in your room.

You'll finally be alone

Often, as the honeymoon begins, newly-wed couples are at a loss. Whether you've known each other since you were children or had a whirlwind courtship, the fact is that in the days or weeks before the wedding your time alone together has probably been minimal, so there may be a moment or two of awkward silence. The best solution for these uncomfortable sensations, should they occur, is to ignore them, to give them a small place in your thoughts. Time alone together will quickly make the feeling go away.

I am in favor of anything romantic: candlelight, champagne, open fires and soft music. I knew a couple · who spent their wedding night in a hotel that had a fireplace in each room. They felt a fire was romantic, and it didn't matter to either of them that it was the month of June!

Have a champagne breakfast!

Be sure to put out your "Do Not Disturb" sign on the door and leave a call for the morning if you have to rise at a certain time to catch your plane or train. It's a nice idea to order your breakfast the night before and have it sent to your room at a specific time the next morning. Have a champagne breakfast if you like. Order things that you enjoy and don't worry about the fact that room service is expensive. You can economize later.

When you arrive at your honeymoon site, it's nice to call or to send a telegram to both sets of parents. Your message need not be long, but should indicate your safe arrival and include your thanks to your parents for giving you such a lovely day to remember.

Being honeymooners is fun!

You are honeymooners now—really married people—and you should not be embarrassed to admit it. People are not going to make fun of you. It's a very special time in your lives, and you should enjoy it fully and openly.

In addition to the sight-seeing and the events which you have planned for your honeymoon, it's always helpful to read the information that is provided for you at the hotel. Quite often they will have lists of places of interest in the area, tours available, nice places to go for meals and such, and it's fun to read through this information and make a list of things that you might like to see and do.

Make friends while you are on your honeymoon. If you meet another couple you like at your hotel, join them for drinks or dinner or share sight-seeing together. You'll have new people to talk to, new things to think about and, who knows—you might make some lifelong friends. Bring along books to read, perhaps reading and discussing the same book at the same time. Plan to do things, things which interest you both and will make your honeymoon even more fun. If you are shy together at first, mutual interests will help ease the way for conversation. Even the most at-ease couples will enjoy sharing their holiday fun with others.

Meet new people; make new friends

It's fun to collect souvenirs of your honeymoon to add to your wedding scrapbook or just to keep in a special place. Photographs, postcards, menus or any small items that will help you remember the things you first shared and enjoyed as man and wife are mementos you will cherish. You might also want to get some small, inexpensive gifts to bring back for friends. A little something that shows you were thinking of them is always appreciated.

Add honeymoon mementos to your scrapbook

When you return from your honeymoon, rested and eager to settle in your new home and to enjoy it together, your husband may carry you over the threshold, a custom thought to have begun with the Romans, who felt that this kept evil spirits away from a new home. Whatever the origin, it doesn't really matter. It's a nice custom and lots of fun.

You can begin arranging your home the way you want it as you unpack and put away your wedding gifts. You may want to return some of the gifts you received, so try to do it as soon as possible, as some stores will not accept returns after a certain length of time has elapsed.

Once you're a little settled, you might want to invite friends and relatives over for coffee and tell them about your honeymoon; you can even show them the pictures of your honeymoon and your first days in your new home. And thus you begin your new life.

With all the excitement of the wedding and reception behind you, you'll soon settle into your new home and your new way of life, and start enjoying being "the newlyweds down the hall."

38

A Bride Forever

YOU CAN BE HAPPY EVER AFTER

BY NOW YOU HAVE NO DOUBT RETURNED from your honeymoon and are happily settled into your new home. You're ready to begin and enjoy your life as a bride and as a new "Mrs." Yes, people will call you a bride for your first year of marriage, but you can be a bride for this first year and forever if you really want to.

Of course, there will be adjustments that you will have to make. It's only natural because you are living with someone new—someone you love—someone who is not only of the opposite sex but who, like you, has his own unique and special personality. So you'll need lots of love and understanding.

Some of your first adjustments will concern learning to share, phrasing criticism, respecting privacy and learning to understand each other.

379

What are you two like in the morning? This is one of the first things you'll find out about each other. Perhaps one of you is a morning person—someone who wakes up easily in the morning—and one of you is a night person—someone who doesn't.

Are you a "morning" person?

You may be the one who is a morning person. You wake up in the morning and you're wide awake—full of energy with a big smile on your face. Then you suddenly find that your husband is just the opposite. He's the one who can stay up for the Late, Late Show, but finds it all but impossible to wake up in the morning. Well, you're different, so you're going to have to adjust to this difference.

You may have to change some

You'll both have to give in a little bit. Perhaps you could regulate your hours so that both of you go to bed a little earlier—this may help him be a little more cheerful in the morning. Or you might make a special effort not to be as cheerful and noisy as you might generally be in the morning. Subdue yourself a little bit, just for the mornings. Let him ease into waking up, and don't play loud music or be too chatty. This will give him a chance to wake up. Remember that your husband, like yourself, must become accustomed to differences in habit and personality. If you are considerate of his idiosyncracies, you will find yourself with a happy husband—and a happy marriage.

He may like to be alone sometimes, too

Try to respect your husband's privacy, and allow him to ease into sharing things. Let him do things his own way—handle phone calls, mail and his own belongings as he chooses. Keep in mind that you have times when you would like to be left alone—perhaps you have something you need to think about or a decision to make by yourself. This can happen to your husband, too. Keep in mind that just as you like to be alone, he may sometimes like to be alone, and you should respect that wish. Don't presume that because he wants to be alone, he doesn't want to be with you. He is still an individual and so are you. This has not

380

changed. The only thing that has changed is that you are now together to share a life, and sharing things comes gradually and at a different rate for each individual; so don't force the issue of sharing if it may be interpreted by your husband as giving up his privacy. Let it happen naturally and slowly.

If your husband does have small habits that tend to irritate you, don't make these large issues. Realize that where he leaves his socks or whether he reads at the table while eating is a small item. Such habits are not crucial, so don't make them too important—in your mind or in your marriage.

Learn how to phrase and express your criticism of his habit in a loving way. One way to do this is to give general praise about your husband's courtesies. Point out the things that he does for you that you like, and praise him for them. During the same conversation mention the small items—his habit—that irritates you, and ask him if he might change that particular habit—it would be so nice if he would.

How to criticize

Let's say for example, your husband doesn't hold the door open for you when you are going into a building or getting out of the car. You might start the conversation by praising him for the special courtesies that he does give you. Mention that you think it is particularly nice when he calls you from the office to say that he is coming home late, that you know many husbands who don't, and that it means so much to you. Mention perhaps how nice he is to you in public, or how nice he is to others. Let's say your husband is the type of person who chats and mingles with all the guests at a party, tries to help people have a good time, starts interesting conversations and is generally enjoyable to be with. Point out these things to him, and in the midst of this conversation say something to the effect of: "You know, honey, I'm sorry to mention this—it's a small thing—but it would be a nice thing if you would hold doors open for me. Your other cour-

Tell him the good things first

tesies are so nice and so thoughtful; and if you could just do this one small thing for me, I would really appreciate it."

This approach, phrased in your own words and brought up at a time when discussions are possible, is, I think, the best way to ask him to change a habit. I know that the wrong approach is to nag or badger your husband, or compare him in a negative way to other husbands or other people that you know, or compare his behavior now with his behavior before you were married.

Don't nag! If you nag your husband—saying things like: "Why don't you open doors for me? Sue's husband does it all the time. I guess you don't care as much about me as you did before we were married"—and make a negative comment, your husband is going to remember it in a negative way, and though he may change the habit, he may resent it. I think it's preferable to approach your husband in a positive way—in the way you would want him to point something out to you.

You wouldn't want him to say to you: "Boy, I wish you could cook like my mother," or "You know, I heard Joe's wife makes Lasagne. I sure wish we had something interesting to eat once in a while." You wouldn't appreciate these kinds of comments, so be considerate of him and make your criticism courteous, loving and gentle.

To fully adjust to your husband, it is necessary to know as much about his behavior as you can. Try to understand what his life at work is like. You may have already found yourself thinking: "My husband really has it easy. He goes to the office, does pretty much the same kinds of things every day, has a nice business lunch, and comes home to relax. But I stay at home, responsible for the whole house and doing all the work that needs to be done—much of which I don't like. I work very hard, he takes it easy."

If these thoughts occur to you, think about what your husband really has to do—try to put yourself in his position. Think of it this way: How would you feel if your husband's boss were to come to your home for dinner. You'd be suddenly face to face with the man whom your husband is responsible to every day of the week. Would this put you in a mild panic? It does many women. Stop and think about it. You'd have to meet his boss and, for an entire evening, please him. Besides preparing a special meal, you'd guide conversation so that it would be interesting and entertaining to him and in general create a good impression of yourself, your home and your husband.

Put yourself in his shoes

While entertaining the boss is an occasion to you, your husband has to do it five days a week. He deals with the boss every day, and if he doesn't please the people he works for, he doesn't have a job. If he's going to school, he has to work hard to get good grades or he'll fail. Your husband has standards and difficulties in his work or his schooling, just as you do in your life—whether you're staying home and managing your household or you're combining your home duties with a career or a job. Keep in mind that your husband has problems too, and try to understand his position.

Don't bother your husband at the office. Think about it this way: If you call your girl friend at her place of business and ask to speak to her, wouldn't it be logical for you to say, "Connie, I'd like to talk to you if you have a minute." You wouldn't presume that she could put down everything that she is doing to talk to you at that particular moment. You might say something like, "Well, if you can't talk now, give me a buzz back later."

Treat your husband the same way. He has responsibilities just as a girl friend in an office situation would. When you call him, ask him if he's busy. If he is, ask him to call you back later, or briefly tell him why you are calling. Or tell him that you called just to chat, and when he has a second, would he call you back. This will help him too because he won't feel pressured to talk to you at that particular moment, and he won't feel bad if he has to call you back later.

Be a good listener. Listen and care about what your husband has to say about his life, his work, his problems. Try to learn as much as you can about your husband. Read about his business, or ask questions about the courses he is taking; care about his progress. Listen to his problems, share his life with him, and he will do this with you. He will lend a more sympathetic ear and have much more understanding of your life and your problems if you show him that you really care about how he spends his day, what he is trying to achieve and what his difficulties might be.

Keep in mind that your husband is struggling and working very hard—whether he's in school or has already taken a job—to achieve success. Yes, it's for his own personal satisfaction, but also for you. The two of you are a family now, and he wants to make your lives as enjoyable as he possibly can. He's trying to make a nice living so that he can provide you and himself with a nice home and some of the luxuries of life. He's trying to make your life together happy; so understand this and encourage him and care about what he is trying to achieve.

You'll talk about his life and yours and about everything and anything that's important to the two of you. After all, one of the pleasures of marriage and the close companionship you have when you're happily married is that you can be yourself with the person that you've married. You can talk with him freely about anything and everything that affects you, your relationship and your life together. Don't fail to take advantage of this. Talk to your husband about all the things that are important to the two of you.

Try to keep your conversations about happy things, and accent the positive things in life. Don't

"Listen to his problems, share his life..."

He's working for both *of you*

384

dream up or dwell on problems, or moan and nag about things. These kinds of feelings have no place in your conversations. Try to center and concentrate your conversation with him on the positive, happy, important things that are worth discussion.

Talk about happy things

You should be honest about things with your husband. Tell him everything. I don't think it's good to keep secrets from each other. This burdens both of you. He can't understand why you feel bad about something if you don't explain to him what's happened. He can't understand and share your happiness in something if you don't tell him why you're happy. Talk to him frankly, even if you're in a situation where perhaps you've dented the fender on the car and it really, really upsets you to have to tell him about it. Don't keep it inside yourself—tell him. It's difficult to confess such things, that's true; but he loves you—he married you because he loves you, because he thinks you're the most wonderful person on this earth. He's going to understand how you feel and why you feel the way you do. He's going to try to help you in your life. You two are sharing a new life and it's best to begin by being as close as possible. This closeness and companionship will strengthen if you are both open and honest with each other. This includes discussing major and minor decisions thoroughly with each other. Neither one of you should take the responsibility of making decisions alone. That's one of the pleasures of being married—you don't have to make decisions by yourself anymore.

When you are making a decision, it is helpful to write down the pros and cons involved. Pool your ideas and thoughts and come up with the best decision that the two of you can make together; and once the decision is made, it's made by both of you. It's not his decision or your decision, it's the decision that you have made together; and this is what you can act on. And it will be helpful to you, I think, to combine his

Work together for the best decision

385

thoughts and yours to come up with a mutually satisfactory decision, one that you both feel good about.

If you make a mistake—if you do something foolish, or do something that you wish you hadn't done—apologize for that particular thing. Don't apologize for your total existence by saying something like, "I never do anything right." Apologize for the specific thing you did wrong and be honest about your mistake. Don't hold it inside and be too proud to admit that you, like everybody else, have made a mistake.

Discuss everything, and grow together

By discussing decisions, mistakes and many other things, you can help your husband understand himself better and encourage him to help you, too. Many young couples share their observations about each other. The wife points out her husband's good qualities and anything he might change or improve— in a nice way—and they discuss these things. The husband in turn does this for his wife. It is beneficial to both because they learn about each other and they learn about themselves. When a couple does this they seem to grow and progress together instead of growing at their own separate rate—and perhaps growing apart. It's an excellent idea and I've seen it work very well. I can't recommend it too strongly.

Treat him better than a friend

As you learn more about each other you will probably begin to think: "Now that I know him well, how should I treat him?" A general approach is to treat him *better* than a friend. It may seem strange for me to be advising you to treat your husband better than you would a friend, to be nice to him. You may think: "Of course I'll be nice to him, of course I'll treat him better than anybody." But this isn't always what you end up doing. If this is your goal and your general idea, perhaps the specific things mentioned here will give you some idea of how to be as loving to your husband as possible—how to *show* him that you care about him.

Compliment your husband—as you would a friend. If your girlfriend looks lovely in a new dress—

386

obviously beaming about it—you tell her how much you like it. Because it's very important to her, she appreciates and enjoys your comment. The same is true of men. They love to be complimented, just as you do—just as everyone does. Make it a point to tell him the things that you like about him; and compliment him when he looks nice and when he does something that's meaningful to you. It's especially important, I think, to compliment your husband in the morning as he goes to class or to work—even if you go to work, too. Say something pleasant to him, even if you're the type who finds it very difficult to wake up in the morning and you've only got one eye open. Take a second to think about him, a sentence. Tell him, "You really look nice in that blue suit," or "Have a good day," or "I love you more today than I did yesterday"—something nice. It will make his day easier and more enjoyable and it will start him out on the right foot, which is very important.

Many women realize what a morale booster it is for them to go to the beauty parlor. Having their hair cut and set is something they love to do. They get out of the house, and they come back feeling and looking much happier and more attractive. The same is true of men, too. Your husband may say that he doesn't like to have his hair cut, that he just doesn't have time or it's not important to him; but it really is. Try to encourage him to do things for himself; to treat himself well; to go to the barber shop; to care about his appearance; to keep his clothing in good order. This shows him in a very concrete way that you care about him, and he's going to know it; he's going to appreciate it. Your husband may not be too verbal about saying thank you, or perhaps letting you know how much it means to him, but believe me, it does mean a tremendous amount. It will mean as much to him and his morale as doing such things for yourself can mean to you.

You should be nice to your husband, definitely, but don't forget yourself in the process. One of the

Encourage your husband to treat himself well

ways you can be nice to yourself is to care about your physical appearance. I recently overheard a woman talking to a newly-wed couple and she said: "You know, you two are really remarkable—you've gotten better looking and more attractive since you've been married. I've never heard of such a thing. Usually couples let their appearance go, and some even become sloppy and don't care after they're married. What's your secret?" Well, their secret is simple: She cared about her appearance because she wanted to be attractive to him and he cared about his appearance because he wanted to be attractive to her.

Because you're really in love, you will have a glow about you for all of your married life. This couple had that glow, but they also made it a special point to consciously improve their appearance.

Your look is a matter of attitude

This care about the way you look is a matter of attitude; it's not always a matter of finances. You can look very attractive in a simple cotton dress if it's clean and pressed and of a flattering color. It doesn't have to be expensive. You don't have to spend a lot of money on clothing and cosmetics to be attractive, but you do have to try to learn about yourself. Learn what cosmetics make you look attractive; what colors are most becoming to you and most pleasing to your husband; and learn about yourself in general. Care about yourself and constantly try to improve your appearance.

Don't retire at 23!

When you get up in the morning, make an effort to be attractive. Put on a clean housecoat, a little bit of powder and lipstick, and a smile—that's all that's necessary. The few minutes it takes to make yourself attractive are well spent—you'll feel better and look better, and you'll both benefit from it. It's very important for you to stay active as well as attractive. Don't make the mistake of "retiring" at the age of 23. Or think that becoming a Mrs. is your cue to sit down, to take life easy and just turn yourself off. This is true whether you have a career or you don't; whether you manage a home and plan to have children; or whether you have a career or job of your own. It's very important to you as a person to keep yourself active and happy. You can't make someone else happy unless you're happy yourself. You've got to begin at the beginning. You've got to be happy, and he's got to be happy. So when the two of you are together, you will share happiness; and it will grow and multiply and become better and better.

Be active and involved with your life. It will make you a happier and more interesting person. Cultivate new ideas, new interests. If there's something you've always wanted to do, do it. If there's some kind of a sport that you or your husband have always been interested in—perhaps he's always wanted to play golf—give it a try. You can always rent the equipment if it is too expensive to buy. Enlarge your areas of interest and find activities that you can share with him. Finding things that you will both enjoy will help you grow closer together; and it will help you experience fully all the things in life that are even more fun when shared.

A good way to develop your area of interest—and perhaps to find a more interesting you—is to pick one thing—anything—and become expert at it. Choose whatever you like—painting, flower arranging, reading, skating, interior decorating—even going back to school—and concentrate on it. Your activity can be very rewarding and, who knows, it may open up an entirely new career idea to you. And once you feel that you've learned all you want or need to know about a subject, you can move on to other areas. Continual learning will keep you alive and interesting—and exciting. The more you learn, the more you grow; and sharing these experiences with others will be very rewarding—both for you and for those you love.

Another major area of interest for you will be your new home. It will give you lots of new things to

Enjoy life; you'll be happier

think about—and do! Yes, you are now a home manager, and it will be up to you to decorate your home, choose the furnishings that you like and manage your complete household—including cleaning, meal planning and keeping the finances straight. Also, it is up to you to create a pleasant mood for your new home.

A home, like a person, is unique, with its own personality. Your home reflects you and the type of person that you are. You've probably had the experience of walking into someone's home and getting an instant impression of the people who live there by seeing the kind of furniture they have, the way it's arranged, whether the home is neat or not, the lighting bright or subdued and the music soft or loud. All of these things create a mood in a home, and it is up to you to select the one you want.

It's particularly important for yourself and for your husband to have a calm, relaxed atmosphere in your home. You can be active and happy; you should enjoy things and be exuberant in your home. But think of your home in terms of a haven—a place where you can go to relax, to enjoy your husband, to enjoy living together, to share experiences with him and with friends—a special place for both of you. Plan for it, and create the mood for your home that you've always wanted.

The pleasant mood of your home can be disturbed by the mismanagement of your household finances. Some wives are puzzled by this, but you don't need to be. Ask your husband's help, and be frank about it if you don't understand how to manage money or balance a checkbook. Ask him if he can help you so that you can do it on your own—or perhaps he will want to handle certain aspects of your family finances.

If you're both in the dark about managing money, get advice from someone else. Consult a friend who's good at finances, someone who works at your bank, or your parents—anyone you think would be

There will be lots to think about—and do

Your home—a special place for both of you

Puzzled about finances?

helpful to you. And read books and magazine articles to find out what other families have done about their finances and how they budget their money. Get ideas on how to set up a family budget and what you allow for different items.

Once you have worked on and set up a general budget with appropriate amounts to spend for necessary and luxury items, try to live within that budget. Don't overextend yourself—particularly at this point in your life. You'll have plenty of time later to buy things that you need. You've got a lifetime of shopping ahead of you, so take it easy and go slowly. Decide what it is you want, and work out a practical solution to get it.

By now you have some idea about how to manage your money and make your home a happy one, and you can begin giving some thought to sharing your new home with some new friends. As a new couple, you'll want to begin looking for friends among happily married young couples like yourselves—preferably those who are in your same income bracket and who share your interests. And you will want these friends to be guests in your home—for whatever type of entertaining you enjoy and your budget permits.

Share your new home

Entertaining can be easy if you remember to be inventive. Serving interesting foods and planning unusual features will present a challenge and will give you the chance to prove yourself a good hostess.

To be a well-prepared hostess who serves interesting menus, collect recipes and party ideas from your favorite cookbooks and women's magazines. Then try them out—well in advance of serving them to your guests. Encourage guests to "just drop by" by having a supply of items that are fast and easy to prepare. Frozen or canned hors d'oeuvres and desserts are just the answer. Your friends will soon know that you like them to come by—and that you also have good refreshments to enjoy when they get there. With a little care—and

It's fun to have friends "just drop by"

a fun-filled spirit—your guests will come to feel as at home in your house as you do.

* * *

Just as I hope this book was a help to you when you were planning and enjoying your wedding, I also hope that the suggestions given in this chapter will help you as you begin your marriage.

Your good attitude and strong desire to be a good wife, plus the love and consideration you have for your husband, are sure to equal a very happy life for the two of you. And you will be a bride forever. And ever.

ACKNOWLEDGMENTS

The photographs in this volume are reproduced by kind permission of the following companies and photographers:

American Stock Photos (Facing Chapters 17, 22); ArtCarved (Chapter 3); Victor Baldwin (Facing Chapter 30); Color Spree (Facing Chapters 3, 20, 26, 34, 35, 37); Doves of Happiness (Facing Chapter 27); William Figge (Facing Chapters 6, 9, 23, 24, 38); Florists' Transworld Delivery (Facing Chapter 21); Franciscan table top fashions (Facing Chapter 13); Hansen Cakes (Facing Chapter 30); Harry Langdon Jr. (Facing Chapter 31); Kay McRee (Facing Chapters 1, 2, 4, 5, 7, 8, 10, 18, 25, 29); Walter T. Mynar (Facing Chapter 19); Lee Rhodes (Facing Chapter 36); Rosenthal U.S.A. Limited (Facing Chapter 14); Saks Fifth Avenue (Facing Chapters 15, 16); Wallace Silversmiths Public Relations, courtesy of Hamilton Watch Company (Facing Chapter 12); Wedding Planner Company (Facing Chapter 8); Robert Wightman (Facing Chapters 28, 32). Cover photo by William Figge. Original drawings by Jon Haber.

This book was designed by Kay McRee and typography by Continental Graphics, Los Angeles, California, in 12 point Palatino with 3 point leading. The part headings are in 72 point Typositor Zoom and the chapter headings are in 84 point Typositor Zoom. The text and jacket were printed by offset lithography by Continental Graphics, Los Angeles, California. The text paper is 70# Simpson Lee Publishers Opaque Blue White, and the jacket paper is 80# Lustro-enamel, supplied by Zellerbach Paper Company. The book was bound by Pacific Bookbinding Company, Los Angeles, California, in Kivar 5.